Arthur Granville Bradley

Sketches From Old Virginia

Arthur Granville Bradley

Sketches From Old Virginia

ISBN/EAN: 9783337014421

Printed in Europe, USA, Canada, Australia, Japan

Cover: Foto ©ninafisch / pixelio.de

More available books at **www.hansebooks.com**

SKETCHES

FROM

OLD VIRGINIA

BY

A. G. BRADLEY

London
MACMILLAN AND CO., Limited
NEW YORK: THE MACMILLAN COMPANY
1897

All Rights Reserved

PREFACE

SEVERAL of the enclosed studies have appeared in whole, or part, in *Macmillan's Magazine* at various times.

The following, however, were published in other periodicals, namely "The Doctor," "Mar'se Dab," and "Plantation Memories" in *Blackwood*. An "Old Virginian Foxhunter" and "Quail Shooting" in the *Badminton Magazine*; and "On the Old Bethel Pike" in the *Fortnightly Review*, under a slightly different title.

I have to thank Messrs. Blackwood, Messrs. Longman, and Messrs. Chapman and Hall for their courtesy in allowing me to include the above papers in this book.

The fact of this latter being a collection of studies written, for the most part, independently of one another, and at various times, will, I trust, sufficiently account for an absence of method or continuity that is under such circumstances inevitable.

So far as they go, however, they recall, I think, many of the characteristics of a generation that is rapidly passing away, and has at any rate long ceased to represent modern Virginia.

They relate chiefly to the period covered by the fifteen years or so following the war, when the whole adult population had been brought up under the institution of slavery, both white and black, while the former almost to a man had actually taken part, as individuals, in the great struggle that terminated it.

The Civil War, with its far-reaching consequences, succeeded in utterly dislocating the rural economy of the South, but it could not change the personalities, the habits, the traditions, and methods of thought of the men who had grown up under the system it destroyed.

I offer, therefore, no apology for the comparative remoteness for the most part, of my period. Indeed, this appears to me to furnish a perhaps somewhat needed excuse for the republication of these slight illustrations of it.

For what neither war nor legislation could accomplish of a sudden, time with its slower and surer hand has effectually done. Another generation, who have no personal knowledge of the slavery and ante-bellum period, has arisen. Its members have had to adapt themselves to the ways of life followed by other democratic communities engrossed in trade and agriculture. Virginia, in short, no longer possesses any particular social features that would make it of special interest to an outsider; to one from Europe at any rate. Its material progress has happily been considerable, though not so great as some of its Sister States further South or that its friends and well-wishers had perhaps hoped for having regard to its central position and former predominance. But this is a matter wholly alien to the point of view from which these Sketches were written. So I do not think I need offer any excuse for having allowed, what seemed to me during a residence of a great many years in the Old Dominion, and several subsequent visits, the more picturesque, humorous, and pathetic side of its life to find expression in the studies here collected.

One word in regard to the dialect passages. I have purposely avoided any elaboration in spelling the vernacular, whether of negro or "poor white" where such occurs, but have endeavoured to give the general sound and sense of this without taxing the application of readers who, as a body, are showing, I am told, unmistakable signs of revolt at being referred to appended glossaries even by distinguished and popular authors.

A. G. B.

CONTENTS

	PAGE
INTRODUCTION	1
THE DOCTOR	41
AN OLD VIRGINIA FOXHUNTER	70
ON THE OLD BETHEL PIKE	90
PARKIN THE SADDLER	111
THE "POOR WHITES" OF THE MOUNTAINS	136
THE VIRGINIA QUAIL	157
MAR'SE DAB AFTER THE WAR	179
TWO EPISODES ON RUMBLING CREEK	212
SOME PLANTATION MEMORIES	241
A TURKEY HUNTER	265

SKETCHES FROM OLD VIRGINIA

INTRODUCTION

BEFORE introducing to the reader, to the English reader at any rate, so many old friends and well-remembered scenes from Virginian life, it seems to me that it would be not wholly amiss to give some slight historical account of the Old Dominion itself. I am perfectly aware of a certain incongruity in prefacing sketches of so light a character with anything in the shape of a historical essay. An author, however, may be allowed perhaps some license in this particular so long as he distinctly labels such a chapter with an unmistakable title. For no reader of a light work, I take it, considers himself bound to read the introduction. And that there is perhaps even less occasion than usual in this case, so far as the continuity of this little book is concerned, I will frankly admit. Having thus, I trust, made my peace with those who have no curiosity whatever regarding the past history of Virginia, I will remind those who have that this state and Massachusetts are not merely our two most ancient and interesting colonies, but from their loins have sprung, not wholly, but in a great measure, those two diverse types of Anglo-American known as Northerner and Southerner. The Western type, it is true, has lately appeared upon the scene, and has partially diverted both attention and significance from the old line of cleavage. But this is a mere detail when one considers that only thirty years ago as many millions of men, representing on the one side the traditions of Virginia, on the other that of Massachusetts, with more or less fidelity, shook the world for four years with the bloodiest strife of modern times.

Nothing, however, could well be more different within the limits of a single race than the men who originally settled Virginia and those who undertook the sterner task of subduing the cold soils and facing the fierce climate of New England. The latter were not merely Puritans, but aggressive and intolerant Sectarians. Politically, too, they were republicans, and never even professed a partiality for kings and princes. They developed their country upon lines that were both democratic and gregarious; social equality, or something like it, survived longer than probably it has ever done among educated communities in the history of the world. To public opinion, dominated by a Calvinistic Church, every man had more or less to submit himself or go. The time that was not spent in extracting a living from a not too generous soil, or in fighting Indians, was given over to the hearing of interminable sermons and of religious exercises, in which the Old Testament in its literal sense was the daily model. The high average of character and education, of industry and vigour, tell their own tale, and the history of New England is perhaps more really interesting than that of Virginia. But to the modern Englishman there is something unspeakably distasteful in the narrow religious bigotry and tyranny that seemed to stamp every bit of colour, every spark of gaiety out of life. One renders ungrudging respect to the sturdy pluck and industry, and admires the hardihood which, even in the seventeenth century, swept with home-built ships the distant shores of Africa, or landed the produce of America in Spanish and Italian ports. The one was slave-hunting and the other was smuggling, it is true, but what a relief, after all, it must have been to get away from those village deacons for so long a period. And when, too, one thinks of that audacious attack of volunteer soldiers and sailors upon Quebec, bearding the redoubtable Frontenac himself in his own impregnable stronghold, it is all very inspiring; and so is the thought of the first capture of Louisburg and the legions which so cheerfully poured out to battle in later days when the French were on the warpath. One is almost tempted to entertain flippant and unworthy suspicions that the alacrity with which the colonial New Englander was ready to go to the ends of the earth was not wholly unconnected with the restrictions and the gloom of his home life. There is really good authority for supposing that when away upon these jaunts the excellent Yankee made up for lost time. From the militia camps upon Lake George, in the Seven Years' War, the chaplains complained in letters, still extant, that the swearing was terrific, learnt no doubt from the British regiments, who had in fact just come from Flanders. Wolfe also testifies that his sturdy New Englanders were incorrigible should a cask of rum accidentally fall in their way. But to be serious and to return to the subject in hand, how wholly different was the early settlement and after development of Virginia! Of the first failures to establish a colony, few people know much. Of Captain Smith, however, and John Rolfe and the romantic episode of Pocahontas which mark the second and successful effort, almost every one knows something, though of the number of Virginians who to-day boast of the blood of the Indian Princess, no one has ever pretended to an accurate knowledge. This of course all happened in the opening years of the seventeenth century. By 1640 or thereabouts, when the early struggles were well over, life in Virginia had become quite easy, save for an occasional Indian war. Almost from the first, under the rule of the London Company, and afterwards under the crown, the development of the colony ran strictly upon English and even aristocratic lines. Practically all the colonists were Englishmen, and, nominally at least, members of the English Church. Among a majority of plain folk went a fair sprinkling of cadets, beyond a doubt, from good English families. A legend exists among the more uninformed circles of modern Virginia, that quite a considerable portion of the population are, in some mysterious fashion, sprung from the loins of the "British nobility." I only mention this as a curious and ineradicable superstition that the stranger would be quite sure to encounter frequently during a sojourn in the country. And sometimes the superstition would appear in most humorous garb. It is not unnatural that a people who have been now for some generations out of touch with England and English social life, should have a confused notion of what were the privileges and position of the very small band which formed the British peerage in the seventeenth century. That a nobleman's son (except for an occasional freak) would bury himself permanently, even when ruined, in the American wilderness, or place the Atlantic between himself and those hundred paths to fame, distinction, or at least a congenial competence in Europe to be had in those days for the asking by the higher aristocracy, is a fallacy of course too absurd to traverse.

The squirearchy of the Stuart period were of course quite another matter, and the origin of the fable is no doubt due to the considerable number of gentlemen born who were among the earlier settlers. How these fared in the first hard struggle for existence with their more numerous companions of other classes no one really knows. We do know, however, that towards the middle of the century there were a large number of colonists owning considerable estates, and lifted above the common herd, both in social esteem and influence. The natural desire of Englishmen to surround themselves with broad acres and found families had a great opportunity in Virginia, and the early Virginians took full advantage of it. The authorities encouraged the tendency, and everybody connected with the colony wished to make it as nearly like England as possible. The English Church was jealously established, and the law of entail and primogeniture took firm root. That no Englishman of distinction left the country for a permanent settlement in Virginia we know of a certainty from our English records. So it really seems to me a very unimportant matter as to what proportion of those who early acquired land and influence were related to country squires and what were not. One of the seventeenth century governors writes home complaining of the mania for appropriating the title of gentlemen prevalent among people of no former account who had acquired estates. The fact remains that something like an aristocracy very rapidly came into existence, and was constantly being reinforced; and, moreover, that the seventeenth century is quite sufficiently remote to give most respectable antiquity to those families who were gentry then, whether natural or self-made, and have been so ever since. And these survivals, moreover, are nothing like so numerous as a stranger might be led to infer, if, in his simple innocence, he believed all the claims to ancestral dignity that he heard. The real old meaning of the terms F.F.V. (first families of Virginia) was limited, and entitled to every consideration. The modern adaptation is sometimes elastic enough to make the bones of such departed worthies as Mr. Byrd of Westover, or Colonel Randolph of Tuckahoe, or Mr. Carter of Shirley rattle in their coffins. The influx of Royalist settlers into the colony after the downfall of Charles the First, though many returned at the restoration, gave fresh impetus to conservative

English notions. Those that came were of all conditions, but many gentlemen were among them, as well as others who had sufficient money saved from the wreck to purchase land. An entire regiment, indeed, of eighteen hundred men crossed the Atlantic in a body. Virginia was not without people who sympathised with the parliament, or thought it would be safer to appear to do so, and throughout the war the colony had been greatly disturbed by the squabbles, occasionally bloody ones, of the rival factions. The support of the English government with occasional warships, it should be said, gave strength to the small commonwealth party, and made converts. The restoration, however, was hailed with rapture and great demonstrations in Virginia. Amid the firing of cannon everybody shook hands, and the quasi-parliament men were forgiven, returning readily to that faith in kings and princes which was the natural creed of Virginia. A robe of home-spun and home-grown silk was sent over to the Merry Monarch for his coronation, the arms of Virginia were quartered on those of Great Britain, and every one was happy. A rude awakening came, however, to these enthusiastic loyalists beyond the sea when one day the news arrived that their loving monarch had made a present of most of the colony to a couple of court favourites, Culpepper and Arlington, who seemed to be under the fond belief that these sturdy squires and yeomen, these patriarchs of the woods, would recognise them as the overlords of their estates. Great was the uproar. A deputation went to England, and the easy-going king, who would have parted with half the British

Empire for a little money or a new mistress, was quite surprised at the storm he had raised. With characteristic indolence, however, he revoked the whole business, and only wished to hear the last of the matter. But the Virginians had received a lesson they did not forget. Few people, very few indeed in England I am sure, remember that a few years after this, and exactly a hundred before the American War of Independence, the colony of Virginia rose in arms against the government of Charles the Second. The rebellion was fomented and led by a young English gentleman, a Mr. Bacon, who had purchased an estate upon the present site of Richmond, was son of the squire of Friston Hall in Norfolk, a graduate of Cambridge, and highly connected in the colony itself. The ostensible grievance was the refusal of Sir William Berkeley, the governor, to grant him a commission to fight the Indians who had been murdering settlers, his own overseer among others, but the real causes of discontent lay deeper. There is no space here to speak of them, but it is sufficient to say that if it had not been for Charles the Second's monstrous conduct and flippant ingratitude towards the colony, and for Bacon's great talents and ambition, no movement would have been dreamt of. As it was, the whole country, from its western frontier to the sea, was in arms. The governor had behind him some of the highest, and many of the lowest, of the population. The mass of freeholders, however, sympathised with Bacon, and great numbers joined his standard. The Indians were first defeated, and then loyalists and rebels confronted each other. There were several thousand well-armed men, horse and foot, in the field, and the militia of the various counties under their lieutenants either demonstrated in force or joined issue on one side or the other. Jamestown, the capital, was besieged and burnt, and Sir William Berkeley driven across to the shores of Accomac. Bacon, however, at this critical moment died of fever, and with his death the spirit of rebellion, which had only aimed at putting down abuses, withered. Berkeley got the upper hand, and on the arrival from England of a mixed battalion of the Coldstream and Grenadier guards the colony was easily pacified, and this really dramatic and significant incident closed. The old governor, whose vehement loyalty to his king had urged him to the impolitic course which so disturbed the colony, got little thanks from his master. Having hanged in chains a number of the most prominent revolutionists, he left for England, amid the execrations of the Virginians, to claim his reward. The king refused even to see him, merely remarking, "That old fool has killed more men in yonder naked country than I have for the murder of my father."

The "old fool," who for thirty of his thirty-five years' rule had been immensely popular in the colony, died a few months afterwards of a broken heart. He it was who, in a notable memorandum, thanked God that there were no printing presses or schools in Virginia. In his day, and for a long time afterwards, the Colonial Council, or Upper House, wore red robes of state, while the House of Burgesses sat in the same building, and on occasions of moment were summoned to the Bar, while old Governor Berkeley, from his

throne beneath the royal arms, thundered his
sentiments at the whole assembly. His widow, Lady
Berkeley, married again in Virginia, and her name
may still be seen upon the fragments of a tomb
beneath the ruined tower that almost alone marks
the site of Jamestown. Long before the close of the
seventeenth century, Virginian society had settled
itself upon permanent and established lines. Tobacco
was the one great article of export and commerce.
The large planter was the unit around which everything else revolved. His existence had been made
possible by the large importation of labour, both of
convicts and of respectable indented servants from
Britain, and still more as the years went on, by the
purchase of African negroes brought to his doors
by British or New England traders. Below this
aristocracy came a much greater number of mere
farmers or yeomen, men owning land and perhaps
some servants, white and black, but possessing no
social advantages or education. Below these again
came the landless whites, servants, small tenants and
others, and lastly, as a caste apart, the negro slaves.
The cleavage between the gentry class and the rest
of the community, was emphasised by the entire
absence of popular education. The sons of the former
went very largely to the English universities, or failing
that were taught by imported tutors. But for even
the middling sort there was, till much later times,
no education at all, while the retention of land in
large tracts was fostered by primogeniture and entail.
Counties were created on the seaboard from the very
beginning, and were multiplied as settlements crept

inland. Each county had its lieutenant, its militia, and its magistrates, organised upon English principles. The whole early settled portion of Virginia was intersected with navigable creeks and rivers. The great planter had his special wharf upon his own plantation, up to which every year sailed an English ship bringing necessaries and luxuries from his commission merchant in London, Bristol, or Glasgow, and returning with the year's crop of tobacco. The face of this Eastern country was gently undulating and fairly fertile, the climate genial and healthy, save for the agues, to which after all Englishmen at home were more or less accustomed in those days. Nearly every crop which could be grown in England, grew then in Virginia with equal excellence in addition to the native products of maize and tobacco. The latter, however, became an absolute passion from the earliest times with the Virginians, to the great detriment of all other industries. Fine horses, however, besides other cattle were imported, and horse-racing became the stock amusement both of the country gentry and the lower classes. All the old English games too were played at country gatherings, while the deer and the fox were hunted, and fighting-cocks were part of every planter's establishment. The big plantations were like oases in the vast wilderness of forest with which primitive Virginia was clothed. The tidal rivers served as highways, while only bridle paths led through the woodlands that often intervened for miles between each estate. The more considerable houses were built of brick imported from England, and were upon the style of the smaller manor houses of the period. The majority, however, were of wood, but in either case were surrounded by quite a village of outhouses and negro cabins, interspersed with orchards and paddocks. After Bacon's rebellion the capital was moved to Williamsburg, which during the hundred years of its supremacy, till the war against England, that is to say, never rose to be more than a large village of one wide street. Here, however, was the governor's palace and the House of Assembly, and hither during the session flocked the aristocracy of the colony; the burgesses to quarrel in the house, as they invariably did, with the royal governor, and the ladies to dance or show off the latest fashions sent from London at the viceregal routs. Strong churchmen in a political sense as were the Virginians, in the actual practice of their religion circumstances have for all time been greatly against them. Counties were divided into parishes, in each of which a church was built, and endowed with a tax laid upon the population, and payable like everything else in tobacco. Churchwardens, vestrymen, and clerks, were all there in full dignity of office, but the great difficulty was the parsons. These were sent over ready made from England, and were of the most dubious description, and lived chiefly at free quarters in the planters' houses. As boon companions, or even as instructors to the children, they seem to have been more edifying than in the pulpit of their rustic churches in the woods. Early in the eighteenth century the great inconvenience incurred by native candidates for orders, and by the imported clergy awaiting priest's orders, in having to cross the Atlantic for ordination, stimulated the new large and flourishing colony into a desire for a bishop of its own. With this in view a deputation was sent to England to wait upon the minister of the day and lay the case before him. The great man seems to have kept the delegates cooling their heels in his ante-room for several days, and when at last, as the story goes, he admitted them to an audience he received their appeal in a most crushing and contemptuous fashion. At length one of the Virginian spokesmen plucked up courage, and asked him if he thought that Virginians had not souls to be saved as well as Englishmen. "D——n your souls!" was the exalted person's reply, "go home and grow tobacco."

So the bishop question was disposed of, and postponed *sine die.* In spite, however, of the slovenly condition of the Church in Virginia, the ruling classes were as bitter as ever against dissenters till, as time went on, such opposition became useless. Those of the common people who had any sense of religion at all, drifted away from a Church that had no vitality, and was, moreover, so entirely aristocratic in tone. Among a population, too, scattered, such as this was, over so wide an area, laws of this kind could not be enforced, and in course of time became a dead letter, except in so far as the collection of tithe was concerned. Nor must it be supposed that what I have called the aristocracy of Virginia were as securely placed or as humbly deferred to by the yeomanry and lower class as the squirearchy of Great Britain. There was, in fact, a great deal of democratic feeling below the surface and beyond a doubt much jealousy. The poor were taxed much more highly than the rich, though the latter were the beneficiaries of such taxation. For it was they that chiefly filled both houses of the legislature, whose members were not only paid most liberal salaries, but often got allowances for the keep of servants and horses as well. There were numerous government offices, too, all highly paid, many of them sinecures, but all enjoyed by the ruling class. Upon the top of this came the Church dues, and lastly, though only landholders were allowed to vote, land itself was held comparatively free of all taxation. A safety valve, however, for what discontent this state of things created, and we are speaking of nearly two hundred years ago it must be remembered, lay in the great back country which intervened between the older counties and the Alleghany Mountains. A better climate and generally richer soil too, made this a refuge not merely for the discontented and the lawless, but for young men of good birth who, under the laws of primogeniture, were constantly pushing westward, with little or no patrimony, and were a valuable element in the rougher and more democratic communities, out of which these back counties were originally formed. So Virginia, from Bacon's rebellion in 1676 onwards till the revolutionary war in 1776, led upon the whole a placid, happy, prosperous existence, rich rather in the material things of life than in actual money. Population increased, chiefly from within, for with the exception of indented servants and African negroes, immigration was inconsiderable, save for one notable exception. Of this last I must crave permission to say somewhat more than a few words, seeing that it was part of a great movement which left an indelible mark both on Great Britain and America. The immense emigration of Irish Roman Catholics to America is quite a modern affair. It had not begun in the eighteenth century, nor did it reach serious proportions till after the famine of 1849. Though land hunger was its catch word in Tipperary and Mayo, it has had little hunger for the rich lands of America. No class of emigrants indeed to the United States have ever done so little pioneering or so consistently flinched from facing the prairie and the forest. It is in towns the modern Irish emigrant is chiefly to be found, and greatly dominating the sort of local politics under which Americans for two generations have groaned. About the year 1720, however, another class altogether of Irish emigration was moving in. It came from the north-east, was wholly Presbyterian, and by blood chiefly Scottish. These people were of a kind who cared nothing for towns and little for politics, as understood by the modern Irish, and whose mission was to colonise the wilderness. They had already, indeed, tamed one wilderness, for in a little over a century they had transformed Ulster from a semi-barbarous waste into a well-cultivated, thriving province. They had also proved an invaluable bulwark of the English power in Ireland ; the famous Siege of Derry being, of course, the most memorable instance of their heroism. And they were now to have their reward. It will be remembered how secure was the Protestant ascendency throughout most of the eighteenth century in Ireland. Bitterly as the

Catholic Celt felt his position, his power of resistance had been crushed at the Boyne, and he lay practically supine for nearly a century beneath the heel of the Protestant gentry and the Irish Church. The latter was at this time one of the greatest ecclesiastical shams to be found perhaps in history. There were more bishops in proportion to communicants, and bishops, too, with very large incomes for which, as a rule, they did almost nothing, than in any Church that has ever been known. Pluralism among the incumbents, too, was rampant; and when one of these by interest or jobbery had secured a sufficient number of livings to give him a comfortable income, he was accustomed to take himself off to Dublin, Bath, or Tunbridge Wells, leaving an unfortunate curate on a miserable pittance, to grapple with the work of two or three parishes, often many miles apart. It would be interesting to know what precise fraction of the money wrung from Roman Catholics was actually paid to the men who vainly but honestly endeavoured to do the Church's work. The Government's attitude towards Papists and potential rebels was at least intelligible. But it now seemed to most even of the dominant party a grievous scandal that the loyal Presbyterians of Ulster should still be debarred the rights of citizenship because they adhered to a creed which the British Government actually upheld by law as the established Church in Scotland. A bill to grant them equal rights with their Episcopal fellow countrymen was brought in with the general approval both of Ireland and England. But to the dozen or fifteen sainted men who enjoyed the fat bishoprics of this remarkable establishment, it seemed a terrible thing that a Presbyterian should sit in Parliament or hold a commission in his Majesty's service. That these were the men who had defended Derry, that they were passionately loyal, God-fearing, and law-abiding above all other Irishmen, and of most vital necessity to the country, was nothing. These absentee bishops of absentee rectors and tumble-down half-empty churches, thought that the very heavens would fall if such a fearful thing came to pass. They mustered thick in the Irish House of Lords, and they threw their very souls into the righteous crusade. Wonderful things were sometimes accomplished upon College Green as we all know, and the bishops upon this occasion in the teeth of public opinion carried the day. The Protestant Nonconformists who had even before this begun to flit, took the verdict as final, and prepared to leave their homes by thousands. It is said that in twenty years a hundred thousand of these virile Puritans crossed the Atlantic, with what effect on Ireland's future who, indeed, can estimate. They sailed by shiploads to Philadelphia and Charlestown, avoiding with singular consistency the Puritan commonwealths of New England. For half the century they kept pouring their steady stream through these two seaports. They did not stop, however, about the towns, but worked their way, for the most part, through the settlements to the Alleghany mountains, which like a lofty wall, formed the western barrier of every colony, from Pennsylvania to Carolina. These mountains were then the extreme limit of Anglo-Saxon enterprise. No settler's axe had yet touched those virgin forests, and the dreaded Indian still looked upon them as his happy hunting ground. The Scotch-Irish exiles, however, seemed determined not to place their liberties a second time in the power of any government, and threw themselves with consummate courage upon those romantic highlands that had even by the colonial backwoodsmen been hitherto regarded as beyond the pale of safety. And all along the fertile foothills and valleys of the great range the northern immigrants spread southward; while the southern immigrants, who had traversed the Carolinas, spread northward, till in the course of years they joined forces and were clustering more thickly on the western frontier of Virginia than at any other point. Here in the beautiful Shenandoah valley, between the Blue Ridge and the Alleghanies, long before Virginian settlement had reached it, were scattered the lonely clearings of the Scotch-Irish, and the German Lutherans, who followed in their wake. A second generation became the best Indian fighters and hunters on the continent, and it was they who opened the way to Kentucky, who founded Tennessee, and who were first upon the banks of the Ohio. Equally handy with axe, plough, or rifle, rough and uncouth, thrifty and close-fisted, they differed as much from the easy-going Virginia squire, as men who speak the same language could very well differ from each other. These, however, were the first settlers of the western parts of the colony, and upon it they set their stamp so indelibly, that to this day, within a morning's ride, you may find two people and two counties scarcely more like each other than are

Limerick and Antrim, Devonshire or Durham. East of the Blue Ridge everything even now is characteristic of the old Virginian traditions: big dwelling houses and poor ramshackle farm buildings, uncared-for roads and a beautiful country, sadly scarred on the surface by generations of slovenly treatment. You will find too on the one side an easy-going, somewhat thriftless, but generous, well-mannered, and hospitable people. Yet within ten miles, though an integral part of Virginia and for a hundred years intimately associated with its trials and triumphs and institutions, you will come upon a district whose people live for the most part in unpretentious houses, but whose farm buildings are large and well-painted, roads excellent, and fields well tilled. A thrifty and industrious folk, whose manners are as nearly ungracious and whose habits as far removed from hospitality as could very well be possible in the Southern States. This great valley is to-day by far the finest portion of Virginia, and this is partly due to the fact that it was one of the great nurseries of that virile Scotch-Irish race whose qualities their neighbours regard with more respect perhaps than actual affection. The active part these people took against the mother country in the War of Independence is of course a matter of history. Washington had an immense admiration for the hardy borderers with whom he had camped and hunted, and fought so much in his youth. But a small portion, however, of these mountaineers were available as a matter of fact for Washington's armies. Fortunately for him another method had just been discovered in Ireland for expelling the cream of her population and sending them over to fight against England in America. The crippling of the linen trade was of course England's crime, but every student of Irish history will also recall the lamentable clearances by Lord Donegal, and other large proprietors, when their long leases fell in during the middle of the last century. It will be remembered how they turned out hundreds of Scotch Presbyterian tenants to make room for western Celts who promised higher rents, or would pay bigger fines. Whether indeed these short-sighted landlords or the frenzied bishops of former days conferred the most lasting injury on their country, is of no consequence here.

Virginia, at any rate, together with the rest of North America, benefited enormously by the influx of this hardy race, over whose movements I have, perhaps, already lingered too long.

The Seven Years' War began prematurely in America, and, after a few preliminary skirmishes between Washington with his Virginia riflemen and the French, was formally inaugurated by Braddock's fatal fight in 1755. That Isandlwana of the eighteenth century paralysed Virginia from end to end, and staggered even England. British regiments, for the first time since the former century, had landed in the colony, making love to the ladies, and somewhat damping the loyal ardour and friendly feelings of the gentlemen by the hauteur of their bearing and their misplaced contempt for provincial soldiers. When the shattered remnants of Braddock's beaten army came staggering back over the Alleghanies, leaving the bones of the stubborn bull-dog who commanded them, and of sixty officers and seven hundred men, to be picked by wolves on the banks of the Monongahela, there was great dismay, both in the log homesteads of the back counties and in the far-off manor houses of the Tide water region. Washington, as every one knows, had been there at the head of five hundred Virginia riflemen, the only men upon that fatal field who understood the game of war as played in the American woods, and whom Braddock, with loud oaths, and a free use of the flat of his sword, tried to beat into close formation, as he had beaten his poor red-coats. Most of the Virginians fell; Washington's coat was shot through in several places, and two horses killed under him, but he was reserved, as we know, for greater things. The Indians, egged on by the French, swarmed over the western frontier of Virginia, and, amid scenes of fire and blood, swept through the clearings of the bold Scotch-Irish borderers, crossed the Blue Ridge, and fell upon the back-counties, that had almost forgotten what Indian fighting was like. Even the planters in their distant manor-houses began to think the days of their grandfathers and great-grandfathers had returned, and trembled. Two years of terror and bloody skirmishing reigned upon the border. But as soon as French Canada saw that it was no longer a case for aggression on the English colonies, but a matter of fighting for its own existence, the tide of battle rolled northward. Wolfe and Quebec fell together, and a great sigh of relief went up from Virginia. Its borderers reckoned up their dead by hundreds—men, women, and children.

The squires and farmers of the old settlements, who had not taken much part in the great struggle, while thanking God that they were Englishmen at such a glorious moment, gave thanks also that they would be harassed no more for supplies, and waggons, and contributions from the British Generals at Philadelphia, and rejoiced that they had heard the last of the French.

The white population of Virginia was by this time something like a quarter of a million, while the negroes, who had increased with great rapidity, were not, perhaps, very far short of that number. And the scattered method of Virginian settlement filled up, after a fashion, the whole space between the mountains and the sea, which constitutes, even to this day, the entire region that is typically Virginian in character and tradition. The manner of life had in no way altered. There were more squires and more yeomen, more "poor whites" and more negroes. That was all. The upper class had gained something in dignity, from long privilege, and from their constant connection with England had kept abreast of the times to an extent that surprised the few European travellers who personally witnessed the isolation of their lives. The middling class, the ordinary farmers, had gained somewhat, perhaps, in education, but were the strange mixture of roughness and courtesy, shrewdness and simplicity of kindliness and barbarism that puzzled Captain Anburey, who lived two years among them in 1778, and elicited, a few years later, almost the same expressions from that observant traveller, Mr.

Weld. The lower class were almost unredeemed savages. Their chief pastime was in personal combats of a sort in which biting and kicking and gouging were the main methods of attack. Many of these rustic ruffians trained their nails to a prodigious length, and sharpened them at the ends, with a view to gouge out their opponent's eye more neatly and deftly. Biting off the nose, too, was another test of skill, and worse performances, which will not bear relation. Nor were these isolated instances of barbarity, but the common habit of the lower classes. No court-day or race-meeting would have been complete for these folk without one or more edifying spectacles of the kind, which were carefully arranged beforehand. The gentry had, of course, no part in such matters. They did not interfere, because it was not their policy to trouble their heads in any way about the habits of their inferiors with a white skin, nor was their position of that secure kind in which such interference would have been tolerated.

These savage performances are the theme of every contemporary writer who has given us pictures of the southern colonies in these days. I have, indeed, myself talked to numbers of old men who can remember these barbarous fights which, in the mountain counties, lingered on far into this century.

Then there were the Scotch-Irish and those who had rallied round them, far away upon the frontier, who though politically in Virginia, were practically at this time beyond both her laws and social influence. These men had brought with them a keen sense of religion and a respect for education. Their descendants, in spite of a certain ferocity and lawlessness engendered by the hardships and dangers of their daily lives, had by no means wholly lost this. Their ministers girded up their loins and went out to battle with their flocks. In their rude log houses, thrust far into the forest wilderness, the family Bible found a a place among the long rifles, and deer horns, and Indian scalps, that decorated their walls. A story describes two of these daring hunters in the wilds of the then scarcely trodden Kentucky forests, reading *Gulliver's Travels* to one another by the camp fire at night.

The immense increase of the negroes was already beginning to be something of a problem to the more educated of the class who owned them. It was not customary, nor at that time very easy, to sell them, nor was the price as yet very tempting, while on many plantations, even then, there were a greater number than were required to do the work.

Now, however, came the great War of Independence against the mother country which, for the time, upset all minor considerations and disposed of all domestic questions.

Except for the fact that they had been so closely allied with the English troops in the late French wars, separation from the mother country implied no very great wrench to the men of New England. But the sentiments of Virginia had always been so very different, that neither a close study of the facts, nor a knowledge of the people, seem to me to fully explain the leading part they took in bringing on the war. If the middle and lower classes had inspired the movement, and compelled their superiors to follow, the situation would be much more readily conceivable. But it was the aristocracy of Virginia that led, and the others followed, willingly enough no doubt, but that is not the point. The opening of the revolution found Virginia, if not actually the largest or wealthiest colony, the most influential at any rate, and most certainly the leader of opinion in the south. Nowhere else, either north or south, was there such a numerous class of educated gentry. The first orator, and the first soldier in America, were both Virginians. And the famous Patrick Henry, who swayed men in such a fashion never before or since equalled, upon the western continent, threw his whole power against the mother country in the councils and on the platforms of his native colony. He was sufficiently well connected to be not wholly distasteful to the upper classes, and at the same time sufficiently needy and plain of speech and garb, to pose as a man of the people. Possibly the Virginians might have risen in any case, but in the forefront of all their consultations is this tall, gawky country lawyer, with his flashing eyes and hawk-like face, holding them spellbound, and urging them with impassioned eloquence to draw the sword. The most sacred spot in the modern Richmond, is the old wooden church, which the negro hackman still points out with his whip to the inquiring tourist as "de place whar old Partick Henry spoke de famous piece of liberty or def." Of the first few years' fighting, Virginia took a comparatively small share. War, for a long time, was waged almost wholly in the north, and it was only the Virginian troops that actually marched to join Washington's army, who came in contact with its horrors. The greater part of the people, at any rate, stayed at home, and learnt what it was to have no market for their tobacco, and be forced to receive payment of dues in paper money that sank dangerously near to the point of worthlessness. What men on their lonely plantations thought in their heart of hearts as the war progressed no one will ever know. Some were, beyond a doubt, uncompromising rebels, others equally stubborn Tories. It is probable that a far greater number between these two extremes were doubtful or indifferent, nor is it possible that both in Virginia and Maryland there should not have been an undercurrent of profound regret and sadness at the rupture, and this of a kind more widespread and more deep than was called for in the northern colonies.

Yet when the war itself with heavy and devastating hand fell on Virginia, we hear of fewer active loyalists, by far, than in either New York or in the Carolinas. There is, indeed, no doubt that the revolution struck a blow at the old colonial aristocracy, from which it never recovered; a certain number were of course loyalists whose estates were ultimately confiscated and themselves driven penniless into exile, while many were permanently ruined by the destroying hand of Cornwallis' armies. At the same time Virginia came out of the conflict as one of the first and most patriotic States in the new Confederation, with her great son Washington a head and shoulders above any engaged in that unhappy struggle. And by

Washington's side stood most of the leading men in Virginia. This was no class war. The province had fought against alien armies under the leadership of its natural chiefs. There was nothing internally subversive whatever in the movement. Yet close upon its heels there followed a democratic wave which seemed aimed at the very class who had furnished the most prominent patriots. Primogeniture and entail were swept away by the Virginian legislature, likewise the Church of England as an establishment. These measures taken alone were perhaps not unnatural, but it does seem extraordinary that the upper classes, who had no intention whatever of turning Presbyterians or Methodists, allowed their parish churches to be infamously desecrated, the communion plate stolen, and the whole machinery of the episcopal Church paralysed for nearly a generation, because the mass of the people looked on it as symbolical of English ascendency. Public worship in Virginia from the earliest times to the present day has been singularly lacking in beauty and vitality. But this episode in its history is peculiarly discreditable, both to those who were the aggressors, and to those who tamely suffered such things to be.

When the war was over society shook down again into something like the old lines, though an independence of manner was assumed by the common people which, if neither offensive nor aggressive, was yet a marked change from the Colonial period. The aristocracy grew more numerous, less relatively wealthy, and less exclusive. For great numbers of new families sprang from " plain people " into " quality " as prosperity returned. This new blood, with the admirable example of the old colonial families as its standard, did not greatly turn from its old grooves a society which, if in some ways singularly narrow and provincial, evolved out of its picturesque simplicity a remarkable list of able men. It is worthy of note that in the period following the war Washington, Jefferson, Madison, and Patrick Henry, all men of world-wide fame, were living on their estates in Virginia at the same time. The centres of population and influence had shifted westward somewhat. Even thus early travellers tell us of old manor houses on the eastern shore standing deserted amid worn-out wastes of broomsedge, sassafras, and scrub pines.

Jamestown, the first capital, had been long given back wholly to the wilderness. A ruined church-tower, a few broken tombstones, and the remains of a powder magazine, alone mark the spot upon the banks of the broad James, where the first English parliament met upon American soil.

Williamsburg, too, with its single street, was soon politically deserted, and had little left to boast of but the college of William and Mary, a foundation second only to Harvard in antiquity, but distinguished for nothing else. This reminds me, however, that the Virginians at last got their Bishop, and it was at this college he first took up his residence. Richmond, nearer the centre of the state, had become the capital, perched upon high hills at whose feet the broad James, after some miles of rocky rapids, subsides into a tidal river. Its site has been the admiration of many travellers, and the centre, as we all know, of some of the heaviest fighting of modern days.

Life in Virginia during the early part of this century did not greatly alter under the new dignity of the foremost province of a rising nation. The State had passed, it is true, through a short "silly season" just after the French revolution, for Jefferson, with all his ability, was crazy on some points, and this same French revolution was one of them. He entertained feather-headed French republicans, and even encouraged Virginian freeholders, of all people upon earth, to don caps of liberty and cut capers, till Washington almost wept with vexation that any of his countrymen could be persuaded to make of themselves such lamentable buffoons. Jefferson, though a respectable landowner of Albemarle county and most influentially connected, and withal a scholar and familiar figure in Parisian society, was a prodigious democrat and in many ways most unlike the typical Virginian of his class. His knowledge, however, was most wide and varied, and he was a great promoter of education. At Charlottesville he founded a state university, which has ever since held a good provincial position, and been a great boon to poor students beyond a doubt, if a dubious one to the wealthier who had hitherto been compelled to go to the great universities of Europe or the North.

The period which followed the achievement of independence was a stirring and stormy one for Virginia. Bankruptcy, chaos, disintegration hung for years over the new and still doubtful union. The new constitution had been made and fought over. The relationship of the young republic to European countries, who were by turns cajoling and threatening her, had to be adjusted. A hundred problems that required statesmanship to solve had to be solved, and this, too, while the world was in an electrical condition with the wars following on the French revolution. It was not till after the close of the wanton war with England, into which the third Virginian president, Mr. Madison, had plunged the nation while the mother country was in her great life and death struggle with the tyrant of the world, that the Americans really settled down to their own affairs. The pretext for this war was the impressment of American seamen by British warships, one good enough for a patriotic school text-book perhaps, but by no means so plain to a serious student of that period; nor was this *casus belli* even mentioned in the treaty of peace two years later. To half America, at any rate, including New England, this war seemed a monstrous and wanton act. One party, however, for various reasons, wanted it, and I am sorry to say that Virginia led that party, and Mr. Madison, as chief magistrate of the great liberty-loving republic of the west, extended a helping hand to the enslaver of half Europe and the would-be enslaver of all of it. Canada, however, was the immediate object of attack, in whose forests thousands of expelled American loyalists had taken refuge and begun life afresh with extraordinary courage and fortitude. Seldom surely in history was defeat so richly deserved, as in the series of very ignominious ones the American armies that fell on Canada received from the small handful of settlers and soldiers who defended it. These little-known campaigns are quite curiosities of military history, while the extraordinary bombast of the invading generals' proclamations to their troops are probably the most humorous things of their kind now extant in print. It is no wonder that the bravery with which the Americans fought their naval duels and repulsed the attack by land on New Orleans is generally made to obscure the greater and more important operations in the north which for the most part so signally failed. The war of 1812–14, however, was not without good effects; for it cleared the air at any rate, and the country settled down again to its own domestic concerns.

Life in Virginia went on very much upon its old lines. Its leisured class continued to supply not the giants of former days perhaps, any longer, but many leading politicians to the national councils. It produced also some distinguished lawyers, and a large number of excellent officers to the army and navy of the United States. The towns continued to be small and unimportant, and trade, excepting the manufacture of tobacco, and banking, to be carried on chiefly by the Jews or foreigners. Country life still continued to be everything in Virginia, and as the estates of the gentry class, owing to subdivision, were smaller than of old, and consequently nearer together, social intercourse grew more and more the passion of the Virginian's life. He travelled very little, and all social touch with England was destroyed by the revolutionary war, and was never afterwards even to the slightest extent regained. Yet, in spite of the political antagonism to Great Britain which Virginia generally manifested from the revolution onwards, in private life, paradoxical though it sounds, the better people still cherished much of the old affection for the mother country, and nowhere in America would an English visitor have been more welcomed than in the Old Dominion. Most of the middle and lower class belonged now to other denominations, but the upper had got their episcopal Church back again, though it had of course to be supported by voluntary contribution. The clergy, if they were not very vigorous or accomplished, were profoundly respectable, and lived upon sufficient incomes in comfortable rectories surrounded by glebe lands, with not very much to do but officiate on Sundays and eat a friendly meal from time to time with their hospitable and prosperous parishioners. Negro slavery, as I have said, was inherited by the Virginians. Whether they liked it or not, they had to accept it. By about 1830 thinking men were getting somewhat anxious on the subject, for these coloured dependants had increased so immensely in numbers that it seemed likely they would soon eat some of their masters out of house and home. Land, upon the other hand, had generally been deteriorating in fertility through the reckless cultivation of tobacco and its subservient crops, accompanied by the exigencies of negro slavery. In semi-tropical or tropical countries, especially where there was not much conscience, this form of labour was cheap. But in a temperate climate of moderate fertility it was most uneconomical. The Virginian was saddled with his negroes, among whom were many useless old men and women, as well as crowds of young children. He had to feed, clothe, house them, and call in the doctor when they were sick, to say nothing of occasional presents of money, which was the customary habit with good masters; nor could men of character, without losing caste, sell their own people. These latter represented capital, of course, but locked up, unavailable capital. They conferred dignity no doubt, if owned in sufficient numbers, but it must be remembered that the slave-owners were not a special class in a social sense. Both the gentry and the plain farmers owned slaves, though the former in much greater numbers. In 1850 out of 347,000 slave-owners in the whole South, only 8,000 owned more than fifty negroes, or, roughly speaking, ten families. While 174,000 owned five negroes or less, or, by the same estimate, one family. A hundred head of all sexes and ages would have represented the belongings of a gentleman of substantial property, though there were exceptional instances of five or ten times that amount. About the period I have mentioned things were in fact getting somewhat strained in Virginia; not in the Scotch-Irish districts to the west, where tobacco was little grown and negroes not widely owned, but in the old planting country between the Blue Ridge and the sea.

The better-class were careless, perhaps, rather than actually extravagant. Things were left chiefly to overseers, though the Virginian country gentleman was an intelligent, capable man, ready-witted, and quite equal to most emergencies, as circumstances have proved. Slavery, however, in a region really unsuitable for the institution, made him the failure, as a rural economist, that the face of his country has always, more or less, plainly shown him to be. Though almost everything was grown or made within the plantation fence, a lavish hospitality, however, simple, makes inroads upon a property worth only a few thousand pounds, and, except in the Shenandoah Valley and a few other favoured districts, the bulk of the land was only worth, at a rough average, some £3 to £5 an acre. About 1830, however, unlooked-for conditions arose that had a most stimulating effect upon Virginia, namely, a large demand for negroes from the states to the southward, such as Georgia, South Carolina, Alabama, and Mississippi. This was chiefly due to the cotton-planting industry, now developing at a great rate. In these regions, for the most part, negroes were not the hereditary appendages of families as in Virginia, where the comfort and well-being of their slaves was a matter of wholesome pride. In fact, much of the country was comparatively new, and the men that worked it new men. In the cotton country, as well as in the sugar and the rice fields, slave labour was extremely profitable, and those who had negroes worked them more after the hard fashion of the story books. Down south the overseer's whip really cracked, and the flogging-post was a very prominent institution. Slaves grew old quickly, and died. Even Sundays on the Mississippi was not always a holiday. With the exception of certain notable districts the planters, as a class, were immeasurably inferior in traditions and habits and civilisation generally, to those of Virginia and

Maryland. The demand for negroes from these states grew brisk, and continued so till the civil war. When one part of the country was overburdened with labour it did not quite know what to do with them, and another part wanted it badly and had the money to pay, the result was inevitable. But it must not be for a moment supposed that respectable Virginians put their surplus negroes up to auction and sold them away down south. The feeling against deliberate sales for money remained as strong as ever. But still, paradoxical as it at first sounds, Virginia became the chief of what was known as the "raising" States, and a large revenue flowed in every year in return for strong, healthy Ethiopians, who went down to toil in the cotton fields and the sugar estates of men whose aims and instincts were wholly commercial, whose breeding was generally common, and who had little or no regard for public opinion. A very different matter these poor fellows found it from working corn rows or harrowing wheat land, splitting fence-rails or burning plant beds, with much sociable conversation in the wholesome fields and woodlands of easy-going Virginia.

How it came about that this steady export of negroes was maintained requires some telling.

In the first place it had always been considered legitimate to sell a negro who was incorrigible, and one impervious to punishment. In former days it had not perhaps been always easy to do so. Now, however, any sort of a man who was capable of work fetched a fair price; and they had a system of discipline in the far south which made personal character a matter of comparatively little moment. Then again the slave dealer was everywhere in evidence, getting "bunches of hands" together to take south, tempting slave owners and paying far higher prices than had ever been paid before. There were of course, too, unscrupulous men in Virginia as everywhere else, who cared nothing for other people's opinion, and would sell anything that fetched a price. There were many, also, who were desperately pressed for cash, and had not principle enough to resist the money bags shaken in their faces, for negroes that were of no equivalent use to them. Lastly, there was one very common source, though an unintentional and lamentable one, by which Virginian negroes found their way south in considerable numbers, and brought a large amount of money back into the state. Slaves had by this time become much the best security for money in the south, better even than land, for they were instantly convertible into cash or could be always hired out for their wages, whereas land in Virginia could not even in the palmiest days be readily disposed of at short notice, for there was so much of it, and could rarely be satisfactorily let.

The land-owners as a class were inclined to exceed their income, and borrowing became fatally easy when slave property increased so much in value. Confidence in paper, based on land and negroes was absolute. But like mortgages in all countries the unexpected would often happen, and foreclosure would bring an estate, negroes and all, to the hammer. Neighbours would, it is true, on such occasions, buy in the slaves if possible, and then little hardship was

INTRODUCTION

incurred. Indeed individual sales were constantly made with the slaves' consent, or often at their own wish, to suit their convenience, or matrimonial views. But in these sheriffs' sales there was not always money to put up against the brisk bidding of the dealers, and there were sad scenes all round, among both black and white, over which we will not linger.

In the fifties began the mutterings of the storm that broke with such terrific fury in the following decade. The southern people had dominated national politics at Washington for most of the century, and Virginia had led the south. When at length, however, they found themselves being overwhelmed by the numerical and industrial growth of the north and their power slipping away, it caused irritation, natural enough, if illogical. Much friction had been engendered between the two sections by their directly conflicting interests and their different views generally of life. The brotherly feelings of 1776 had absolutely vanished. The two sections, speaking generally, knew astonishingly little of one another, and what they did know they did not like. Slavery, though abolition was not then thought of as a political question, was an unceasing bone of contention. As civilisation swept rapidly westward and new states and territories were opened out, the burning question arose whether it was to be permitted in them or not. No impartial person who had ever looked upon an old free state and an old slave state side by side from an agricultural and economic point of view, could possibly have two opinions on the subject.

The northern settlers who were pushing westward held naturally only one, and that very violently, and of course this view was the right one. The Virginians and other southern slaveholders, however, maintained that the soil of the United States belonged as much to them as to New Yorkers or New Englanders, which was undoubtedly true; nor did they see any reason why they should not carry their domestic institutions with them. And this was an important matter, as slave-holders were constantly emigrating from the worn-out lands of the older states to the fat prairies of the new.

The personal rancour created by all these questions counted for almost as much as the questions themselves. Such an amount of bad language has never probably been used in the history of journalism as these two sections of the now dis-united states showered on each other, for many years previous to the war, and the venom was extended to social and political intercourse in the only city, Washington, where the representatives of the two parties met. Virginians, who had been by no means, as we have said, enthusiastic for slavery, got tired of being vilified at home and abroad for holding opinions which, as a class, they did not hold, and for committing atrocities that they did not commit. They were worried, one might almost say, by intemperate abolitionists into becoming ardent champions of an institution of whose drawbacks they had formerly been outspokenly conscious, and had been more than once almost ready to abolish. So, on the other hand, the old families of New England, the most cultivated class in America, many of whom came down from an unbroken line of well-educated and distinguished ancestors, grew tired of being stigmatised as low-born shopkeepers by vulgar tobacco-chewing editors in the swamps of Mississippi or Arkansas. Nor could the men of a race, who had done more hard fighting in their history than any other in America, remain wholly impervious to such epithets as "white-livered curs," or "chicken-hearted cowards," which were being continually showered upon them. Virginians, perhaps, did not take much part in this besotted nonsense. Nor by any means did they howl for war like the hot-heads of South Carolina and her sister states. Virginia as a matter of fact was divided within herself upon the subject. But all her best people had a profound reluctance to draw the sword against the Union which their ancestors had done so much to establish, and in whose government they had taken so prominent a part. Numbers of her sons were in the United States army and navy. They were, it is true, then as always, Virginians first and Americans afterwards, and whatever steps the government of their native state elected to take, her children, east of the Alleghanies at any rate, would follow almost to a man, and we all know the decision that was come to. But none the less there was real grief among nearly all of those whose opinions were most worthy of respect, that things had come to such a pass. Possibly, too, Virginia better understood the formidable nature of the contemplated struggle than the federation of states to the south of her, who forced on the issue.

Neutrality, however, was impossible to the Old Dominion, for she lay between the combatants. The time came when she was compelled to take the field. Her soil became the cockpit of the contending armies, and was ravaged from end to end, and her slaves forcibly freed. But her sons covered themselves with glory, and if one may say so, out of a host where all were valiant, will be for ever remembered as the bravest of the brave.

THE DOCTOR: AN OLD VIRGINIA FOX HUNTER.

Now the Doctor was a Southerner of the old school. Nor was he merely a North Carolinan, a Tennessean, a Kentuckian, or a Georgian—not any, thank you! No; our friend was a Virginian—a real "old-fashioned, blue-blooded, whole-souled, open-handed Virginian." And this he was by virtue of eight or nine generations of forebears who had fought, physicked, speechified, fox-hunted, raised negroes and tobacco, in that immortal commonwealth. No day passed but the Doctor, in his simple fashion, unconsciously thanked God that he was a Virginian. For did not virtue, valour, honour, gallantry select the Old Dominion in the days of the Stuarts as their special depot, from whence, in modified streams, these qualities might be diffused over the less fortunate portions of the Western world? To the unsophisticated Englishman, to the ignorant Frenchman or German, an American is an American. If he is not rampantly modern, sensationally progressive, and furiously material, he is nothing at all. But the Doctor would scarcely ever speak or think of himself as an American, except in the same sense that an Englishman might call himself a

European. The Doctor was, every moment of the day, and every day in the year, a Virginian above everything; and, as I have already said, he felt thereby that a responsibility and a glory above that of other mortals—American mortals, at any rate—had been conferred upon him by the accident of his birth. I may add, moreover, that he was unquestionably non-progressive, that he was decidedly not modern, while to the end of his days he was so reactionary that the sound of a railway irritated him; and, finally, that he was, beyond a doubt, eminently picturesque.

The Doctor was about sixty-five at the time of which I write. He had never set foot outside Virginia, and never wanted to. That a country, however, or climate, or people, or scenery existed that could be mentioned in the same breath with the old Cavalier colony, never for one moment was accounted within the bounds of possibility by that good and simple soul.

And yet, paradoxical as it may seem, the Doctor was proud of his descent from pure English stock. "None of your Scotch or Irish, or Scotch-Irish, for me. No, I thank you, sir. My folks," he was fond of relating, "were real English stock, who came over 'way back in early colonial days, and settled on the York River. They were kin to the nobility." Whatever may have been the accuracy of this last claim the Doctor's patronymic in Virginia genealogy was above reproach. Nor should I like it to be supposed that my old friend was given to blustering about either his State or his descent. Your fire-eating, blowing, swaggering Southerner belongs either to a lower social grade, to the more frontier States of the South, or, to a greater degree perhaps than either, to the fertile imagination of the writers of dime novels. The Doctor was a Virginian. His thoughts and his habits, which were peculiar and original, were simply those of Virginians of his class and generation somewhat strongly emphasised. He was just and unassuming, kindly and homely. There was about him a delightful old-fashioned, if somewhat ponderous suavity of manner, that the rest of the Anglo-Saxon race have long, long out-grown. To even hear a married female that was not black addressed as otherwise than "Madam" positively pained him. As for the children, the Doctor had a separate greeting for every one of them, let his host's quiver be ever so full. Ay, and generally something more than that; for the Doctor's capacious pockets were known by the little ones to be almost as inexhaustible in the way of chincapins, hickory-nuts, and candy, as his well-worn saddle-bags were of less inviting condiments.

The Doctor's belief in his country (and by his country of course I mean Virginia) was the religion in which he was born. He would never have dreamt of intruding it on you. International comparisons he could not make, for he had never been out of the State. I feel perfectly sure, however, if the Doctor had travelled over every corner of the earth, that his faith was of that fundamental description which was proof against mere sights and sounds. He would have returned to the shade of his ancestral porch, temporarily staggered, perhaps, but still unconvinced that any land or any people could compare with old Virginia.

Once more in his cane-bottomed rocking-chair in the shady porch; once more within sight of the blue mountains, the red fallows, and the yellow pine-sprinkled sedge-fields of his native land, he would quickly recover from the temporary shocks that had irritated him. The sublime faith in "the grand old Commonwealth" would return, and he would thank God more fervently than ever he was a son of Virginia: not because of her present or her future—for he considered the Virginia he belonged to died with slavery—but on account of her people and her past. The Doctor, happily, had been spared all these trials, and his faith remained pure and unimpaired. The only capital he had ever visited was the charming little city of Richmond, where every third man or woman he met was his cousin; where most of society in his day called one another by their Christian names, dined in the middle of the day, and sat out on chairs in the street after supper. Richmond was a snug and pleasant place no doubt; but its atmosphere would have tended to confirm, not to shake, the Doctor's homely faith.

He had only a moderate property—two farms—of which we shall speak anon. But then he was a Patton; and as everybody south of the Potomac knows, the Pattons are one of the first families in the State,—none of your modern and self-dubbed F.F.V.'s who make the term a laughing stock are they, but real old colonial people, whose names are written on almost every page of their country's history. Besides this, Judge Patton, the Doctor's father, was one of the greatest jurists south of Washington—"in the world," Virginians said; but as a compromise we will admit he was one of the first in America, and quite distinguished enough to reflect a social halo over his immediate descendants, supposing even they had not been Pattons.

The original Patton mansion was burnt down in 1840. Nothing was left but the office in the yard, where in those days our friend the Doctor pursued his medical investigations and entertained his bachelor friends. The judge was a busy man, and much absent. He was always "laying out to build him a new house"; but death "laid him out" while the scheme was still in embryo. The Doctor, who, as only son, became proprietor, had his hands too full, what with negroes, and farming, and physicking, and fox-hunting, to carry it out till the war was upon him, and with its results put an end, as he thought at the time, to everything which makes life sweet.

It must not, however, be supposed that the Doctor and his father had gone houseless or camped out since 1840. Not at all. From the old brick office whose isolation had saved it from that memorable conflagration, there had grown—I use the word, advisedly, as applicable to Virginia architecture—there had grown a rambling structure, whose design, rather than whose actual weight of years, gave it an appearance venerable enough to command the respect and admiration of summer tourists from New York and Philadelphia. It was not often such apparitions passed that way, but when they did, they would almost always pull up at the Doctor's front gate and gaze through it with that admiration and respect that Northerners are inclined to pay to anything in their own country that recalls the past.

"Oh, isn't that too quaint for anything!" the ladies that sometimes accompanied them never failed to remark. "That's a real old ramshackle Virginia house, by thunder! and a pretty heavy old fossil inside it, you bet!" said the more observant of the gentlemen.

The Doctor would have gloried in such criticism had he heard it. He hated Yankees; he hated your new-fangled houses; he hated railroads; he hated towns; he hated breech-loading guns: sights and sounds and things that he was not familiar with at five-and-twenty, he would have none of when he was between sixty and seventy.

The Doctor's house was unconventional to be sure, while weather and neglect of paint or whitewash had given it an air of antiquity to which it had no real claim. It lay a hundred yards back from the road, and appeared to consist of four or five small houses of varying dimensions, and occupying relationships towards one another of a most uncertain kind. Two of these leaned heavily together, like convivial old gentlemen "seeing one another home." The rest lay at respectful distances from each other, connected only by open verandas, through which the summer breeze blew freshly, and lovingly fanned the annuals that spread and twined themselves along the eaves. Almost every style of Virginia rural architecture found place in this homely conglomeration of edifices which even "old man Jake," the negro, who has for twenty years looked after the Doctor's horses and stolen his corn, used to describe as "mighty shacklin', and lookin' like as if they'd bin throwed down all in a muss."

It was, however, a real old characteristic Virginia house of its kind. There were squared chestnut-logs, black with rain and sun, against which the venetian shutters of the windows banged and thumped in gusty spring days as against walls of adamant. These same logs were got out of the woods and squared, the Doctor would tell you, in days "when men had plenty of time and plenty of 'force' (*i.e.*, slaves) to do those things properly." Then there were walls of pine weather-boarding, erected at a period when, the same authority would have informed you, "folks began to saw and season their lumber five or ten years before they started to build." There were roofs of wooden shingles slanting and sloping in every direction—black, rotting, and moss-grown here, white and garish there, where penetrating rains had forced the slow and reluctant hand of repair. Dormer-windows squinted at you from above, patched as to their shattered panes with local newspapers of remote date, and speaking of stuffy attics behind, where hornets, yellow-jackets, and "mud-daubers" careered about in summer-time over the apple-strewn floors. Then there was the old brick office before mentioned —relic of a distant past: of a period when the Virginia planters, though surrounded by the finest clay, were so absorbed in tobacco that they sent to England for their bricks. It is probable, however, that these particular bricks were produced upon the spot. At any rate, their comparative antiquity and presumably mellow tone have been ruthlessly effaced, for this is the only part of the Doctor's mansion that he has selected for a coat of whitewash. It is used for professional purposes, and is known by the Doctor's patients as the "sujjery." I know it is hopeless to try, by a bald description of timber and bricks and mortar, to give any idea of how the Doctor's rambling homestead appealed to the sense of the picturesque, and to the affections of those of us who were familiar with it and with its inmate. Nor should the surroundings be forgotten. The stately oaks that towered high above the quaint low buildings, and covered with leaves and *débris* the greater portion of that domestic enclosure which in those parts was known as the yard. The straggling branching acacias that grew close to the house, and spread their tall arms above the roof, littering it in autumn with showers of small curly leaves, and choking the wooden gutters (for the Doctor considered tin piping as a modern heresy) with fragmentary twigs. The fresh green turf that had matted and spread for 150 years around this house and the more imposing one that preceded it. The aged boxtrees that had once, no doubt, in prim Dutch rows lined some well-tended gravel-path, but now cropped up here and there upon the turf, like beings that had outlived their time and generation. The clustering honeysuckles, bending their old and rickety frames to the ground. The silver aspens before the door, whose light leaves shivered above your head in the most breathless August days. The slender mimosa, through whose beautiful and fragile greenery the first humming-birds of early June shyly fluttered ; and the long row of straw hives against the rickety fence, where hereditary swarms of bees—let well alone—made more honey than the Doctor and all his neighbours could consume.

The Doctor's front gate too! How well I remember it! And the short avenue of stunted cedars leading across the turf to where the front porch of the old house once stood. I speak thus feelingly of the gate because it was such a real old Virginia arrangement, and in fruitless endeavours to open it I and my horse have so often had to jump—for our skins, if not our lives, as it suddenly collapsed and fell forward with a prodigious crash on to the high road. The Doctor's gate had no doubt commenced life with two hinges and a latch. Most of the time I knew it, however, it was poised upon a single hinge, and that the lower one, and was kept upright by two ponderous twelve foot fence rails being leaned up against it. To look at that awful barrier you would have supposed that the Doctor was the most inhospitable instead of the most sociable of men. To achieve a passage through that gate with dignity and safety required assistance. Most of the Doctor's friends—nobody walked, it must be remembered, in Virginia—used to hang about outside and shout till some of the hands came and removed the obstacle. You couldn't have left your horse outside and walked across the lawn, for the "guard dog" was a fearsome feature of Virginia rural life, and of the Doctor's premises a whole pack of hounds, if they were at home, regarded themselves as the responsible custodians. All the years I knew the Doctor he was going to fix that gate—and I believe he woke up every morning with the fullest intention of doing so. But he never did it. One or two of his intimate friends used to pull the snake fence down on one side and ride through as a protest, declaring it was a much easier matter than opening the gate. But it was no good. Of course the Doctor's attitude towards his gate was merely an exaggerated form of the attitude taken up by many of his neighbours towards dilapidations in general ; just as his reactionary tendencies were those of most of his contemporaries only emphasized with undue vigour.

It must not be supposed that the Doctor's establishment, though strongly typical in a sense, resembled to any extent the real old Virginia mansion. The Pattons, it will be remembered, had been burnt out, and the present pile had been originally intended only as a makeshift ; but it was such a makeshift as would perhaps be seen nowhere out of Virginia. Of the more substantial family mansions there were several crowning the hills in the Doctor's neighbourhood. Square blocks of brick, some many-windowed and green-shuttered, with heavy porticoes supported by rows of white fluted pillars stretching along their face. Great wooden barns others, with acres of roof and rows of dormer-windows, and crazy crumbling porches, and stacks of red-brick chimneys clambering up outside the white walls at the gable-ends, or anywhere else where they come handy for that matter.

There were plenty of these within range of the Doctor's house and the limits of his practice, and to the proprietor of almost every one the Doctor was related. The stages of this relationship varied from the unquestioned affinity of cousins and nephews, to that which is described in Virginia by the comprehensive and far-reaching appellative of "kin." To be kin of the Pattons, moreover, was in itself a desirable thing in Virginian eyes. Though the Doctor lived in such an unpretentious residence, and worked day in and day out as a country practitioner, there were people in the neighbourhood holding their heads pretty high, who were always pleased to remember that their father's first cousin had married the old Judge's brother.

With all the Doctor's quaint ideas and strong prejudices, I have said that he was a thorough gentleman. He was of the kind meant for use, and not for show. Good heavens! what would your dashing British Æsculapius, in his brougham or well-appointed dogcart, have said to my old friend's appearance when setting out for a long winter day's work? I can see him now, riding in at the gate on some wild January day, bringing hope in his kindly face, and good conservative time-honoured drugs in his well-worn saddle-bags. A woollen scarf is drawn round his head and on the top of it is crammed an old slouch hat. A long black cloak, fastened round his throat with a clasp, and lined with red flannel, falls over the saddle behind. His legs, good soul, are thickly encased in coils of wheat-straw, wound tightly round them from his ankles upwards, a special patent of his own. In his hand, by way of a whip, he carries a bushy switch plucked from the nearest tree, and upon one heel the survivor of a pair of spurs that would have scarified a rhinoceros had they been sharp.

The Doctor had been a widower since the first year of the war. After a fashion not uncommon, he had buried his wife in the orchard. A simple marble shaft in that homely quarter spoke of her virtues and her worth to the colts and calves that bit the sweet May grass around her tomb, and to the encroaching swine that crunched the rotting apples as they fell in autumn from the untended trees. The Doctor had had two sons but both had fallen in the war. Who he would "'ar [heir, as a verb] his place to" was a common subject of discussion among the negroes on the property. His profession, no doubt, was his first care; but his heart was with his farms and his foxhounds. The Doctor had practised over, or, as we used to say there, "ridden" the south side of the county for nearly forty years. He had studied medicine with the intention only of saving the doctor's bill in his father's household of eighty negroes. He had soon, however, dropped into a regular practice, and for the last five-and-twenty years, at any rate, no birth or death within a radius of ten miles would have been considered a well-conducted one without his good offices. The Doctor's income, upon the well-thumbed scroll of hieroglyphics that he called his books, was nearly three thousand dollars a-year. He collected probably about fifteen hundred. A considerable portion, too, of this fifteen hundred was received in kind payments, not conveniently convertible, such as bacon, Indian corn, hams, wheat-flour, woollen yarns, sucking-pigs, home-made brooms, eggs, butter, bricks, sweet-potato slips, sawn plank, tobacco-plants, shingles, chickens, baskets, sausage-meat, sole-leather, young fruit-trees, raw hides, hoe-handles, old iron. To utilise these various commodities, it would have been necessary for the Doctor to have had a farm, even supposing he had not already been the fortunate proprietor of two. Indeed, a farm to a Southern country doctor is not only necessary as a receptacle for the agricultural curiosities that are forced upon him in lieu of payment, but for the actual labour of those many dusky patients who can give no other return for physic and attendance received. You could see a bevy of these Ethiopians almost any day upon the Doctor's farm, wandering aimlessly about with hoes or brier-blades, chattering and cackling and putting in a happy and a pleasant day.

The Doctor might have been called a successful physician. He had no rivals. There were two inferior performers in the district, it is true, who were by way of following the healing art—small farmers, who were reported to have studied medicine in their youth. One of these, however, had not credit sufficient to purchase drugs, and the other was generally drunk. So it was only their near relations, when not dangerously indisposed, who patronised them—or some patient of the Doctor's now and again, perhaps, who took a fancy the latter was too "aristocratic," till he got badly sick, and returned with alacrity to his allegiance. There is no doubt, I fear, but that the Doctor practised on the lines of thirty years ago. Tory to the backbone in every other department of life, it was hardly to be expected that he should have panted for light and leading in that branch of learning in which he had no rival within reach. Papers or magazines connected with the healing science I never remember to have seen inside the Patton homestead; and yet, after a great deal of experience of the good old man's professional care, I have a sort of feeling that I would as soon place my life in his hands as in the hands of Sir Omicron Pie!

What time the Doctor had to spare from physicking, I have said he devoted to farming and to fox-hunting. I should like to follow him for a bit on his long professional rounds, and listen to his cheery talk in homestead and cabin; to help him fill his long pipe, which he draws out of his top-boot when the patient has settled down to sleep or quiet; to hear him once again chat about tobacco and wheat, politics and foxes. I should like, too, to say something of the Doctor's farming—heaven save the mark!—on his two properties; the one " 'ard " him by his father and the other one, the quarter place near by, that " cum to him with his wife, ole Cunnel Pendleton's daughter."

I must only pause to remark, however, that the Doctor farmed, as he did everything else, in the good old Virginia fashion—or in what is now irreverently known as the "rip an tar [tear] principle." He didn't care anything about acres or estimates; and as for farm books, his professional accounts pestered him quite enough. Of rotations, he neither knew nor wanted to know anything. His chief aim was to plough and sow as much land as he could scuffle over with all the labour he could scrape together. Of manuring, clovering, or fertilising he took little account. If only he "pitched" a big crop, he was a proud and happy man. When each recurring harvest brought results more insignificant than the last, a temporary disgust with the whole business used to seize on the old gentleman, and he would swear that the wheat crops had been of no account since the war; that tobacco had gone to the devil, and that he'd quit fooling with a plantation for good and all. In the eyes of those who knew him, however, such tirades meant absolutely nothing. A Virginian of his sort could no more have helped farming than he could have altered any other of the immutable laws of nature. A younger generation, and many indeed of the older one, have learned wisdom and prudence in the management of land since the abolition of slavery. The Doctor, however, and the few left like him, were bound to be land-killers of the genial good old sort till they were laid under the once generous sod they had so ruthlessly treated.

The Doctor's first care was of necessity his patients: but there is no doubt, I think, that his real affections were divided between his farms and his fox-hounds. That he did his duty by the former was amply testified to by the popularity he enjoyed. That he signally failed in the treatment of his lands was quite as evident. For while he healed the sores and the wounds of his patients, the sores, the wounds, the storm-rent gullies, the bare galls in his hillsides, grew worse and worse. The maize-stalks grew thinner, the tobacco lighter, the wheat-yield poorer, year by year. One has heard of famous painters, who perversely fancied themselves rather as musicians—of established authors, who yearned rather to be praised as artists. So the Doctor, who certainly had no local rival in his own profession, seemed to covet fame rather as the champion and exponent of a happily departing school of Southern agriculturists. In this case, the income derived from the profession just sufficed to make good the losses on the farm. So, though the Doctor, in spite of his household expenses being trifling, could rarely lay his hand on a five-dollar bill, he managed to keep, upon the whole, pretty free from debt. With a scattered practice, and an agricultural hobby extending over a thousand acres, including woods and old fields "turned out" to recover, it may be a matter of surprise that our old friend had leisure for a third indulgence, especially one like fox-hunting, which is connected in the British mind with such a large consumption of time. Nevertheless, the Doctor, like most of his compeers, was passionately fond of the chase, and, in spite of the war and altered times, had kept hounds round him almost without a break since he was a boy. It will be seen, however, that fox-hunting, as understood and followed by the Doctor, was by no means incompatible with his more serious avocations.

Now, if the fashion in which the Doctor pursued the wily fox was not orthodox from a Leicestershire point of view, it was for all that none the less, perhaps, indeed, so much the more genuine. Fox-hunting, for two centuries, has been the natural pastime of the Virginia gentry; but they imported the chase of the fox and the customs pertaining to it from the mother country at a period when such things were conducted in a very different style from what they now are.

The hunting of the fox, as carried on in England early in the last century let us say, offered, I take it, a very different spectacle from that seen in the elaborate and gorgeous cavalcades and the rushing fleet-footed hounds that race to-day over the trim well-drained turf of the shires. No foxes were killed in those days in forty minutes, I'll warrant. Men started their fox at daybreak, and pottered along, absorbed in the performance of their slow hounds, over the rushy, soppy, heathy country, from wood to wood, for hours and hours. They were lucky then, no doubt, if Reynard succumbed in time to admit of their punctual appearance at that tremendous three-o'clock orgie, which the poet Thomson has so graphically laid before us.

In England nowadays, except among a chosen few who understand and enjoy the science of hunting, horsemanship is the alpha and omega of the chase. With a large majority the latter is but a modified form of steeplechasing when indeed it is not pursued from motives wholly alien to a real love for either horse or hound. With the Virginian, who was simply a survival of other days, it was nothing of the kind. The Doctor knew nothing of bullfinches or of post and rails or five-barred gates, in a sporting sense; but what he did not know about a fox was not worth knowing at all. As for his hounds, he could tell the note of each at a distance when the music of the whole pack was scarcely audible to the ordinary ear.

As far as I remember, the Doctor generally used to keep about five couple of hounds. It is needless to say he always swore they were the "best stock of fox-dogs in the State." Jim Pendleton, his cousin across the hill, and Judge Massey, on the north side of the country, who also kept hounds, were quite prepared to take an affidavit of the same kind with regard to their own respective packs. The Doctor's hounds lived as members of the family. A kind of effort was spasmodically made to keep them from appropriating the parlour, and so long as the weather was mild, they were fairly content to lie in the front porch, or in one of the many passages which let the air circulate freely through the Patton homestead.

If the weather was cold, however, and the Doctor had a fire in the parlour, the older and more knowing dogs seldom failed to eventually gain a lodgment. By persistently coming in at one door, and when kicked out by the long-suffering M.F.H., going round the house and slyly entering at the other, they invariably conquered in the long-run, and established themselves on the warm bricks of the hearth before the great white-oak logs which blazed on the bright brass andirons.

Of course it was not often that the Doctor and his hounds were all at home together on a winter's day. If the latter were not hunting with him, they were out upon their own account—for, be it noted, they were absolutely their own masters, as is the way with Virginia fox-hounds. If the Doctor chose to accompany them and do a great deal of tooting and some holloaing, I have no doubt a certain amount of satisfaction animated the breasts of the pack. But it made no difference whatever to the sporting arrangements they had planned among themselves, or to their general programme. Whatever happened, they were bound to have their hunt. As the Doctor's pride and joy was not in his own performances in the saddle—for he never attempted any—but in the achievements of his dogs, this want of discipline and respect was no drawback whatever to his satisfaction.

The Doctor, I have remarked, could combine his favourite sport with the exercise of his profession. That is to say, if he were going out in any likely direction, he would manage to keep his hounds around him till he had dispatched his lamp-light breakfast, and they would all start together. The pack, moreover, was easily increased, for the Master had only to step round to the back porch, which looked across the valley to Cousin Jim Pendleton's place, and to blow lustily on his tremendous cow-horn.

A very little of this music was sufficient to bring the greater part of the rival pack scrambling in a half-guilty way over the garden-fence. After a little growling and snarling and snapping, the strangers would settle down among the Doctor's hounds as if they had been raised on the place.

See the Doctor attired for the chase emerging with his hounds from that awful front gate of his, which is being held up and open by the combined efforts of two stalwart negroes. It is a mild and soft February morning, at about the hour when the sun would be

seen mounting over the leafless woodlands to the
east of the house, if it were not for the dark banks of
clouds chasing one another in continuous succession
from the south-west. The Doctor is not quite such
a scarecrow to-day. The weather is mild, and he
has left the coils of straw behind, having his stout
legs encased in grey homespun overalls. The long
Mexican spur is on his left heel. The black cloak
with the red lining is on his back. The slouch hat
upon his head, and spectacles upon his nose. A
high stand-up collar of antique build and a black
stock give the finishing-touch to a picture whose
"old-timiness," as the Americans say, would have
thrown a New England novelist into convulsions of
ecstasy.

The Doctor this morning is combining business
with pleasure. He has to visit the widow Gubbins
who fell down the corn-house steps the week before
and broke her leg. But he has had word sent him
that there is a red fox in the pine-wood behind the
parsonage, hard by the Gubbins domicile. I need
not say the saddle-bags and the medicine bottles are
there; but besides these, there is the great big
cow-horn which the Doctor carries slung round him,
and blows long blasts upon as he goes titupping,
down the muddy lane. These blasts are rather with
a view of personal solace than from any definite
aims. The Doctor loves the horn for its associations,
and goes toot-tooting down the soft red road, and
waking the echoes of the woods and fields mostly for
his own personal benefit and refreshment. Hector
and Rambler, Fairfax and Dainty, and the rest—little

wiry lean fellows of about two-and twenty inches—hop over the big mud-holes, or creep round the dry fence-corners waiting for the first bit of unfenced woodland to trot over and commence the day's operations.

The Doctor, however, is determined, if possible, to keep them in hand till they reach the haunt of that aforesaid red fox who is said to be lurking in the parson's wood. He hopes to be able to exercise authority sufficient to keep these independent dogs of his from getting on the trail of a ringing, skulking grey fox in the first ivy thicket or open bit of forest they come to. It is no manner of use, however. The rutty, soppy road, soon after it leaves the Doctor's estate, straggles unfenced through half a mile of mazy woodland. Though it is a turnpike of old coaching fame—a road the memory of whose once bustling gaiety well-nigh brings tears to the eyes of the old inhabitants—it is scarcely visible to the rare waggoner or horseman in these degenerate times, on account of the wealth of autumn leaves that hide its rugged face. Into the wood plunge the eager and undisciplined hounds, the dry leaves crackling and rustling under their joyous feet as they scamper and race amid the tall oak and poplar trunks, and one by one disappear beyond the very limited horizon. The Doctor toots and toots till not only the forest but the hills and valleys beyond echo to the appeals of the familiar cow-horn. Mighty little, however, care the dogs for such tooting. They look upon it as a harmless sign of encouragement, a pleasant accompaniment to the preliminaries until the more serious work begins. Nor do they care in the least when the Doctor drops his horn and begins to holloa and shout and storm—not they. He might as well shout and storm at the wind. The Doctor gets very mad. He doesn't swear—Virginians of his class and kind very seldom do—but he uses all the forms of violent exhortation that his conscience admits of, and that belong to the local vernacular. He calls the whole pack "grand scoundrels and villains." In a voice grown husky with exertion, he inquires of their fast-fading forms if they know " what in thunder he feeds them for?" He roars out to little Blazer, the only one left within good speaking distance, that he'll " whale the life out of him ;" whereupon little Blazer disappears after the rest. So he finally confides to the sorrel mare, who is ambling along under him at the regulation five-mile-an-hour gait of the Southern roadster, that those dogs of Cousin Jeems (the Doctor says " Jeems," not because he doesn't know any better, but because it is a good old Virginia way of pronouncing the name) are the hardest-headed lot of fox-dogs south of the Potomac river.

But hark! there is a boom from the pine-wood, the deep green of whose fringe can be seen far away through the naked stems and leafless branches of the oaks. The Doctor pulls up; he "concludes he'll wait a while and see what it amounts to, anyway. The scoundrels are probably fooling after a rabbit, or, at the best, struck the tail of a grey fox" (the most common native breed, that won't face the open or run straight). The Doctor draws rein at the edge of the wood where the straggling forest road once more becomes a highway, fenced in from fields of young wheat, pasture, and red fallow. He thinks the Widow Gubbins can wait a bit, and that old red fox at the parson's can lie over for another day.

"That's old Powhatan, cert'n and sure; and that's a fox of some sort, I'll sw'ar," remarks our old friend to the sorrel mare, who pricks up her ears as another deep note comes echoing from the valley below.

It is late in February; and though February in Virginia is practically the same dead, colourless, leafless, budless, harsh winter month it is with us, yet there are sometimes days before it closes that seem to breathe of a yet distant spring with more witching treachery than the greatest effort that period can make in our more methodical clime. And this is one of them. The soft and balmy air is laden, it is true, with no scent of blossoms or opening buds. The odour of smouldering heaps of burning brush and weeds, or of tardily burnt tobacco plant beds, is all that as yet scents the breeze. But after a month of frost and rain and snow and clouds, the breath is the breath of spring, and the glow of the sun, now bursting through the clouds, seems no longer the sickly glare of winter. The soft Virginia landscape, swelling in gentle waves of forest, field, and fallow to the great mountains that lie piled up far away against the western sky, is naked still and bare, save for the splashes of green pine-woods here and there upon the land. But there is a light in the sky and a feel in the air that seems almost to chide the earth for its slow response. The blood courses quicker through the veins of even easy-going Virginia farmers at the thoughts of seeding-time. The negro's head comes up from under his shoulders and his hands from his pockets, where they have each respectively spent most of the winter, and the air becomes laden with those peculiar dirges that mark the Ethiopian's contentment of mind at the prospect of warm weather and of his limbs once more becoming "souple." The soft breeze begins to coat the tops of the damp furrows with a thin powdery crust that in a few days' time will be converted into that March dust so universally beloved of farmers. The young wheat, smitten and scorched and beaten almost out of recognition, lifts its head once again and spreads a carpet of tender green to the sun. The early lambs, beginning to think that after all they were not sent into the world to shiver behind straw stacks, frisk and gambol in the fields. The blacksmiths' shops at the cross roads and the Courthouse villages are thronged with coloured labourers and tenants, whose masters, now seeding-time is upon them, have suddenly remembered that every plough in the place is out of fix, and not a harrow has its full complement of teeth. The light breeze from the south-west moans softly in the pines; but among the deciduous trees not a withered shred of foliage is left for it to stir, and the silence is complete. The freshly awakened sunlight streams softly down between the leafless branches and the rugged trunks of oak and chestnut, hickory and poplar, and plays upon the golden carpet of wasted leaves that hides the earth beneath them.

The Doctor, as he stands at the edge of the forest, would ordinarily upon such a day be deep in agricultural reveries of a most sanguine nature. But he is now waiting for one more note of evidence that there is a prospect of what he would call "a chase"—hesitating as to the Widow Gubbins.

Suddenly there is a great commotion in the wooded valley beneath, and in a few seconds you might be in a Leicestershire spinny, so busy and joyful are the little pack with their tongues. "That's a fox, any way," says the Doctor to the sorrel mare; "and, likely as not, a red." Two small farmers, jogging down the road, pull up their horses and yell with the peculiar shrill scream that is traditionally as much a part of Virginia fox-hunting as the familiar cries of the British hunting-field are with us. The Doctor, though his voice is not what it was thirty years ago, catches the infection, and, standing up in his wooden leather-capped stirrups hallooes at his hounds in what he would call "real old Virginia fashion."

"By G—d! it's a red," says one of the small farmers, who has perched himself on the top of the fence, so as to look down over the sloping tree-tops on to the opposite hill.

"The dogs are out of the wood, and are streakin' it up the broom-sedge field yonder—dawg my skin if they ain't!"

This is too much for the Doctor.

"Pull down the fence, gentlemen, for God's sake! and we'll push on up to the old Mathew's graveyard on top of the hill. We shall see right smart of the chase from there. I know that old fox; he'll go straight to the pines on Squire Harrison's quarter place."

F

The four or five top rails are tossed off the snake fence; but the Doctor can't wait for the remaining six. The long spur is applied to the flank of the sorrel mare, the apple switch to her shoulder. Amid a crashing and scattering of rotten chestnut-rails, the Doctor, cloak and spectacles, saddle-bags, pills, medicine-bottles, and overalls, lands safely in the corn-stalk field upon the other side. The two farmers follow through the fearful breach he has made, and they may soon all be heard upon the opposite hill cheering and yelling to the hounds, which by this time are well out of reach of such encouraging sounds. Neither the country, nor the horse, nor the Doctor, are adapted for riding to hounds; nor, as I have before intimated, has the latter any idea of doing so. The good man wants to hear as much as possible—to see as much as possible—of the chase; but when he neither sees nor hears a great deal—which, when a strong red fox goes straight away, is generally the case—he will still take much delight in collecting the details from other sources.

If his hounds eventually kill their fox half-way across the country, friends and neighbours, who became accidental witnesses of various stages of the chase, and each of whom did their share of hallooing and cheering, will send round word to the "old Doctor," or "call by" the next time they pass his house, and cheer his heart with praises of his dogs. The Doctor will probably have bandaged Mrs. Gubbins's leg, and be half-way home by the time the death-scene takes place, in some laurel thicket, miles and miles away from the corner where we left our friend bursting through the fence. Not more than half-a-dozen, probably, of the fourteen or fifteen hounds with which the Doctor started, will assist at the finish. Two or three of the puppies will have dropped out early in the day, and come home hunting rabbits all the way. Three or four more are perhaps just over distemper, and will fall in their tracks, to come limping and crawling home at noon. Rambler and Fairfax, however, having assisted at the finish, and being perhaps the most knowing old dogs of the lot, will have trotted round to old Colonel Peyton's close by. They are mighty hungry—for Virginia hounds won't touch foxes' flesh—and they succeed in slipping into the log-kitchen in the yard, while Melindy the cook is outside collecting chips, and abstracting from the top of the stove an entire ham. The said ham was just prepared for the Colonel's supper; but in foxhunting all is forgiven. So after a little burst of wrath he reckons they are the old Doctor's dogs, shuts them up in the granary, and gives them a cake of corn-bread apiece. The following day is Saturday, and the Colonel's son, home from school for a holiday, thinks it an opportunity for a rabbit-hunt in the pines behind the house not to be missed. So Rambler and Fairfax are introduced to the proposed scene of action in the morning. After condescending to an hour of this amusement, they hold a canine consultation, and start for home, where they finally arrive about sundown, to be made much of by the Doctor, who has already heard of the finish from a negro who was splitting rails close by.

The Doctor's satisfaction is quite as great as if

he had cut down a whole Leicestershire field in the fastest thing of the season. His heart warms towards those under-sized, harsh-coated, slab-sided little friends of his as he stands watching the negro woman breaking up their supper of hot corn-bread with buttermilk as a treat—on the back porch. They have all come in by this time, and scuffle and growl and snap around the board as the food is thrown to them.

The knowing ones take advantage of such an evening as this to assert, with more than usual assurance, their right of entry to the house. The Doctor has had his supper, and hopes that no ominous shout from the darkness will, for this night at any rate, call him to some distant sick-bed. He has drawn up his one-armed rocking-chair to the parlour fire, and by the kerosene lamp is poring over the last oration on free trade by that grand old Virginia gentleman and senator, Mr. Jefferson Randolph Beverly Page. Conscious, as it were, that some extra indulgence is deserved on this night, the dogs begin to crawl in. One by one, beginning with the oldest and wiliest and ending with the timidest puppy, they steal into the room and become grouped in the order of their audacity from the glowing bricks of the hearth outward to the door. Nor to-night has the Doctor kicks or cuffs or anathemas for the very worst of them.

The log fire is crackling in the wide chimney, and the light of the flames flicker over the quaint low-ceilinged room with its whitewashed walls, black wainscoting, and homely decorations; over the antlers on the door, that recall some early exploit of the Doctor's in West Virginia wilds; over the odds and ends of old silver on the sideboard, that have been saved from the wreck of the Patton grandeur; over the big oil-painting of the famous jurist, and the dimmer, smokier visages of less distinguished but remoter ancestors, who believed in the divine right of kings and knew nothing of republics and universal suffrage. Here, however, surrounded by his dogs, we must take leave of the Doctor, or rather I should say of this picture of him, for the good old man himself has been laid this many a year by his wife's side under the orchard turf. Nor do I even know to whom he ar'd his place. But on whoever or whatever this dubious blessing may have fallen, I will undertake to say that he bears very little resemblance to his predecessor, who was the product of a social condition that has for a generation ceased to exist and of a period that is irrevocably dead.

AN OLD VIRGINIA FOXHUNTER

WHILE the Pattons, as I have already indicated, were indelibly associated with Berkeley County and have lived there ever since it was created in Queen Anne's reign, everybody knows that the older and more easterly county of Sassafras has never been without Broomsedges since time was in Virginia. It was a Broomsedge indeed who was county lieutenant of Sassafras during Bacon's rebellion and took the county militia out with him against poor old Governor Berkeley, who, when he got back into power again, hanged so many leading Virginians, including Colonel Broomsedge, that even his master, Charles II., for whose sake he had done it, called him an old fool for his pains.

The present Colonel Broomsedge of Locust Grove, whom I propose introducing to the readers, had also tried his hand at rebellion, as will be shown, and a very much bigger one, but he had come out of it with a whole skin if with a very much reduced estate. It was not, however, as a retired military man I wished to introduce the Colonel, but as a foxhunter of a still more serious and ardent description than the Doctor himself. For the Colonel gave himself up wholly to the sport and made it in fact the business of his life; troubling himself about little else. He was probably the last landowner in Virginia that after the war continued to devote himself so entirely to the Sport of Kings.

Now there have been two schools of foxhunting in America, and these are as widely sundered from each other in origin and method as the Poles. The one is exotic, a modern importation, and greatly flourishing; the other is ancient, comparatively indigenous, and practically extinct. The latter had been from remote times a part of the social life of the older slave States; the former has its habitat in regions more or less contiguous to the great cities of the North, whence it draws its supporters and devotees. The hounds, the huntsmen, the whips are English; the whole turn-out is as faithful a reproduction of Leicestershire or the Blackmore Vale as circumstances will allow. The gentlemen are irreproachably clad by London tailors or by tailors imported from London, and are admirably mounted; and that a goodly proportion of them are bold and accomplished horsemen is universally conceded by adequate judges who have seen them race over the adamantine pastures and stiff timbers of Pennsylvania or New York. Ladies, too, in such gatherings are as much to the fore, both in numbers and even in equestrian skill, as their British sisters; and there are drags and smart traps galore at the meets, and dapper grooms with second horses. Nothing, in short, is wanting—not even, as some ill-natured curmudgeons would, perhaps, like to suggest, the desire and the ability to go.

Upon the rapid and successful development of foxhunting in the Eastern States, American society is upon every account to be congratulated. But my old friend Colonel Broomsedge, of Sassafras County, Virginia, had no sort of congratulations for his fellow-sportsmen at the North—a section he had never visited, and had no desire in the world ever to visit. He used to sniff and snort and almost rage at the pictures of the Genesee or Long Island meets in that most admirable and sport-encouraging journal, *Harper's Weekly*, which we used to take him over—not, I am afraid, without some spice of mischief in the intent. "D—d Yankee contraptions!" "Thunderation tomfoolery!" were the mildest terms the Colonel could find relief in. And he was churchwarden, too, and read the lessons in the Episcopal Church, and was anything but what Uncle Ephraim, his huntsman, called a "swarin' man."

The violence of the Colonel's epithets was due chiefly to political and social hatred, and to have fully understood it a knowledge of the Virginia of twenty years ago would have been necessary. But, putting this aside, if you had been privileged to see the Colonel, as I have so often seen him, jogging out at daylight on a wintry morning with his five or six couple of weedy-looking little hounds, and tooting on his big cow-horn to let the odd members of the pack who lodged about in the neighbourhood know he was on the warpath, you would have understood, I think, why he pitched the *Harper's* about the verandah, and blew such fierce clouds of smoke from his long reed-stemmed clay pipe.

It was soon after the close of the war that I first knew the Colonel. On the strength of his former militia rank he had held a command at the opening of that great struggle. But his ardour, I was always given to understand, exceeded his discretion as a strategist, and his years, which were even then in their sixth decade, furnished the authorities with a good excuse for relegating him to the safer shades of the commissariat department.

At the surrender of Lee, however, he sat himself down in his old home of Locust Grove, and on the 1,500 acres of very indifferent land which surrounded it. And when he did so, the Colonel, like most of his friends, thought that the world, so far as he was concerned, had practically come to an end.

He had owned about a hundred negroes, more or less, and it was they rather than the ancestral acres on which he supported them that constituted his chief wealth. And now they were gone; that is to say, as a moneyed property they were gone. Otherwise, most of them remained as freemen in the same cabins they had inhabited as slaves. It is doubtful whether, when their chains were struck off by Lincoln's proclamation, they or the Colonel were the more bewildered. The latter, as was customary with most of his class in Virginia, had been the most benign of masters. If there had been any tyranny on the plantation at all, it was old Uncle Gabriel, who had been a sort of house steward ever since the old Judge's days, that was the tyrant, and its victim had been the

Colonel. The word "freedom," indeed, as applied to Gabriel, would have been an immense joke; and his master was accustomed to declare that, when he called all the negroes together and told them they were free, the only genuine throb of liberty which was felt in the assemblage was felt beyond a doubt by himself in relation to the long tyranny of Uncle Gabriel.

But the Colonel's joy was premature. Old Gabriel stuck to him, and lectured him, and tyrannised over him, and called him "Marse' Bob," till he died, and had the biggest negro funeral I ever saw, with the Colonel as chief mourner, looking five years younger than he had done at any period since the war.

When, in 1865, the ruined South began life afresh, none of the Colonel's people wanted to leave him. A free nigger, to them, had been a stray nigger without a master—an object of contempt to such as belonged to a family of quality like the Colonel's. Such ideas were very soon modified; but, for a time at any rate, there was little migration. Formerly the Colonel had found them in food, clothes and medical attendance, not to speak of small presents of money from time to time. Now, however, the estate was parcelled out among the various families, and conducted upon what political economists denominate the Metayer system, but what the Colonel's negroes called "wukin' on sheares."

This arrangement suited the Colonel down to the ground. It would furnish, for his time at any rate, the actual necessaries of life. He had no children. His wife, good soul, had had a long innings of both the social pleasures and domestic burdens of the slavery period. For it was upon women of her position that the latter fell most heavily; and, altogether, "the Colonel's lady" was perhaps not sorry to be able in her old age to relinquish them.

During those horrid years of war, when half a million of men were butchering one another on the soil of Virginia, and when even the quiet shades of Locust Grove were startled from time to time by the distant roar of guns or the red light of battle in the sky, there was not much foxhunting, as may be well imagined. The pack, which had been the pride of the Colonel's heart, and the terror of Sassafras County foxes, had sadly decayed: four or five old dogs and a few riotous young ones, to whom fox, rabbit, or coon came equally handy, were all that remained. But by the time I first knew the Colonel he had resuscitated his pack, and had discovered that life, after all, was still worth living. If half of his neighbours had been killed or crippled, and all of them ruined by the war, he found that he, at any rate, could scratch along somehow, and devote himself much as of old to the absorbing pursuit of his life—that of foxes. His wants were few, and the system of agriculture pursued by his Ethiopian tenants didn't fret him in the least; for was he not a Virginian of the good old sort, who could see a hungry field grow hungrier—even to starvation point—under half a dozen successive crops of grain without the faintest twinge of his agricultural conscience?

Moreover, the leaden hail that had wrought such havoc upon men and horses, and indirectly even upon hounds, had created a veritable heyday for foxes, and they had thriven so vigorously in Sassafras County that a sore and bitter cry went up from the newly restocked poultry yards and sheepfolds. So when the Colonel settled down to devote the remainder of his days to the pursuit of Reynard, he had the satisfaction of feeling that he was at the same time a public benefactor of the first importance.

In former days there had been at least half a dozen packs of hounds in Sassafras County. Fox-hunting had, in fact, been the chief sport of the gentry in East Virginia since the early part of the eighteenth century, by which time a squirearchy of English blood, surrounded by well-cleared estates, had taken the place of the once trackless forests. Fox-hounds and even foxes were imported from England to fill the measure of that rural life which, thanks to slavery, had become so rudely comfortable and uneventfully pleasant. The English red fox was imported perhaps a little later, when the indigenous gray species was found to be but a second-rater, clinging to the woodlands, and with all the "ringing" instincts of the hare. The imported varmint throve and multiplied, though never interbreeding with the native, and maintaining to this day those straight-going qualities which have made him at once the delight and the despair of so many generations of Virginia sportsmen, with their slow hounds and rough country. The gray fox, however, which always was, and still is, in a majority, gave very fair sport to men whose whole thoughts are centred in the doings of their hounds, as were the thoughts, no doubt, of English squires who hunted foxes in the days of Walpole and the elder Pitt, and didn't ride, I will dare swear, with anything approaching the impetuosity they are made to do, for instance, in the Christmas numbers of the London weeklies. With these gray foxes also, the Virginian hounds got plenty of blood, and maintained thereby a stout heart in those long all-day runs after the scarcer red fox, which so often failed to end in a kill. But all the more on these latter occasions was the ambition of the Virginian M.F.H. fired to achieve success. And when his wiry little favourites fairly raced an "old red" down after a four or five, or perhaps even a seven or eight hours' "chase" (as he called it), there was no prouder or happier man between the Alleghanies and the Atlantic. He didn't often see very much of these big performances himself, but he plodded along on his slow, soft-conditioned, long-tailed horse over the deep corn fallows and rough broomsedge pastures and open leaf-strewn woodlands, listening with delight and keen knowing ears to the fast fading music. And when his hounds had swept beyond both sight and hearing, he would tit-up along, picking out the line from labourers in the fields or travellers on the roads, who would have often holloa'd themselves hoarse as the hounds passed in sight. He would have felt too, would this primitive sportsman, just as much elated at the fashion in which his hounds were pushing this old fox along, though he was not with them, as if he were a Thruster of the first water showing his heels to a whole Leicestershire field. Washington, for example, when he was at home at Mount Vernon, was a most enthusiastic foxhunter. His diary takes careful note of the days he hunted, which were many, the sport he had, and often the company he hunted with. He took immense pains with his breed of hounds, which were famous in Virginia for long afterwards. And he seems, moreover, to have kept several horses for hunting purposes only. His diary, too, seems to indicate that his lady guests —and his house was generally full—sometimes hunted with the gentlemen, but, as a matter of fact, Southern women, though they could all of necessity ride, took very little interest in sport.

I don't know whether it may not have been to some extent the force of association, but there always seemed to me something entirely delightful about these old-fashioned Virginia homesteads, with all their contempt for comfort and convenience.

The ancestral halls of the Broomsedge family were in excellent keeping with their master, and both were eminently picturesque, perhaps, rather in a social than a purely artistic sense—and in a fashion peculiar to Virginia. The date upon the chimneys was 1769; but Broomsedges were there fifty years before that, at least—in a former house, as the gravestones in the walled burying-ground across the fence would tell us, even if the Colonel had not been sometimes given to making his ancestry the burden of his conversation. The bricks of the present structure, under a climate of comparative extremes, had assumed a really venerable aspect, and the narrow windows with their small panes suggested the fashion of other days. Nor were signs of dilapidation and decay wanting to give the necessary touch of sentiment to the stronghold of a race whose doom, both as individuals and as a class, had been sounded. For no country houses such as this will ever again be built in Virginia for gentlefolk to live in from generation unto generation ; city merchants will erect convenient villas, and farmers will build farmhouses, but even the latter will be what the Colonel called "Yankee contraptions." No present or future architect, for instance, will ever contrive such a porch as that which towered above the front door of the Broomsedge mansion. Its roof was on a level with the lofty eaves of the house, and the tall columns which supported it supported also two landings, an upper and a lower. The upper landing opening from the bedrooms was convenient for the airing of mattresses. Upon the lower one before the front door, when the heat was too great for his favourite tree, or when it was raining, sat the Colonel, with two or three of his most favoured hounds at his feet.

From the back of the house innumerable outbuildings of various dates and in all stages of disrepair staggered away in quaint procession towards the huge barns and stables, and on either side a row of negro cabins told a significant tale of other days. Much cherished oaks of giant stature threw their limbs heavenward, and buried in grateful shade the whole easy-going colony beneath them. In front of the house upon the lawn, however, there were only ornamental trees—maples, mulberries, silver aspens, and mimosas—and these the Colonel had taken good care should not obstruct his view of the high road, which was barely fifty yards away. For the old gentleman had a passion for conversation even above the passion of the average Virginian, which is saying much indeed. And as he sat upon the porch or with his chair tilted back against his favourite mulberry-tree, he kept his eye fastened on the road. And the traveller who was shouted to by the Colonel to "lite and sit awhile" and could resist that tone of hospitable command, must have been an individual wholly unsuited to dwell upon Virginian soil—some despicable pettifogger who carried a watch about and grudged an hour or two for genial interchange of views on politics, or farming, or the war, much less for a homily on foxhunting. For the Colonel could talk well on anything from the British Constitution, of which he was an ardent admirer, to local agriculture, in which you might have supposed he was a shining light if you had heard him hold forth on curing tobacco or fallowing for wheat, and did not at the same time know his habits, or I may add his farms.

But it is the Colonel as a man of action, the Colonel in the winter season, and above all upon hunting mornings, that I should like to be allowed to recall. These hunting days of his, I need hardly say, were nothing in the shape of fixtures. No local papers advertised his meets, no sporting correspondents chronicled his doings. No rendezvous or prearrangement was of any use, for no neighbours ever any longer joined him as they had often done before the war—in the brave days of old—bringing their dogs to run against his, and dining together afterwards, and talking politics and foxhunting and wheat and tobacco till all was blue. The Colonel hunted now for himself alone, and by himself and just when he felt inclined, which was about three days a week, perhaps, when the weather was propitious.

Sometimes, too, he hunted, as it were, under compulsion—that is to say, he might have himself made other plans, but his hounds would occasionally break out upon their own account, and he had of course to go with them. For only some of his small pack were regularly kennelled, and that often in some empty tobacco barn, beneath whose logs with a little industry they could generally scratch their way out. The rest lay around loose, and spent their days upon the porch, or under it, or in the dining-room till they were kicked out. And in the nights if the weather were cold or rainy they not infrequently crawled through convenient draught holes in the wall, and found snug domicile in the gloomy caverns that intervened between the floors of the house and its foundations. It was by no means unusual while seated at supper round the Colonel's hospitable board to be conscious of fearsome sounds beneath your feet, which seemed to come from the very bowels of the earth, but as a matter of fact were nothing more than a portion of the Colonel's pack contending for bone or bed.

But not all the terror of the Colonel's boot or Uncle Ephraim's lash could deter them from taking now and again, as I have hinted, a day's hunting on their own account. Indeed, on more than one occasion when staying with this fine old sportsman, I have been waked in the dark of a winter morning by the sound of heavy blows upon the Colonel's door, and old Uncle Ephraim shouting at him somewhat after this fashion:

"Marse' Robert! Aw, Marse' Robert!"

"What's the matter?"

"Dem ar dawgs is off agin, I hearn 'em runnin' fur all they's wurth at the upper een of old man Daniel's cornfield."

Then there would be the sound as of a heavy body falling, and the old house would shake almost to its foundations as the Colonel rolled his 200 lbs. avoirdupois out of bed, and roared out of the window for his horse and down the stairs for his morning "julep."

In ten minutes he would be on his horse, thoughts of vengeance and chastisement having alone consumed him while hustling on his clothes. But by the time the old gentleman has got clear of the yard, and cantered out past the stables and barns, tobacco houses and negro cabins, he can hear the hounds still running, and thinking that an illicit hunt is better than none at all, he begins to blow loud blasts on his big cow-horn, relieving himself of his anger thereby, and fetching out from various shelters far and near those of the pack that had not played truant.

But these after all were but occasional irregularities. The Colonel upon most hunting days sallied forth with dignity and in order—a good breakfast in addition to his early "julep" beneath his generous breadth of waistcoat, and his pack, small, wiry, wizened little fellows of two or three and twenty inches perhaps, following demurely at his heels as if they had never done such a thing in their lives as take "bye days" upon their own account. The Colonel knew nothing of eleven o'clock meets, except from those accounts in the New York papers which, as I have hinted, brought him within measurable distance of apoplexy. His rule in winter was to throw off (though he didn't use that term) before sunrise, and his horn sounded along the country roads as often as not before the first streak of day had broken. Old man Ephraim still sometimes went with his master, mounted on a plough mule all rubbed and chafed by collar and trace chains, and the two might have been heard as they splashed along the muddy road talking somewhat after this fashion.

"I reckon we'll see if we can't scare up that old red that beat us last week from the Doctor's pine wood."

"Thar's two or three grey, Cunnel, 'twixt here an dar in dem ivy thickets, an if de dawgs strike ther trail they's gone fur sho, and thar ain't no fence to de road neither."

"That's so, Ephraim; we'd better get out here and cross old man Caleb's wheat, and down over the Doctor's cornfield."

And as old Ephraim rolls off his mule to let down the slip bars for the Colonel and his hounds to go through, it would have been light enough to enable us to make a note or two upon the former's appearance, which, to put the matter mildly, is unconventional to a degree. There is not much Melton Mowbray about the Colonel, that's quite certain. From his slouch hat to his wooden stirrups, from his gray homespun coat to his rusty boots, there is nothing that would not absolutely outrage every tradition of a sportsman's "turn-out." A pair of high old-fashioned stick-up collars fastened at the back with string indicate in a measure the depths of Conservatism that lurk within the breast of their wearer, while with his honest rosy face and white moustache and snowy bushy hair (which his wife cuts twice a year) he looks the thorough good fellow he is and the well-bred gentleman withal, in spite of his astonishing rusticity of attire. As if too he flouted almost by design every conventional decency—though as a matter of fact he really knows nothing about such things—the Colonel carries the sprout off an apple tree for a whip, and wears a spur upon one foot only, and that too a weapon of antique design, which, moreover, cannot possibly have been cleaned since the war. But the Colonel wouldn't care a blankety blank what anybody thought of his appearance, and would wonder what in creation his clothes had to do with hounds or foxes. Even John Peel, though his methods were probably not unlike the Colonel's and the hours he kept were very similar as we know, would have been shocked, I think, at the Old Virginian's attire. But the latter, as I have said, would upon his part entirely fail to comprehend the point of view.

When the Colonel and Ephraim reach the Doctor's pines there is very little ceremony in the way the eager hounds anticipate their movements and throw themselves into the ten acres of green woodland through which a stream fringed with now naked alders winds its way. The two old sportsmen, the Anglo-Saxon and the African, master and ex-slave, united by their lifelong passion for the chase, take up their stand outside and wait for that music which to each of them is the sweetest sound in life.

There have been whimpers already from the covert, but the old Colonel knows the language of his hounds as the parent does of his children, and which of them it is talking and what it amounts to, whether it is Trumpeter "foolin' after an ole har," or Beauregard "triflin' on a possum trail," or Rattler with confident and trustworthy note proclaiming the presence of nobler game. And sure enough on this occasion, too, it is this celebrated hound who wakes the Colonel and Uncle Ephraim from their reverie, and in a few moments the whole pack have answered to his well-known summons.

There is then great music for a space, and it grows greater, and the two old men outside the wood listen to it in silent rapture.

"Cunnel," says Ephraim as the situation intensifies, "that ar ole red'll hev to quit, I reckon." And even as he speaks a big red fox breaks covert not a hundred yards from the corner they are standing at, and faces the open with an air of confidence in himself and contempt for the Colonel's already defeated endeavours that warms up that old warrior mightily.

"That's the gentleman that beat us, Ephraim; that's him! I'll swear I know every hair on his durned hide."

Then indeed is the time to see this veteran pair, perhaps at their very best, and hear a notable duet. Old man Ephraim is standing in his stirrups—one of them, by the way, hung on with a rope—and at the very top of his power and lungs is giving the shrill

Virginia hunting cry that there does sole duty for each stage of the chase, with his hat in his hand and his bald black wrinkled head fringed with a circlet of short silvery hair, and his mouth wide open and his withered frame shaking with excitement. The Colonel at his side has got to work on his big cow-horn, and with cheeks puffed out and the colour of a ripe tomato is filling earth, air, and sky with its strenuous blasts.

Out come the hounds on the line one after the other and in straggling fashion, but none the less keen and always full of music. It is nothing from their pace that the sturdy fox who has just disappeared over the top of the wheat field has to fear, but they may wear him out, and run into him at midday or even in the afternoon, for the tenacity and hardiness and scenting powers of the Colonel's hounds are remarkable if they have little speed. Old Ephraim, whose powers of sporting narrative have been the delight of two generations of loafers at the village post-office, whence he fetches the Colonel's letters daily, has some most fearsome stories of long runs in the days of old. That celebrated hunt which took place in Christmas week 1831, when "the Jedge, Marse' Roberts' pa, kep' de hounds," is known to every one in Sassafras County. We were never tired of making Uncle Ephraim tell that story, for the old man had come to believe in it himself most firmly for the last half-century or so; and I think, upon the whole, it was the most magnificent lie I ever heard recited in cold blood and in detail, and by a member of a church too. "Yes, suh, fo' Gawd I's tellin' you de solemn troof. Dem ar dawgs run dat ar ole fox fur two days an' two nights clar through. . . . It wur de day befo' Christmas, dey struck dat ar fox's trail, and when de Jedge quit off hunt'n at sundown he done tell me ter foller dem hounds and see whar they's gwine ter. Well, suh, I follerd 'em all dat night. I follerd 'em all Christmas Day and all dat night too, and when I caught up wid 'em jes as sho' as yo' born, suh, it wur over in Hanover County about'n hour after sun-up, and fo' de Lawd de fox was *walkin'*, and de hounds was *walkin'*, dey was all *walkin'*, widin a few yards of one nur'r."

How this old sinner gathered up the emaciated voiceless hounds and the exhausted fox and put them all in a two-horse waggon and drove them home, I always suspected was a comparatively recent addition. But Ephraim invariably recited the legend with his hat in his hand, as if baring his head for the vengeance of heaven to descend upon it—as, indeed, he frequently invited it to do—should he deviate one hair's-breadth from the " solemn troof."

From what has been said in an earlier part of this paper it will be readily understood that there was no eager shortening of stirrup leathers or cramming on of hats with the Colonel and Uncle Ephraim as the hounds went away. At the same time the red dirt flew for a brief space from the Doctor's wheat field in a fashion that testified to the ardour with which these veterans, lying back in their saddles with their legs thrown in Southern manner straight forward, sent the long-tailed half-bred and the plough mule up the sticky slope. It is only, however, a spasmodic burst of excitement. There is a snake fence on the ridge, and as Ephraim rolls off the mule to throw down a panel he finds breath for two or three more holloas.

"Praise de Lord, Cunnel, I kin holler good on a fox chase yit, tho' you is got me down as mighty nigh eighty on de book."[1]

But the Colonel only waits for the three top rails to be pitched off, and then there is a fearful earthquake and scattering of chestnut timbers, as with apple switch and solitary spur he lifts the cob at the remaining five, and, striking them about halfway up, carries the whole panel away with him into the next field.

Space forbids us to follow our old friend as he potters along far in the wake for the present, at any rate, of his hounds. I think, however, from what I have said of the Colonel it will be readily understood, by most readers of the *Badminton* at any rate, that this astute old gentleman, steeped to the lips in the ways of hounds and foxes, will be very apt to see something more of the fun before it is all over. And even should he not do so, and his dogs after all kill their fox on some remote plantation miles away, he will be just as pleased as if he had ridden at their heels to the finish. Indeed, from the Colonel's obsolete point of view, due to habit and circumstances, there is no very clear connection in his mind between foxhunting and horsemanship. I wish, too, we were able once again to follow him home and sit with him for a bit in the old wainscoted dining-room, beneath the stolid portraits of bygone Broomsedges in wigs and ruffles,

---

[1] The old register in which the birth, deaths, ages, &c., of slaves were entered.

and listen to his cheery yarns of hounds and foxes and politics and war, when the long reed pipe is lit and the oak logs are roaring on the big brick hearth.

But this, alas! is, after all, but a retrospect. The Colonel's cow-horn has long ceased to rouse the echoes of the Virginian woodlands. It is five years or more since I stood by his grave, even then not entirely a new-made one. And as I stood there in the old graveyard to the west of the house, amid a scene of ruin and decay, I felt how immense was the gulf between the past and the future in the South, and what a fine race were these Old Virginia squires; and I thought then, as I have often thought before and since, how really lamentable it is they found no contemporary chronicler of fame in whose pages they might live again, and as a type acquire some measure of immortality. None arose, however, and now it is too late—for they are gone.

ON THE OLD BETHEL PIKE

The Bethel pike, or, as it is sometimes called, the "old rock road," runs right through what was once the blackest bit of the black belt of Virginia. This latter term, let me hasten to explain, has no geological significance whatever, but was merely used to indicate that middle region of the State where, in former days, the negro was most thick upon the land. Regarding the second name conferred upon the decayed highway, along which I am going to ask the reader to travel with me in fancy for a short distance, it will be sufficient to say that the remains of the only effort on a large scale ever made in Virginia east of the mountains to macadamize a country road still strew its surface. This memorable achievement belongs to the days of stage coaches sixty or eighty years ago. It took the shape of a narrow causeway of rough rocks bisecting the broad mud track of which the ordinary Virginia road did then and still does consist, and was once regarded as the wonder of its time. I have seen old pictures—mostly advertisements it is true—of the stage coach flying along this crude embankment behind four horses all extended to a gallop. But ever since I can remember, the chief aim of the declining traffic has been to dodge the fearsome causeway by hugging first one fence and then the other, according as weather and circumstances permitted. Nowadays, indeed, you may travel for miles along the Bethel Pike without meeting any traffic whatsoever, whether horse or foot, and this not because the road has relapsed into a state of nature, for that is the normal condition of most Virginia roads, but because there are scarcely any people left to travel on it. The country hereabouts is hilly, but the old road crosses it with a disregard of gradients and of everything else except mathematical precision such as would have extracted admiration (at a respectful distance) from an ancient Roman. Indeed I have often thought that a thousand years hence possibly—for nothing short of dynamite will ever make any impression on this old road—some enthusiast may arise and declare that even Virginia was not exempt from the tramp of the Roman legions.

Whatever things may look like a thousand years hence, there is to-day no more pathetic sight of the kind to be seen perhaps anywhere than that presented by large districts, nay, whole counties, in this same black belt of Virginia. In regions nearer home it is true the deer may wander or the sheep nibble over the vanished habitations of an expatriated peasantry. But in such cases it is rather the triumph of economy —if in some eyes an undesirable triumph—over sentimental poverty. The human occupants must have lived perpetually upon the borderland of want: their four-footed successors are at least the symbol of wealth and the pastures they wander over are of greater, not less profit to their owner, than before. But here over large districts of Virginia everything has gone or almost everything—squirearchy and peasantry alike—and they were not miserable and poverty-stricken, but happy and prosperous. Nor is there here any stock to take their place, for stock would starve upon the briars and broomsedge that run riot over the deserted fields. And these people, let it be remembered, lived here, not for many centuries it is true, but for more than two, and this for the purpose in hand is much the same as twenty.

The leading cause of this desolation, it need hardly be said, was the civil war and the collapse of negro slavery. But it was by no means the only one. The recent history of the South is on the whole one of progress. Those districts that were naturally rich in soil or mineral wealth, have maintained or vastly improved their former position. Those which are naturally poor have retrograded, with still greater rapidity, and it was upon these latter that the most patriarchal establishments in the old slavery days were very largely to be found. For the last few years it has been all that the keen Yankee or thrifty German can do to hold his own upon the richest lands of America. The fight of the easygoing and somewhat shiftless gentry of Virginia upon some of the poorest ceased long ago, and was a foregone conclusion, though hardly at the beginning of the seventies a foreseen one. For I remember very well about that time how people in those parts felt and spoke regarding the future. A large number of the gentry and practically all the yeomen or middling class remained upon their farms after the war. They could not all go to Baltimore and become lawyers and insurance agents, though so many Virginians did fly to that then almost sole harbour of refuge, as to create a grievance among the natives not yet quite forgotten. By the close of the decade which saw the war, almost every landowner remaining on his place, and these were many, had contrived to collect sufficient implements and stock wherewith to cultivate his lands. The latter, carrying good houses and what local custom considered good outbuildings, were at least his own, if sometimes encumbered. The negroes had virtually not moved, and could be hired at wages which, compared to the rest of the continent, were very low. The Southerners are constitutionally a sanguine people, and the Virginian, when he had recovered from the shock of war and reconstruction, and had fairly settled down at home again, was by no means unhopeful of his future as a farmer. He was poor of course, and had little or no credit, for his negroes had been his security, while now they were free men and his labourers. But with very few exceptions the Virginian gentleman had never tasted luxury as the word is commonly understood. Of the many daily necessities of an English landowner or gentleman of most moderate means he never dreamt. In his establishment there had been a plain abundance, but in its appointments and fittings, except that everything was clean, and that it was distinctly the home of a gentleman as opposed to that of a mere farmer, there was no approach to the sumptuousness of the ordinary English country mansion.

An owner of three thousand acres would rank in England among the lesser squirearchs. But three thousand British acres before the recent collapse, and even yet sometimes, would mean £150,000 or nearly a million of dollars. Now half that sum in the palmiest days of slavery would have bought out nearly any of the bigger magnates in Virginia, land slaves and personalty, and few of the country gentry were worth a quarter of it. I mention this because so much rubbish has been written of ante-bellum luxury and splendour by imaginative Americans, either Northerners who knew nothing of the old Southern life, or by untravelled Southerners whose notions of luxury mean abundance of home-grown eatables, a mint julep before breakfast, a black boy to pull their boots off, and nothing to do. Such writers have been taken too literally, and much misconception has arisen both in England and America regarding the actual standard of that happy, careless, and picturesque life, which distinguished the Southern States, and most of all Virginia, before the war.

The Virginia gentry of slavery days lived simply, partly because they had to, and partly because they knew no other life. The cares of a plantation and the ownership of a hundred or two negroes admitted of much leisure, but did not admit of those prolonged absences in which an English landlord can indulge. In some districts that I could indicate there was money made in a modest way by actual farming. In most, however, and in particular such a one as we are now considering, if the estate was self-supporting it was all that could be expected of it. When the domestic wants of the planter's household had been supplied, and the numerous families of negroes fed and clothed, all of which was done with little recourse to the city merchant, there was not often a great deal left for outside needs. Education was, of course, a leading item, but the State University was comparatively inexpensive, nor were there sons in costly regiments, nor wine-merchants' bills worth mentioning, nor did the accounts of tailor and dressmaker make very serious demands on this happy rustic society. Taxes were light, while of those innumerable tributes to his position which, in the shape of local subscriptions, lighten the purse of even the smaller English squire, the Virginia landowner knew nothing. There was no high-class fast life to attract the men folk, either of a sporting or convivial sort, for racing, though popular, was not of a harmful or costly character. Young gentlemen went to the dogs occasionally, as they will do all the world over; but in Virginia they had to go there in a dismal, squalid fashion, amid the atmosphere of provincial whisky saloons and low companions. The tone of society, however, was in general wholesome and excellent, and it matters little if its backsliders had no opportunity of sowing their wild oats like gentlemen, if there be in that any particular merit.

The very simplicity of this old Virginian society was its charm, with its courteous old-fashioned manners and its hearts both stout and kind, and as much education within its ranks as was in those days necessary to ladies and gentlemen living out of touch with the world's great centres. Perhaps the principal domestic extravagance of these days was the annual visit to the Springs, a pilgrimage no properly constituted Virginian family could omit. Here were mountain breezes and healing waters for the sickly; dancing and flirting *galore* for the young; and opportunities for the old of telling stories and cracking jokes and talking politics, such as no local courthouse even could offer. That was a happy day always when the family started in all its glory for the Springs. The wheat harvest was over, the corn was "laid by," the young tobacco plants had "taken holt," and under the hot July sun were dimpling the red hillsides or darker low grounds in chequered lines of green. The negroes were sleek and fat, and happy in the sunshine and the abundance around them. There was a lull in the year's anxieties, and the lord of this strangely constituted kingdom possessed his soul, for once, in peace as the family coach, loaded with trunks and piloted by some ancient retainer, turned off the ruts of the private road on to the ruts of the great main highway. Along the same route, too, went the saddle-horses, bestridden by frolicsome sons or cackling negroes, pacing, racking, or fox-trotting along in the red dust, all bound for one or other of those mountain Meccas of the Virginia pilgrims. This forlorn old rugged, deserted turnpike echoed in former days to the merry tramp of thousands of these light-hearted pilgrims. Now those indefatigable beetles, whose mission consists in rolling the summer dust of Virginia highways into pellets much larger than themselves, pursue their inscrutable calling from morning till night, with little fear of destruction by wheel or hoof. Entertaining, it was true, was the delight of the Virginian, nor were there ever in the world more kindly hosts; but the plantation provided almost wholly for the simple entertainment, and nearly everything was produced that ministered to a guest's wants. The saddle-horse that was sent to fetch him from the station, even the servant that led it there, was raised on the place; the blankets he slept under were woven in the cabins; the mutton, the ham, the fried chicken, the hot biscuits, the batter cakes, and the other simple and admirable condiments that formed the acme of local Epicureanism were all—with the exception of a mint julep in the morning, and a glass or two of Madeira perhaps at dinner—home grown.

I should not, however, have thought it worth while to drop into any financial comparisons concerning the bygone gentry of Virginia, except for the reason that it has always seemed to me a pity that so much florid nonsense about "Barons" and "lavish splendour" and the like should have obscured, not only the truth, but, in a measure, also the chief excellence of this society, which lay in its simplicity. A simplicity, too, of which it was itself almost unconscious, for it knew nothing else, and had no standard of comparison.

As a matter of fact, Virginia had been none too prosperous for the last generation of the slave era. Her lands had been going down, and but for the great demand for negroes occasioned by the development of the new cotton planting industry in the far south, some crisis in her affairs must have occurred thirty years before she was forced into war by her hot-headed sisters.

To come back, however, to the close of the war and the period of reconstruction referred to at the beginning of this chapter. Numb despair had been succeeded by something like hope in the breasts of the Virginians, who still stuck to their homesteads. I well remember the state of feeling upon this subject. The land had never, it was truly said, been reasonably treated under slavery; and upon this every one was agreed. To kindly treatment the exhausted acres and infertile fields would generously respond. So said Yankee farmers who began to put in an appearance, though not a very warmly welcomed one; so said hard-headed Scotchmen and confident cock-sure Englishmen. And so at last came to believe the native owners, though not quite so confident, because they knew them better, of the ready response to improvement of their paternal acres as the strangers who lectured them on the subject, and what was better still, backed their opinion by purchasing for purposes of illustration no inconsiderable share of the country. There was a good excuse indeed in those days for the number of estates that were for sale; and very eligible they appeared. Their buildings were far superior to the ordinary farmhouse of Canada, and there was no suggestion of that backwoods life which had hitherto been indelibly associated both in the British and New England minds with expatriation. The lands were well-watered and lay in gentle undulations ready for the plough. The landscape was not sublime, but it was good to look upon, and still is so for those, if there could be any such, to whom its briery wastes and sedgy fields and rotting fences tell no tales. Stately forests of fine timber covered the unoccupied spaces; prolific orchards of apple and peach-trees bloomed around the homesteads: the climate was the best upon the Atlantic coast. It was, in truth, a region calculated to hold the affection of its sons, and to attract the stranger, particularly the educated stranger, and imbue him with a hankering for country life under such conditions as seemed here to exist. " Here will I live and die," was the resolve of many a New Englander and not a few Britishers as they surveyed the roomy, and even dignified-looking mansion, with its ancestral oaks and broad acres, that had just passed into their hands at a price which seemed to them a bargain, and to those who knew perhaps a little better, quite fair and reasonable. Such prices, indeed, read now like a joke, though in truth a very grim one. "Who can suppose," wrote an English author and authority on such matters about the year 1870, "that these Virginian estates, now freely offered at thirty and forty dollars an acre, will be long in the market at figures such as these." A true enough prophet was our author, but alack, alack, not in the fashion he intended. Far as the eye can see, and that is very far indeed from some high points upon the Bethel Pike, there is scarcely a farm that if put upon the market to-day would fetch, not forty, but *four* dollars an acre. Upon behalf of most I will undertake to say that the auctioneer would expend his eloquence upon deaf ears and shout his laudatory platitudes in vain.

But this is merely the bald financial side of the question, though it may be doubted if pages of description could tell a woeful tale more significantly. I do not know that this is a very interesting, or what would be called a very tragic tale, to the general reader. I am not in a position to judge. It is simply that of the depopulation of a large region, where life for long ages went merrily, but is now silent, or very nearly so, and the feeble sparks that flicker here and there amid the weedy desolation, only seem to accentuate the sadness of the scene.

Every one has gone, not only the old families, but the later ones, who with help and hope and capital, came in a quarter of a century ago to fill up the gaps that war and its consequences had made, and to demonstrate that the poor lands of Virginia only wanted farming properly to laugh with gladness. One after another natives and foreigners gave up the unequal struggle.

The latter soon found that except in the strips of river bottom they had struck land of a poverty beyond all calculation, and through whose too often porous subsoil manures disappeared with heartbreaking rapidity. No natural grass, as in the Northern States, and western counties even of Virginia, grew upon the waste places to cover their nakedness, but broomsedge and briars and thorns and saplings only. To achieve a set of clover required considerable effort, and even then the result was problematical—while winter storms cut deep channels in the soft red hillsides, and summer suns blistered and defertilized the galls and scars that marked their course. In the middle of the "seventies" prices fell grievously. The West, with her overflowing abundance, grew nearer every year. All grades of tobacco but the very best, which was producible only in certain counties, ceased to pay. Growing seven or eight bushels of wheat to the acre, with an occasional twelve, had been possible under slavery, and remained possible, though hardly profitable with the high prices which followed the war, but with the collapse of the grain markets became an absurdity. The fattening of cattle on land that could rarely be persuaded to take or hold grass worth mentioning was out of the question. Guide books and histories, and magazine writers from time immemorial, tell us that all this was because the lands of East Virginia were worn out by repeated crops of tobacco. There is a half or rather quarter truth about this—as every one with a practical experience of this subject knows—that amounts to a fiction. This is what many of the strangers thought who came into the country after the war, and it took them some years to find out that the greater part of the land was "naiteral po' in the woods," as the vernacular had it. The country had been well enough to live happily in and raise negroes. Even after this, till the West came into action, it remained as a sort of possibility. But with the fierce competition of fat prairies and low prices, what could such a region hope for? People cannot live on sentiment or feed on climate. Nor can old associations or tender memories keep the wolf from th door.

Ever since the period following the war it ha been my lot to traverse, at stated intervals, the same twenty miles or so of the old Bethel Pike. And if I take as my text this particular line of road it is only because I know it best, and have been an eye-witness of its slow but sure decay, and have moreover the melancholy satisfaction as I ride along of peopling many of its deserted homesteads and abandoned fields with familiar names and well-remembered faces. For this, after all, is but a fraction of a large slice of Virginia which tells the same sad tale. Nor would it be a spectacle half so pathetic if the country, as here and there is actually the case, had been wholly abandoned to the forests of scrub, oak, and pine, that without intrinsic value of their own would, if unchecked, at least have thrown their kindly canopy over these dismal skeletons of the past. But life, as I have said, flickers feebly still upon these old estates. Heaven knows whom they now belong to. Most of them have changed hands, and that more than once, and always at declining prices, since I can first remember them. Many of them are now hardly worth paying taxes on, and taxes are low. Here and there a surviving scion of some old family may be found struggling with the briars, bearing but little likeness in appearance or education, and still less in the condition of his life, to his forbears. Sometimes the dilapidated acres are still owned by the family, who are scattered in trade or what not all over the United States, while some "poor white" or negro tenant undertakes to pay a rent which theoretically almost nominal is reduced in practice to microscopic proportions. Mortagees own many through foreclosure, storekeepers, perhaps, or lawyers in the local towns, and if they get rent enough to pay the taxes and keep the buildings from actually falling, it is the utmost satisfaction, unless maybe a few days quail shooting in November, that they derive from the acquisition. In some places, indeed, the forests have re-asserted themselves so freely that the very deer, after a banishment of a century, let us say, have found their way back to as great a solitude as that from which they were originially driven. But for the most part the landscape lies as open as of old, and the fields keep their former boundaries, marking them rather by the lusty growth of briars and saplings that have flourished especially along the fences than by the rotting rails they hide. And at the season of the year when, in happier days, the cheery shout of the negro, as he followed his plough or harrow over the red cornlands, and the busy stir of rural life filled the air, the blooms of the dog-wood and the wild cherry and the peach blow over wastes of broomsedge that are in themselves, perhaps, less depressing to look upon than the dismal efforts to fight against fate which break the desolation.

Here is a hillside on whose briery face the withered corn-stalks of two years ago are still standing, telling by their miserable attenuation a tale unmistakable. Here a few acres of wheat thin beyond belief upon the ground, and of a sickly colour, save where some old tobacco-barn or cabin has stood, and a bright, rank patch shows by contrast what wheat should be in April, and what it is not. There, again, a field of last year's corn has been followed in the ordinary local rotation by oats, which amid dead corn-stalks and a promising growth of weeds and bushes is making a desperate struggle for existence. If it achieves this last it may thresh out six bushels to the acre, a miserable output indeed, but one which the sickly wheat-field across the road will hardly run to. Fine horses, as everybody knows, once scampered and whinnied over these now tangled wastes, horses that were the pride of a sport-loving population, whose sires often had borne names of note upon Newmarket Heath and Epsom Downs, themselves distinguished upon Southern race-tracks, and not unfamiliar with the music of horn and hound. It is needless to remark that the Virginia horse, which still enjoys some reputation in America, does not find its model in the miserable drudges that, scarred by collar and trace-chain, toil in these unprofitable furrows, or drag the crazy, half-loaded waggons along the old rock road.

Following along the latter, it carries us every now and again with sharp descent and little ceremony into the waves of some rapid stream that brawls over its pebbly bed with a callous gaiety that seems somehow at variance with the scenes through which it is travelling. As our steed, after the fashion of all its kind in Virginia, stands in midstream and slakes an apparently unquenchable thirst, a pleasant vista unfolds itself to left and right of sunlit foam and gray rocks, and bowers of leaves that willow, alder, beech, and sycamore form with their spreading branches.

Here, too, are some remnants of fertility, and, indeed, all along the tortuous course of the little river strips of alluvial bottom land will be found hugging its banks, which in former days, on the greater estates, made up in some sort for the infertile uplands that spread on either hand. Still in those days such choice bits were treated with some forbearance. To protect them from washing floods at least was the planters' care, and to sow them from time to time in meadow grass or clover. Even such simple operations are beyond the scope of the hungry, shiftless occupier of modern days, whose reckless plough vies with the wayward stream in destroying those few spots where he can still hope to raise some apology for a crop.

But perhaps it is in the homesteads themselves that the contrast between the "then and now" is saddest. Many of them you would hardly notice from the turnpike, for though standing mostly upon hill-tops, those that have any past in a social sense are a long way back from the road, and often hidden by those stately groves of forest trees that throw their protecting arms around every well-constituted Virginia rooftree.

Here is one that, even after the war, remained for long a type of that simple, gracious, old-fashioned hospitality that distinguished the period before it. The track that wandered off the turnpike through the woods to the private entrance was easy enough to overlook even in those days, and now when the dead leaves lie upon it, undisturbed by passing wheel or hoof, it is difficult to trace up to the two rotting posts upon which once hung the ever-open and hospitable gate. The house itself in a score of years seems to have lived a lifetime, and to have hastened from cheerful and well-preserved middle age to decrepitude and decay, while the heavy portico over the door, resting, in the English fashion of the Georgian period, on lofty fluted columns, has shed the plaster from its ceiling in big cakes upon the rotting steps. The windows have mostly fallen out, and a battered shutter hangs here and there by a single hinge from the sash to emphasize the woe-begone aspect of the walls. And these again are scarred with ominous-looking cracks in the brick that no inmates whose interest in life was vigorous and circulation normal could contemplate without dismay. A family of "poor whites" occupy one wing of the decaying mansion and work their wild will on a portion of the surrounding acres. And the "poor white" of Eastern Virginia is both in appearance and ways of life the most unlovely sample of Anglo-Saxon, of rural Anglo-Saxon at any rate, that an inscrutable Providence has fashioned. To suppose too that a single window-pane would be replaced, a single nail driven into a loose plank, or a gate hung upon its hinges under the auspices of these gentry, would be not to know them. If anything were wanted to intensify the melancholy of this spectre of an old Virginia home the gaunt forms and yellow faces and vacant stare of its present occupants are well calculated to do so.

The Virginia squires troubled their heads little about landscape gardening. An acre or so of old turf shaded with forest trees and sprinkled with a few exotics filled, and upon the whole filled well, every requirement of dignity and comfort. But not even this relic of former days, however, has here escaped the aggressive inroad which nature abandoned to itself makes beneath these Southern suns. For the briars and weeds from the half-tilled fields without have leaped the broken palings of the lawn and are disputing every yard of ground with the old sod that seemed to have in it the resisting power of a century's growth and care.

In the vegetable garden, on which chiefly in olden days the care of the household, and above all of its ladies, used to be expended, the turf walks can still be traced, and the posts and trellis-work over which the grape-vines once clambered with such profusion are even yet partly standing. Out of a jungle of weeds waist-high old-fashioned herbs still push their heads up here and there for life and light, and the box-edgings of the beds have struggled up into rank bushes, stiff and straight amid the chaos.

And yet perhaps it is the inside of the house that awakens the saddest memories. Each chamber in its musty silence has some tale of its own to tell, and the tale told within these particular walls is not that of a single family, but of hundreds—the story of a whole race who once were powerful, were a leading factor in the life, not of a province, but of a nation, and who have within a period comparatively brief passed out of existence. The nails are still sticking in the walls from which used to hang those homely but none the less treasured paintings of gentlemen in wigs and swords, and ladies who danced with Braddock's fated officers at Williamsburg, and as sober matrons turned up no doubt their pretty noses (in secret) at Patrick Henry's rustic eloquence and Mr. Jefferson's dowdy clothes. It needs not the memory of these vanished symbols to remind us how Virginia in prosperity and political influence was once the foremost of American commonwealths, and had much more than her share in a numerical sense, considerable though this was, in guiding and shaping the early history of the United States.

Virginia, nowadays, as a state, is, upon the whole, by no means unprosperous. We have been looking at her moribund and historic part. That other portion, which represents her increase and prosperity, which fattens cattle and grows corn with moderate success, which delves for coal and iron, rears blast furnaces and factories and summer hotels, though beautiful indeed by nature, belongs otherwise to the commonplace tale of modern progress, and has no connection with the point of view from which this chapter is written. But this pleasant and prosperous western half that hugs the foot-hills of the Blue Ridge and lies amid the shadow of the Alleghanies is not, to any appreciable extent, the Virginia of the days when her opinion was listened to by sister colonies and sister states with a deference that reads strangely now.

It is this older Virginia, this famous cradle of the English race beyond the sea, that now, so much of it, lies an almost hopeless desert, or what, compared to any other agricultural country in the Anglo-Saxon world, is practically a desert—and seems likely to remain so. This is not an age when the pressure of population is forcing men on to sterile soils—above all on to sterile soils in America, where migration is so simple and land so abundant. It is all, indeed, that the tillers of fertile farms can do, at this time, to hold their own. The owners of indifferent lands are having an anxious time of it, while those who live upon poor ones, though they may have cultivated them with thrift and energy for generations, are abandoning their homes wholesale, as in New England, for the fatter pastures of the prairies, or the sunny fertility of the Pacific coast; and the abandoned farms of New England were considerably more productive than the mass of middle and eastern Virginia. Even the proximity to markets, which at one time partly neutralised the comparative poverty of eastern lands, has no longer any commercial significance. For purposes of export the railroads have equalised long freights and short ones, while in the matter of home markets the centre of population shifts further westward every day. Nor, indeed, could any advantage of markets assist a country whose means of getting to them are over the worst roads in the world, and that has little chance now of ever having better ones. It is difficult to conceive, for those who really know it, any combination of circumstances that can, within measurable time, arrest the decay of large portions of Virginia east of the Piedmont counties—a region, roughly speaking, half the size of England, and once pre-eminently the England of the New World, where the manners and customs, the sports, and even the prejudices of the mother country were reproduced with a fidelity that in colonial days was almost pathetic, and the traces of which are even yet not wholly extinct.

PARKIN THE SADDLER

THE old store at the forks of the Shiloh Pike is an admirable illustration of the contempt of the South in past days for industrial centres—or shall we say its independence of them? Barkers' has been a spot celebrated in local annals for something like a century. It is marked upon the oldest maps of the district in no uncertain letters, while upon the very latest it is written in characters almost as large as those of the populous towns that have sprung up in comparatively recent days along the nearest railway track. Barkers' consists of a single house and a blacksmith's shop. There is no reason to suppose that eighty years ago there was anything more. The oldest inhabitants have been heard to mutter about the place "going down." But oldest inhabitants are nothing if not pessimists; and this matter on being investigated reveals no more than the hazy tradition of a wheelwright's shop having once stood upon the other side of the road. There are no Barkers left now, in the neighbourhood at any rate, to tell the tale of the enterprising ancestor who immortalised their name. The store itself has run to a third or fourth edition. Two great fires at least mark the local calendar. The present edifice dates from before the war, and by a careful abstinence from paint looks venerable enough to harmonise with the traditions of the spot. An uninitiated traveller would pass by Barkers' almost without noticing it; such notice as he might spare would probably be of a most contemptuous and uncomplimentary description. His conclusions, however, like those of many passing travellers, would be erroneous, for Barkers' in commercial circles is regarded as one of the best country "stands" in the state. It is twenty miles from a town or a railroad, quite a novelty nowadays in the civilised parts of America. But from the high red ridge on which it is perched it overlooks a community of farmers that in the days of slavery were very prosperous and even now are fairly so.

Barkers' is of course a post-office, and has been a voting-centre from those blessed days when freeholders alone held that privilege to the degenerate present when the negro crowds to the polls. Congressmen and legislators, would-be congressmen and would-be legislators, temperance orators, revivalists, preachers —all, in short, who, within the memory of man, have wished to capture the votes or influence the opinions of the district, have taken their stand under the big white-oak tree which stretches its broad arms over the store on one hand and over the blacksmith's shop on the other. Men have gone to battle from Barkers', not in ones or twos but in whole troops. A hundred and fifty years ago small companies of adventurous settlers in moccasins and hunting-shirts marched from a few scattered clearings to join the frontier levies against the Indians beyond the mountain. A generation later sturdy farmers, who knew little of the red man or his ways, hastened northward to don the blue coat and three-cornered hat of Washington's Continental Line. And in recent years the fiery cross of the Confederacy found in the whole south no prompter response than among the freeholders who voted and traded and gossiped at Barkers'.

To-day there is nothing moving. It is hot July and it is not mail-day. Even the negro blacksmith has gone to tend his crop, for farmers and horses and ploughs are all hard at work among the tender spreading leaves of the freshly-planted tobacco and the lusty, growing corn. The broad stretch of road around the Tree of Liberty is untenanted save by industrious "tumble bugs," who roll their burdens backwards and forwards through the dust as if secure to-day at any rate from the ruthless waggon wheel. Sometimes a score of horses stand hitched along the fence. To-day there is not one, and the ground squirrel scuttles fearlessly over its rails, and the lizard scrapes and rustles in the heaps of last year's leaves that still lie in its corners. The woods upon the adjacent hillside are motionless in the simmering, breathless heat. Not even a distant waggon is to be heard jolting and bumping over one of the four rough and rutty roads that meet at Barkers'. Even the worthy merchant who is generally to be seen on the rickety porch calling to passing wayfarers to "get down and hitch up awhile" has succumbed to the inevitable and retired to a *siesta* beneath his counter. No sign of life is to be seen, but the buzzard swinging far up in the blue vault above, and below the subject of this sketch—commonly and somewhat quaintly known as Parkin the Saddler.

This is, perhaps, rather an elaborate setting for the picture of a lank and homely man seated on an empty dry-goods case before the store door, solemnly whittling at a chip; but Parkin is a notoriously difficult man to "to catch up with," and almost the only chance of doing so without tracking him through the mountains, the woods, and the fields, is to seize upon, what for him alone, probably, in the district of Barkers', is a dead season. No trout to-day will be feeding in the streams whose course can be traced by the dark hollows in the great masses of blue mountain that lie piled against the western sky. The wild turkey will to-day be leading her tender, fluffy brood through the sequestered shade of the pine woods that clothe the spurs and foothills; and the cock quail pipes forth his lay from the fence-top with a confidence that would secure his safety from the veriest poacher, much less from such a sportsman as Parkin the Saddler.

So far as Jim Parkin is concerned there is nothing to be done at such a time but the comparatively unimportant occupation of hoeing corn and ploughing tobacco. But for farming, though he owns a bit of land, Jim, to use his own vernacular, "has mighty little use," and that is a bold assertion at Barkers', where the entire community think, move, and have their very being in agriculture. This, by the way, is not because his heart is in saddles and bridles, as might be inferred. Jim will make you a bridle or a set of waggon-harness, it is true, but the order would be an act on your part of pure and simple philanthropy. Your troubles instead of being then over would only have begun. You would certainly have to advance the money to purchase the leather, and would probably have to lend him a horse to ride into town upon. Jim is as honest in intention as the day, and upon the whole is a sober man. But the unwonted stir of the city might create in him an unwonted thirst; or at any rate he might meet with long-lost friends, and begin telling big stories of fish and bear till the ten-dollar bill began to burn a hole in the pocket of his shabby coat. He would get home with the horse late the next day perhaps, having been compelled to pledge your credit for another five dollars for leather. Repentance is no word for the state of feelings which would then rend the breast of Parkin the Saddler. His remorse would be so profound and sincere that you would begin to feel yourself almost a brute for not paying him two dollars a day for the time he spent in frolicking, and he would go to work upon the job with almost feverish energy. If no fishing-day interfered and no turkey-tracks in the woods pressed themselves too forcibly on his attention, or if his dogs did not happen to get on a fox on the way home, or if there was no swarm of bees within five miles that required coaxing, you would eventually secure a really admirable article.

It is not, however, in his capacity either of agriculturist or saddler that I wish to recall this simple, kindly, shiftless son of Nature, but as a sportsman of the first water, a poet unconsciously, a naturalist half consciously, and a gentleman entirely. Perhaps, as we are speaking of a poor uncouth fellow of dilapidated appearance and no education worth mentioning, conventionality will be less outraged if we substitute the term "Nature's gentleman." Jim Parker is in truth no beauty, but he has a pair of big gray eyes that tell of kindly virtues worth a deal more. He may be fifty and is slightly lame, though you would not think it to see him travelling down the mountain side after a wounded turkey—for he was shot through the thigh in the war. His peculiarities as a local character are of course his own, but still they are the result of a particular civilisation. From a mere business point of view he is an excellent type of the old-fashioned rural mechanic of the South. Under the patriarchal dispensation of slavery there was so little use for white artisans that the supply was of a most extraordinary description. It rendered its services on the principle that if you could not give a man work for his whole time he would retaliate by doing what he did get when he chose and how he chose, and the custom is not yet dead. The country carpenter, wheelwright or saddler in the South was generally a member of the plainer farming-class; sometimes he owned a small farm himself, and in former days possibly even a negro or two. Jim was one of the latter stock—which indeed was very numerous round Barkers'—and nearly everybody within ten miles called him cousin. He had jolted off the track somehow or other, for neither land worth mentioning nor negroes had ever come in his way. "Too fond of huntin' and ramblin' round," people said. He had acquired, however, with his wife a farm of some thirty acres, on a steep hill-side with a snug three-roomed log house at the foot of it. If the property was not very valuable it was at any rate close to Barkers' and handy for hearing the news, which suited him well. To see Jim at his best it will be necessary to put the dial back to the early days before spring has melted into summer, and to recall one of those May mornings on which the trout in the Virginia mountains may be surely counted on to feed. Jim has planted his corn patch, and thinks with a sigh of relief that there will be no more farming to be done till he has to plough it, and thin out what the crows from the mountain will leave him to thin. This morning he is up and has fed his mule and had his breakfast before the first gleam of day. With a big fishing-basket on his back and a mustard-tin full of worms rattling about inside it, a twist of tobacco in his breeches pocket and a line wound round his old felt hat, he is ambling along the big road leading to the mountains before the first rays of sunlight have reached the valley. Ah! those May mornings in the mountains of Virginia! How vain with feeble pen to attempt those memories of bloom and blossom, of glistening dewdrops and fresh unfolding leaves, of glowing mountain peaks and white torrents leaping into soft oceans of unruffled silent woodland. In the still morning air the tramp of the Saddler's mule sounds hard upon the beaten red road.

The sun has just risen over the distant plains of East Virginia, has shot his rays over the intervening mountains, and lit as with fire the peaks of the Blue Ridge towards which Jim is hastening. Every crag and every scarred cliff, bared by the winter winds of the struggling growth which even at that great height strives to hide them, catches the golden glory. The gray mantle of the dawn that has lain over everything,—from the rank dew-laden wheatfield by the roadside to the farthest pinnacle of the western peaks—yields and flushes as the broad band of gold comes creeping down the mountain side. The sombre wall of woodland that fills the western sky springs into life as the gleam catches the varied verdure of oak and chestnut, gay-leaved poplar and solemn cypress, or the flash of a mountain stream down some gray water-worn cliff.

Jim was born, and his fathers before him, under the shadow of these majestic hills. He is only half conscious probably of the part they played in his existence. He only knows that during the war, the sole occasion on which he was out of sight of them, he was terribly homesick. Just now, however, he is consumed with anxiety lest Mose' Davis, his great and only rival on the creek, should get ahead of him, and rake with his early worm those boiling eddies and heaving pools which Jim hopes to have the first chance at. The venerable and faithful mule, his sole prop, is urged to the utmost speed attainable, and a queer pair they make. Jim, on an old cavalry saddle, leaning back as stiff and straight as a pair of compasses from the top of his head, where some of his erratic locks have escaped through a hole in his hat, to the point of his toe in the wooden leather-capped stirrup; and the old mule, galled and seamed by years of collar-work on its withers and shoulders, and rubbed almost bare on its sides and legs by the trace-chains of many owners. Jim's flowing locks, the fishing-basket with the rattling mustard-tin inside it, and the long, frayed tails of the old green coat, all flap in unison as the patient beast, urged by unwonted pressure, breaks into a canter that threatens a dissolution of the whole outfit. Numerous are the remarks made by the Saddler's friends and relatives now stirring about their fields and homesteads as they catch sight of his familiar figure bobbing up and down behind the gray fence rails of the turnpike. "Well, it does seem to me mighty strange folks can trifle roun' like Cousin Jim these hard times," says Madame Cornstalk, a third cousin once removed, as she throws the remains of the breakfast to the chickens in the yard. "I declar' if that ain't Mar'se Saddler Parker travellin' fur all de world as if he war ridin' fur the doctor!" exclaims sable Uncle Archie to his dusky spouse, as he pitches an armful of stove-wood down before the log kitchen in the yard. "Hello, Cousin Jim!" sings out the burly owner of six hundred acres from the porch of a big brick house. "You seem in a powerful hurry this morning. Fishin', I reckon. Well, leave some for seed anyhow!"

The foot of the forest-clad mountain is reached before the sun is half an hour high. The world with all its works, its taunts and its cares, is left behind and Jim plunges into the forest. Pressing the pace is no longer possible. The red road becomes a steep track strewn with slabs of slippery rock and loose boulders, that yield here and there to stretches of black mould deep in last year's leaves. A grist-mill marks the line between the world and the wilderness, the mountain and the plain. From a loophole somewhere up in the dank and weather-stained walls the miller can't resist the joke. " Hello, Jim, you'd best hurry up! Uncle Moses' jes gone up the creek."

"Dawg my skin!" This is all Jim says, but he "thinks a heap" as he pushes on. If he could only know it, Uncle Moses is at this moment profoundly indifferent to life in general and sleeping off the effects of a business-expedition to town on the previous day. The unsuspecting Jim, however, curses his luck, and pictures every favourite hole and eddy in the stream searched by the skilful hand of his loving relative, who is popularly supposed to spend about two-thirds of his waking hours on the banks of Buffalo up which Jim is now travelling.

How these Blue Ridge streams leap and Tumble and flash and roar! How clear, how fresh, how crystal are the white churning waves that in the hottest days of summer send cool spray-laden draughts down the leafy avenues through which they riot! Above such cataracts you would look for beetling cliffs and sterile crags and rugged nakedness. The cliffs and crags indeed are plentiful enough, but it is only here and there they pierce through the wilderness of leaves that clothes the mountains as with a mantle from their summit to their base. But

Buffalo Creek is not all turmoil and foam. Sometimes its course is checked by a natural dam of rock, and lingers in a pool so deep and black that no shadow even in the sunniest days can flicker on its gloomy face. Sometimes it courses smoothly down some wide half-open glade where an old clearing has run to turf kept sweet and short by the cattle that roam in summer through the mountains. Where the rocky road dips into a glade such as this, Jim dismounts from his mule and hitches it to the swinging limb of a sycamore tree. The depressing spectre of Uncle Moses taking all the best water ahead of him weighs heavily on the Saddler's spirits during that brief period of expectancy which with the ordinary sportsman would be occupied in putting his rod together.

Jim, however, has no rod to put together. A "jinted pole" has been his life's ambition, or the object at any rate of his heart's desire. Since the gun-maker at Shucksborough, where he buys his powder and shot, put up a case of these "Yankee faldangles" in his window some six years back, Jim has been trying to persuade that worthy man that his rods are worth a little less than half the price he puts upon them. The latter has never seen his way to adopting the Saddler's views, and a compromise seems as remote as ever. Jim, in the meantime, clings to the homely sapling of his youth, and prides himself vastly on his selection of young pines and hickories, and their preparation for "fishin' poles." It is not too much to say that the banks of the stream, from its source to where it leaves the mountain and ceases to be a trouting-water, are lined with Jim's poles. Almost every cluster of rhododendron bushes, every thicket of ivy, every pile of brush or bed of weeds, conceals in its depths one of those tremendous weapons. The hiding-place that has not been monopolised by the Saddler has been seized upon by his relative and rival, for the jealousy between these two great sportsmen extends even thus far. The former, on this occasion, having looked carefully round to see that no crafty mountaineer is taking stock of his movements, plunges his head and arms and the greater part of his body into a neighbouring ivy bush, and after a few seconds' scuffling emerges holding on to the point of what ultimately develops itself into a hickory sapling of at least eighteen feet in length. To the end of this he ties with knots of primitive simplicity six feet of gut and whipcord line, and to the end of the gut there is attached a hook that is known in the mountains, for the sake, I suppose, of distinguishing it from the new-fangled "tricks" from Baltimore and New York, as the " Old Virginia " hook. The peculiarities of the latter will be of more interest to the unfortunate red worm that is soon struggling on its fearful shank than to the reader. When Jim has unearthed from the depths of his breeches pocket the big twist of home-grown tobacco, bitten off a piece about the size of a tangerine orange and deposited it in his left cheek, he is ready for the fray.

Where he is standing is just the sort of place that no trout-fisher could pass by. A gravelly beach shelves by degrees into the bright gliding water which under the further bank deepens and darkens as it swirls under hollow sycamore roots covered with green and dewy moss and overhung with banks of fern. All up and down the river-side masses of rhododendrons blaze in the first freshness of their bloom. From among the waves of blossom spring, tapering upward, smooth stems of beech trees and gnarled trunks of maple and chestnut breaking with their thick canopy of leaves the beams of the now risen sun. The Saddler is in his glory. He is no mere brutal slayer of game. Like most good anglers he is full of the poetry of the sport, and his rude being is as profoundly influenced by its associations as the most cultivated of its devotees, though he could not perhaps find words to express his feelings. "I suttn'ly do love to be on the crik on this yer kind o' spring mornin'," is probably the limit of verbal enthusiasm to which he would commit himself, as he poises his tremendous pole for a moment over the broken water at the pool's head and drops the worm into its tempting depths.

I will not enter into a disquisition on clear water worm-fishing, but I feel tolerably certain that the experienced angler, after watching Jim at work with his pole for a while, would decide that he was not a very deadly performer. But the experienced angler, like many other experienced persons, would be mistaken as he would probably find out if he took the Saddler's standing offer, made nearly every time he goes to Barkers', to fish any one in the United States for a new hat. I have spent many a long spring day in the lonely woods on Buffalo with Parkin the Saddler, and in spite of such debasing advantages as

Baltimore hooks and Yankee snoods (as Jim always called casting-lines) and a "jinted pole" and an average amount of skill, I never could get much ahead of my ragged companion on the day's count. That I used to kill as many weighed upon his gentle soul with a weight that, in spite of his supreme good nature and amiable disposition, was at one time almost more than he could bear. The rivalry of Uncle Moses was another matter. They had been rivals ever since the old man had taught him to fish as a boy ages before the war, and they had been together the great exponents, the great patrons of trout-fishing in that little corner of the globe. The low-country farmers that on a general holiday or a slack time come up once in a while to "try the trout" are quite unambitious tyros, who take our friend along with them to make up the basket while they flounder round upon the slippery unaccustomed rocks within comfortable distance of the lunch-hamper. The occasional "city fellah," who penetrates as far as Buffalo Creek and takes Jim of course as his gillie, is more persevering, and is also well armed by the Shucksborough tackle-maker aforesaid. According to Jim, however, this class of sportsman always "skeers a heap more fish than he cotches," and the former's supremacy has never, I take it, been threatened on any of these rare occasions.

It was a real blow to Parkin the Saddler when a ready-made fisherman, so to speak, was launched out of space and set down at his very side on the waters he and Uncle Moses had dominated for a lifetime. It was no selfish fear of their special preserves being encroached on that agitated these honest souls, but pure mortification and wounded pride mixed with profound astonishment. It is many years now since they realised for the first time that the trout-producing area of the known world was not limited to a particular portion of the Blue Ridge Mountains of Virginia. This strange belief imparted to my first encounter with Parkin the Saddler special interest. I should doubt if the splinter of shell that knocked him senseless beside his gun in the Richmond redoubt, and partly crippled him for life, was more of a shock in its way than this unlooked for and successful invasion by a foreigner of his particular stronghold. The way of it was this. I was making a preliminary exploration among other mountain streams of Buffalo Creek. An accident had rendered necessary some temporary substitute for a rod. A poplar or hazel switch about eight feet long that was lying handy seemed to suit my notions of brook-fishing better at any rate than the sixteen-foot pole of the country, and working my way up the then strange tangles of Buffalo one April morning I had reached the very spot where we have just left our friend. The fish were biting very freely, and by pitching a long line up stream I had been able to some extent to counteract the inefficiencies of the rustic rod and had basketed a really good dish of trout. The place in question I have described as being both tempting and accessible, and here on that occasion the little silvery quarter-pounders came out one after another in a fashion by no means general in Buffalo or any other stream. The excitement of the moment was great and my absorption in the sport so complete that I was startled and astonished when a hollow voice sounded from the adjoining thicket—

"Dad blame my cats!"

I turned and beheld Parkin the Saddler as he was more than fifteen years ago, looking, so far as I remember, precisely as he looks now. The same old well-ventilated slouch hat, the same sun-cured green-black tail coat, the same yellow homespun pantaloons and knee-boots turned over at the heel, and the same tangled wilderness of beard and hair, and the big wild eyes almost bursting from their sockets with blank amazement.

"Dad blame my cats!" Jim had a wonderful vocabulary for the relief of his emotions, and avoided by all sorts of quaint compromises the large and expressive D. that would have written him down in the Baptist community to which he belonged as "a swearing man." On that occasion I wasn't in a position to realise the shock Jim had received. What accidentally gave it more force was that he had that day, in fly-fishing parlance, "missed the rise." He had wasted precious time in chasing Uncle Moses through the bushes, trying to get ahead of him without avail, and had dropped back with an empty basket in despair to make a fresh start below. It was thus he encountered the startling apparition which "put him right off everything," except talking, for a week, and he spent this period at the store at Barkers' recovering from the shock and relieving his feelings.

But we must return to Jim as we left him carrying,

and apparently carrying lightly, up Buffalo the weight of the intervening years. He has dropped his worm into the head of the pool, and his big wild eyes glare at the point of his long pole as it follows the course of the bait down the eddying, curling stream. The portentous plug of tobacco stretches almost to bursting the skin of his drawn leather-coloured cheek. But his jaws suddenly cease their monotonous working as the electric thrill of a biting trout flashes down the cumbrous sapling to the horny hands that hold it. The trout is checked for a second only in its downward course. Jim still loses his head like a schoolboy over the first fish. There is a scuffling of feet for a moment on the pebbly shore. He staggers back a step or two, as he does when he has poured a double charge of powder by mistake into the old turkey-gun, and a golden-bellied red-finned trout of a quarter of a pound is in mid-air flying into the rhododendrons behind. "Dad blame my cats!" The prize takes some hunting for in the bushes, but is eventually secured, and the Saddler, a little ashamed of himself, puts on a fresh worm, sobers down, and begins again at the head of the pool.

Jim does not always land his fish in this wise, but at the very best he treats them with scant ceremony. As for playing a trout he would scout the notion, though he has read about "such foolishness" in old copies of *Forest and Stream* that find their way sometimes to his cottage on winter evenings. When he fastens in the rare but occasional pounder, or in his own idiom "hangs a whaler," the struggle is apt to be a brief and violent one. Generally the whaler gets what appears to be the best of it, and returns to his lair decorated with a foot of gut and an "Old Virginia" hook in his gills, and a severe pain in his jaw, to swear off worms doubtless for a considerable period. Jim is not a member of any fly-fishing club, but he claims descent from Ananias with the best of them. That badly treated trout swells and grows with each narration of the struggle to unbelieving Philistines at Barkers', till they ultimately settle the question by deciding that it was not a fish at all but a sycamore root or a chestnut log that Cousin Jim "hung."

There is no space to-day to follow Jim up the mazy gorges of Buffalo. Lonely enough so far as humanity goes are these, unless where here and there a rickety cabin stands by the brook's side; or the quaint but dreaded figure of old Uncle Moses looms large ahead, focused against the white veil of a cataract. But surely no solitude was ever so far removed from sadness as this, nor Nature gayer, nor a wilderness more smiling! The stream has its moments of sadness, it is true. Brief fleeting periods of depression, when its joyousness quails beneath the frown of dank and verdureless cliffs, and its sunlit laughing face grows wan and dark in some uncanny hollow where black whirlpools go round and round for ever and sullen backwaters heave and tremble beneath banks of creamy froth. But these are passing moods. The ways of Buffalo lie mostly through caverns to be sure, but the walls of these caverns are of blooming shrubs and flowering woodland trees, of stately, graceful cedars, of sweet-smelling hemlocks. If their roofs are not the unbroken sky, the soft tracery that breaks the blue of heaven is that of the trembling leaves of maple and aspen, of cherry blossoms in their season, and of dogwood blooms in theirs. And on the bank there is the familiar alder with its homely, sombre leaves, catching, as they whisk downward at their appointed times, the Duns and March Browns and stone flies in which Appalachain trout as well as English ones so greatly delight. What music there is too in the tumble of a mountain stream, and none that I ever knew played more witching airs than the streams of Buffalo! What are all the fiddles that ever scraped in South Kensington to the ever-changing melodies, the solemn dirges, the plaintive carols, the sobs, the laughter, the thunder of such a rivulet as this?

In these sounds and sights and solitudes Jim's rough uncultured soul delights. He is no pot-hunter, and in fact has little care for his fish beyond the pleasure of carrying what he calls a "mess" to some sick old woman, and going perhaps several miles out of his road to do it. His neighbours, busy with their corn and tobacco, call him a loafer, a trifler, and a "no 'count fellar"; but for all that there is not a farm-house or a cabin within twenty miles where a knife and fork would not be laid more readily for him than for almost any one. Or if help is wanted at a bed of sickness no name occurs more naturally to those in need than that of Parkin the Saddler.

Jim, too, is almost the only man in the district who can hunt the turkey with success. If he is ever

K

quite so happy as upon the banks of Buffalo, it is when the woods upon the mountain spurs have turned to gold and scarlet, and the young birds are large enough to shoot but not yet endowed with that supernatural astuteness, that enables them later on to defy the wiliest of sportsmen. Jim has found out long before the season opens where the various gangs have been bred, and where they "use." Not a farmer within ten miles drops upon a flock of turkeys in his rounds that he does not send word to Parkin the Saddler. Then Jim starts off in the crisp autumn morning on the same old mule that carries him to Buffalo. And he takes with him his old muzzle-loading gun whose barrels are wearing so thin that his daily dream of a breechloader, though financially as remote as ever, takes possession of his soul with increasing force.

It is not only in the field of sport that Jim is prominent. Almost every event, that has no connection with his own business or personal profit, is graced by his presence. His own hogs have probably come to various and untimely ends long before the acorns in the woods, and the corn on his half-worked patch, are ready to turn them into bacon. But no hog-killing in the neighbourhood would be quite complete without the Saddler was there to crack jokes and tell "bar" stories,—for Jim is something of a bear-hunter too—or to take a hand in keeping the log fire going and the water hot. No coon-hunt, no corn shucking, no house-raising, no outdoor preaching, no wholesale baptising, escapes the personal attention of Parkin the Saddler. If his criticism on such matters is not of much worth, as a chronicler and a local news-bearer he is invaluable.

But the most notable chapter in Jim's life since the war, and most certainly the most notable in the humble annals of the post-office at Barkers', was the year in which he carried the United States mails backwards and forwards between that centre and the county town eighteen miles off. The postal system pursued by Uncle Sam himself, with regard to the rural districts of Virginia, at that time, was sufficiently remarkable. It was always understood that the actual grant allowed by the department at Washington was sufficient to run a daily waggon between Barkers' and the town. But by the time the fund reached the locality, there was only enough of it left to mount an indifferent person upon an indifferent horse three times a week. And the way of it was somewhat thus wise. The original grant for this postal service, grouped together, probably, with many others, was handed over to a contractor in Washington, presumably a politician with a "pull," who was nominally responsible, no doubt, for any vagaries of his subordinate who carried the letters from Barkers' to Bunkerville, and from Bunkerville to Barkers'. But I think, indeed I am quite sure, that a dissatisfied or injured correspondent might just as well, in those days, have addressed a complaint to Queen Victoria or the Pope of Rome, as to those responsible for the matter at Washington. The original contractor, however, had a very simple way of proceeding, for he in his turn sublet his contract, and it was always said at an immensely reduced figure, to another politician nearer the scene of action, and he it was who out of this reduced amount had to apply as little of it as he prudently could to the Barkers' postal route, and as much as he dare for his own pocket. And this class of person dared much in those days, for the Federal officials were bitter Republicans, and practically every white man was a bitter, but a helpless democrat. There was a mighty small margin left, as will be imagined, for application to the original purpose of Uncle Sam. Prices were good in those days, and even small farmers did not care to ride thirty-six miles three days a week in all weathers, for two or three hundred dollars a year. So when Parkin the Saddler put in a bid for the final contract at a lower figure than any one else, and found the necessary security, he was promptly installed as mailrider for the year. It was not, however, without grave misgivings that the neighbourhood saw the excellent Saddler astride of the mail bags. It was not the immediate safety of their letters that anybody felt alarmed about, but the fashion in which they might be delivered.

There were no gentry in the neighbourhood of Barkers', but some of the larger farmers, who took in a newspaper and got two or three letters besides each mail day, shook their heads when they heard Jim Parkin had got the contract. The latter however, who was a poor hand at calculations, has candidly confessed to me since, that he thought he saw his way to a breech-loading gun out of it, or he wouldn't have touched it.

Nobody however got further than shaking their heads and the majority didn't even do that. Some of those indeed who waited for the mail at Barkers' with the greatest regularity, on Tuesdays, Thursdays, and Saturdays, were never known to get a letter at all, other than an occasional advertisement. But these were the days and this the hour the local "gossip" had made his own, and the meetings were often prolonged ones, while the mail rider struggled with climatic or physical difficulties, or waxed too sociable on the way. When Parkin the Saddler took up the contract, these gatherings grew very prolonged indeed, and instead of two o'clock it was often four or past when the United States mail, in the person of that genial, feckless sportsman, rode up to the porch of the store amid the rough chaff of the assembled throng. How indeed could it have been otherwise, when the gauntlet of two other country post-offices had to be run on the way, with all the greetings and the badinage, and the interchange of opinions on men and things that was thereby implied, and that the soul of the Saddler loved? Nor was this all. It was a lonely road for most of the way, it was true. But still there were occasional farmers to be met, ambling along, and hitherto the United States mail-carriers had at least been able to resist the natural inclination to stop and talk with every one of them. But Parkin the Saddler, who knew them all, could not thus wrestle with his natural self. And even when there was no one on the road, there were other things that appealed with equal force to our friend's instincts. Some of his best beats for wild turkey lay in the pine woods that brushed the fence rails of the Bunkerville road in one place, and in the high oak-clad ridges over which it climbed in another. And it happened, not seldom, that the United States mail bags and their four-footed bearer were left in the lane, while the Saddler himself was hunting for turkey tracks in the woods above. Minor checks, too, arrested, each for their few seconds, the spasmodic course of this undisciplined "Will Wimble": the scent of a fox, the distant note of a hound, the spring of a covey, the scuttle of a rabbit. People, however, in those parts took things easily, and were long suffering, to a degree, in matters of this kind. Cousin Jim, in fact, was regarded with much contemptuous affection, and so long as he was happy it was felt by most people around Barkers' that an hour or so wasted three times a week did not amount to very much.

However, at the end of the year a feeling that neighbourliness might be carried too far, was met half way by Jim himself, who found after all that there was no breechloader in the contract. So with a gasp of relief he threw up the irksome obligation, which bound him to do the same thing three days in every week, and retired into private life.

To see Jim, however, at his best on serious occasions is when Senator Tidewater, that good old Virginia representative of Free Trade and States' Rights, pays his annual visit to Barkers', and from the broken verandah of the store appeals to his friends not to let new issues and local questions allow them to forget their ancient faith. In the whole crowd there is no more vociferous applauder than Jim. His wild eyes dilate with excitement, and his leathery face actually glows with indignation and with pity for himself as an honest toiling farmer fast in the clutches of the unscrupulous Yankee manufacturer; and he goes home to dream of a millennium in which breech-loaders and "jinted poles" are forwarded on application with the enclosure of a two-cent stamp.

THE "POOR WHITES" OF THE MOUNTAINS.

The Blue Ridge may perhaps be best described as an advanced outwork of the great Alleghany range thrust just so far forward as to be within easy sight for the most part of the parent chain. With sufficient accuracy for the present purpose this whole mountain system may be said to run a somewhat parallel course to the Atlantic coast and at a distance inland from it of about one hundred and fifty miles.

I have elsewhere indicated the conspicuous part that this same Blue Ridge has played in the past history of the country. How till nearly the end of the Colonial period it was the limit of civilisation, and how the Virginia that grew up beyond it was the creation, very largely, of another race of people, who set their stamp for ever upon a region that of itself differed greatly in soil, and considerably in climate, from Old Virginia.

Time, however, has long robbed the Blue Ridge of all significance but the surpassing beauty of its form and colouring. Hundreds of miles beyond the blue peaks that were once the Ultima Thule of Anglo-Saxons have arisen some of the most populous centres upon earth; and the scream of the iron horse dragging its heavy freights eastward wakes strange echoes in wild upland glens whose solitudes have otherwise defied the march of civilisation. The traveller of to-day on his way south by one at least of the great trunk-lines from Washington will for many hours see the Blue Ridge filling the horizon upon his right hand. He will pass innumerable streams that either bear the names or swell the waters of those eastern rivers that the civil war made famous. Rumbling Creek is one of these, and I mention it particularly for two reasons. The first is that, after crossing the river on a tressel-bridge, the train stops at the station of Tucker's Mills, from which I think the passing traveller gets the best distant view of the mountains to be had from the railway. The second, because it is upon the head-waters of this tortuous and noisy stream that I purpose to introduce the reader to one type, at any rate of that strange specimen of humanity—the Southern Mountaineer.

So far, however, as the station at Tucker's Mills and its surroundings are concerned, the mountaineer population might be in another planet. The river, it is true, races under the railway-bridge with something of the life that marks its earlier career as a foaming trout stream in some dark ravine of the great Appalachian rampart that towers so wonderfully blue into the distant sky. But the landscape all around is of a lowland character; fat cornfields and green meadows with big farm-houses, half-hidden in apple-orchards and groves of oak and tobacco-fields just planted and through all the roseate blush of the red soil from lane and fallow glowing against the rich greenery of crop or woodland. Perfect in outline, and of that marvellous hue which caused the simple name it still bears to burst naturally from the lips of the adventurers of two centuries and a half ago, the Blue Ridge rolls wave after wave along the western sky. It is full twenty miles away, though you would hardly think the distance to be half as great. The road leading thither is of the true old Virginia type, full in winter of mudholes that have absorbed, and have absorbed apparently in vain, waggon-loads of fence-rails and tons of rock: in summer rough and bony, with ruts worn into chasms and slabs of freestone cropping up above the dusty clay. On the subject of roads even the patriotic eloquence of good Virginians remains dumb; though old man Pippin, who lives on the hill-top yonder and is a firm believer in the superiority of the district watered by Rumbling Creek to every other part of the known world, has been heard to maintain the advantages of even a really bad road: "I tell you, sir, them ar' 'cademized roads is mighty hard on a horse; when thar ain't no mudholes and no rocks a man don't know when to pull up, and is mighty apt to go bust'n his horse along till he drap under him."

There is no fear of any one pursuing such a reckless course between Tucker's Mills and the mountains. The road bristles with impediments to which an uneducated steed would probably succumb, though not from exhaustion, if indeed he consented to face them at all. But upon a small active horse to the manner born, the traveller would be indeed hard to please who could not forget the ruggedness of the way in the beauty of the scenes through which it passes. If the pace be somewhat slow, and particularly should the season of the year be May, or early June, who would wish to hurry through such an Arcady? The wheat on the hill-sides is just heading; the early corn in the low grounds is knee-high, and the negro labourers shout their queer spasmodic melodies as they drive their one-horse ploughs along the rows. At one turn the road enters some forest of primeval oaks and chestnuts through whose tops the sunbeams shyly flicker on the fresh green leaves of shrubs and saplings At another it will be separated from the ceaseless babble of the river by narrow clover-fields ripe for the scythe, or long stretches of clean red soil in which the young tobacco-plants are making their first struggle for existence. The log-cabin of the negro is everywhere: on the slopes of the hills, by the roadside, in the depths of the forest. Unpretentious homesteads, suited to the needs of the times, look peacefully down from wood-crowned hills, while here and there some larger mansion, with its brick walls and pillared porticoes, stands among aged and branching oaks as a memorial of the days of slavery. Again and again the road plunges into the gradually narrowing river, and, as your horse pauses in midstream to slake that unquenchable thirst which the Virginia nag so uniformly affects, rare vistas of wood and water opening to the sight tempt you to unconsciously encourage the bad habits of the cunning quadruped. All the familiar trees that love the banks of running streams are here. The sycamore and the beech, the ash, the alder and the willow, spread their branches above the stream, while underneath their shade the kingfisher and the common sandpiper scud from rock to rock till they vanish over the white sunlit rapids beyond. Shoals of minnows race in the shallows under your horse's feet, and a big chub plunges in the still pool above. The deep boom of the bull-frog sounding from some rushy backwater beats time to the ceaseless chorus of the woodland crickets, and as the day wanes the tinkling of cow-bells in the lanes and woods answers to the musical summons of their owners from the hills above.

And in the meantime the massive outline of the mountains looms nearer and larger. The blue veil of distance is lifted and the mighty wall above us becomes one vast screen of rustling leaves. Houses of even a humble kind grow scarce. The stream gets steeper in its fall, and thunders in an angry fashion against the rugged cliffs and moss-grown rocks that hem in its waters. An old mill, its timbers black with time and weather, totters over an idle wheel. It is the last outpost of southern civilisation. The sights and sounds of every-day Virginian life are left behind, the red fallows, and the green maize-fields, the shout of the negro ploughman and the summer pipe of the quail. The mountains begin to close around, and the air is full of the noise of falling waters, the scent of cedars and hemlocks, and the steady moan of mountain winds sweeping softly over many miles of leaves. A change of scene more complete within the same short space it would be hard to find. The red clay road winding so lately through cheery rural scenes becomes a stony track, toiling painfully upwards between the huge trunks of a dark and sombre forest to the now hidden sky-line three thousand feet above us.

Here is the domain of the mountaineer. Not the romantic, ornamental, somewhat glorified peasant that the word is apt to suggest, but merely one branch of that despised and outcast race of white men that Southern slavery begot. The Southern "Poor White," of which the mountaineer is certainly the most interesting type, is not himself the outcast of a recent or a single generation, but is the descendant of those, who in former days, either sunk below the level, or as emigrants began life outside the pale of those connected directly, or indirectly, with the domestic institution, and the landed interest. Such men in the Free States, in the natural order of things, would have carved a road to competence if not to fortune. In the Slave States an emigrant without means or education may have done so, but the chances were that the odds were too much for him, and that his children were driven, not by violence or deliberate combinations, but by the force of circumstances, into the rough and waste places of the land. There they have multiplied and stagnated, illiterate, squalid, poor, unambitious, despised by whites and by negroes alike, clinging together, intermarrying and degenerating physically and morally. Not at war exactly with the world, but going through life with a kind of latent animosity towards it, as if it had used them ill, and a vague idea that their lot is hard and their chance a poor one. And so it is. Not that a pair of stout arms and a stout heart will not still in America bring a labouring man at least competence; but though the stout arms are there, the energy and the brains to direct them seem to have wholly evaporated from these strange specimens of the Anglo-Saxon family.

And yet, even among these people, material prosperity and civilisation varies considerably in different states and regions of country. But there is neither space nor need to examine such details. The mountaineer of the Blue Ridge, who has been entirely surrounded by a lowland civilisation for generations, is on that very account a more curious survival than the better fed hunter, amid the illimitable highlands of West Virginia, or the "Cracker" of the boundless back-country that lies behind the sugar and rice plantations, and the orange groves of the far South.

It is a popular notion that these people are, as a class, descended from the indentured servants, who were shipped to the Southern colonies from England in the seventeenth and early eighteenth century. That there can be anything like uniformity in their origin is impossible. In the ups and downs of colonial and frontier life, men of all sorts must have been jolted off the track, and with the growth of slavery, and the comparative contempt for manual labour that always existed in the South, dropped out of the race, and retired into the forests, to live as illiterate hunters or idlers. The position their descendants occupy is at least unique. They are worse off in every respect, save fuel, than the French or Belgian peasant, while the latter in his turn has a harder struggle for existence than the average British labourer. The squatter on the Blue Ridge cultivates his own land, or land so rough that its owners do not care to interfere with him, and he touches his hat to no one. But even in a democratic country where hand-shaking is a mania and has no social significance, the plainest kind of country farmer does not much care about extending the hand of citizenship to the pariah from the mountains or the pine-barrens. The latter may starve when his meagre corn-crop and his scanty supply of bacon runs out in the early spring, for all the outside world is concerned or is aware of; and if he never actually dies of starvation, there are sometimes weeks in the early spring when his rations are reduced to microscopic proportions.

To look up at the Blue Ridge from its base you would hardly suppose that a vestige of life lurked beneath that vast green canopy of leaves. A familiar eye might detect here and there the corner of a clearing peeping above the shoulders of the hills, and in early spring clouds of smoke, rising from some burning new ground, proclaim to the dwellers in the world below that human life of some sort exists up in those wild woods. This indeed is about all the majority of the community ever see of the mountain man. There are exceptions, however, and Pete is an exception. Pete, indeed, is a veritable chieftain among mountaineers, and is, moreover, well known in the low country for many miles round, while his cabin guards the narrow entrance to his dominions. At the very foot of the "big mountain" (as distinguished from the spurs and foothills), right in the angle where the north and south forks of Rumbling Creek tumble their respective waters together in a churning and boiling pool, stands the mansion of this illustrious man. Here, too, with the dividing stream the rough road divides also, and by the side of these stony tracks and on the banks of these rocky streams, reaching far away up to the highest gaps between the mountain peaks, are scattered at long intervals the isolated hovels of Pete's subjects. Pete's house, as I have said, stands as befits his autocratic position at the forks of road and stream, and no one can get up the mountain on business or pleasure bent without undergoing the scrutiny of his ever-watchful eye. The house is comparatively palatial, and the shoulders of the hills have receded sufficiently at this meeting of the waters to leave nearly two acres of flat ground around it, giving an air of ease, solidity and distinction to Pete's three-roomed house that the ordinary mountain cabin conspicuously lacks. Pete too has sown the flat in clover, a wonderful concession to lowland ideas. He has even planted a dozen or two of young apple-trees, which mark him as a man far in advance of his race. The logs of his house, too, are squared and not merely round poles unbarked, like the architecture higher up the creek. The chimney is also a departure from other chimneys on Rumbling Creek, for it is of rocks, not of sticks filled in with mud.

One other fact places Pete on a pinnacle in his community—he can write This is the last letter he wrote to me:

DR. SUR,—Thars trowte in the Crick by a heap mo' nor lars yer. Cum orn rite soon. Thars tu walers in the hole at the forx. Yrs respcfly, PETE ROBISON.

From this it may be gathered that my acquaintance with Pete and the mountain community on Rumbling Creek, an acquaintance renewed annually for many years, was due to a predilection for the gentle art. No strangers indeed but anglers (and they were scarce enough), unless it were the sheriff or an occasional cattle-dealer crossing the range by this rough route, ever penetrate beyond the forks of the creek where Pete's house stands. And few of these pass his door without alighting. Whether the subject in hand is trout or cattle, horse-thieves or whisky-stills, Pete's countenance and advice is almost indispensable. For our friend is not only an exceedingly smart man in his way, but an original and a character of the most pronounced description. What is more he is known as a "'sponsible mount'n man," a unique departure from ordinary rules, and a much greater exception even than a responsible Ethiopian. Pete has never been suspected of stealing a steer or setting fire to a barn. When he has taken a contract from some lowland farmer for roofing-shingles, or from the miller for barrel-staves, he has been frequently known to carry out his agreement within the appointed time. People have even been known to pay him money on account before the completion of contracts, which with an ordinary mountaineer would be a most fatuous proceeding. Old Judge Tucker, the big man of the country just below the mountains and once Member of Congress, used in former days, moreover, to ask Pete down to play the banjo and tell "bar stories" to the fine folks from Washington staying in his house. For there was no one on the mountain,

L

nor a negro below it, could "pick a banjer" like Pete. Many a night after assisting at one of those mountain suppers that nothing but lusty youth, still further hardened by long days on the rocky streams or in the saddle, could have survived, have I sat and smoked while Pete twanged at his banjo and crooned out his quaint medley of negro airs and Baptist hymns. Strange performances they used to be, with an audience sometimes of wild mountain men, drawn together by the rare news of a stranger's arrival, standing in the flickering firelight, and beating time with their often shoeless feet upon the rough boarded floor; while outside there was the chorus of the frogs and crickets, the intermittent cry of the screech-owl and the cat-bird, the roar and the gleam of the white water, and the flashing of the fire-flies against the black gloom of the night and the forest.

It is a favourite local pleasantry that the Southern Highlander has, through isolation, ignorance and apathy, so lost the human form divine, as to be indistinguishable at any distance in the woods from a cedar-stump or a fence-rail stuck upon end. Pete at any rate represented a very different variety. He was short and thick, with huge long arms. Everything that was to be seen of him, except his eyes, seemed covered with black shaggy hair. If a human being could be like a bear, Pete was that man; while, on the other hand, if all the real bears on the mountain could have been polled upon the subject, they would most certainly have agreed that Pete was their wiliest and deadliest foe. Our friend was thrifty. He had, for instance, a young horse of his own, whereas most of the folks higher up the creek had to be content with a share in an old one. His house outside, as I have said, was quite superior. Inside you would have said it was absolutely luxurious, if you had begun to pay calls at the top of the mountain instead of coming up from the country below. The long Kentucky rifle that the bears had so much cause to dread, and underneath it the banjo, were ranged above the chimney-piece in the living-room. In this apartment, too, was the family bedstead, resplendent with frilled pillow-cases and a patchwork quilt. There was an oak dresser which contrasted oddly with the smoke-blacked logs of the walls, and which Pete used to declare his great-grandfather had brought from "out thar"—a phrase expressing the mountaineer's very hazy notion of the mother country. Pods of red pepper and twists of home-grown tobacco hung from the rafters, while on the walls hung a pedlar's coloured print of Washington on the verge, apparently, of an apoplectic fit, and a somewhat realistic representation of Lazarus emerging from the tomb. Pete also had a guest-chamber, where weary anglers, and an occasional benighted traveller might dispose their tired limbs on straw mattresses of adamantine texture, and resign themselves to tortures from unseen enemies over which memory entreats us to draw the veil.

For land, there were the two acres of clover and struggling apple-trees, and a clearing of twenty acres on the slope of the mountain above. In the latter Pete had grown crop after crop in succession, and was wont to declare that the steadily-shrinking yield was the result of the wickedness of the times generally.

Mrs. Pete, however, insisted it was a sign of the approaching end of the world and that carnival of flame and torture, the contemplation of which so fascinates the mind of the illiterate Calvinist. Pete, moreover, had a cow and a heifer, and several thousand roofing-shingles and barrel-staves cut in the woods, and some hogs running wild on the mountain, that at this season of the year could almost have wormed themselves underneath his front door.

Pete had seen much of life for a mountaineer, for he had been through the war. He was the only man probably on the mountain who had felt the least enthusiasm for the Southern cause, and he had been more than once detailed with a sergeant's guard to hunt up deserters with which the gorges of the Blue Ridge at that time swarmed. Pete knew every cave in the mountains and every trail. He still recounts with much gusto the exciting chases his truant neighbours used to give him in those stormy days. Many a rifle shot they then exchanged is now joked over as they huddle over the winter fire, about as much influenced for good or evil by that great strife as if they were living in the Sandwich Islands.

Mrs. Pete is a typical mountain woman, gaunt of figure, and with a skin like dried parchment stretched over her projecting bones. If there is little of animation in her appearance, there is less in her manner, and her life is a dreary one indeed. A mixture of superstition and mountain methodism seems to dominate her existence. She will sit for hours before the fire in the broken rocking chair, crooning out disconnected lamentations, after some such wise as this—" The

Lord is good! The Lord is mighty good! We're too sinful, too bad to live! Even this yer mountain's too good for such as us!"—Poor woman, very little attraction there has been for her to wander off along the broad and easy road. Her greatest thorn is the wickedness of Pete, who has never even "professed." That Pete is by far the most honest and reliable man on the mountain will, from her peculiar religious standpoint, amount to nothing in the absence of those hysterical demonstrations which she has been taught to regard as the equivalent of salvation.

Following the winding of the narrow valley, sometimes clinging to the wooded hillside, sometimes descending to the level of the stream, toils upwards the rugged, stony track that is the highway of the mountaineer. Little clusters of cabins break at long intervals the rich and varied foliage of the forest. Rude houses enough for the second or third or even the fifth and sixth generation of Anglo-Saxons in the land of phenomenal progress. The roofs are of riven white oak-boards, curled and twisted by the action of the sun and weather; the walls are of rough, unbarked logs, enclosing a single room; the chimneys are of sticks and mud. Round the house there is a small garden-patch fenced in with chestnut rails, where a few common vegetables, such as peas and onions, testify to the richness of the loose black mountain soil. To each house there is probably a cow wandering in the woods, making in summer a tolerable living on the bushes and weeds, but passing every winter through a critical period of want and weakness, when the slender supply of corn-fodder begins to fail. Emaciated hogs stretch themselves in the sun among the warm rocks, lean as greyhounds, whose only chance of making bacon lies in the still unformed fruit of the oaks and chestnuts that spread their branches above them. The women around the settlement will be more conspicuous at this time of day than the men. Nowhere else in the world, I am quite sure, have the Anglo-Saxon race produced such unattractive, such dismal-looking, females. The peasant girl of Europe may not be all that poetic fancy sometimes paints her, but she at least has health and comeliness, a wholesome colour, and a cheerful mien. The peasant of these Southern mountains has health, to be sure, after a fashion, or at least a wiriness and tenacity of life; but she carries no sign of it in her bony figure and drawn colourless face. As for the men in this early summer season, when the rest of rural mankind, both North, South and West, in their very various fashions, are snatching the fleeting hour, they may be in the corn-patch on the mountain above, but are just as likely to be found loafing through the woods in listless Indian fashion, rifle in hand, or wandering by the brooks with their rough rods and tackle. Though trout, squirrels, an occasional turkey, with now and then a portion of a deer or bear in their respective seasons are to be obtained, no dependence can be placed on such additions to the larder of the Blue Ridge mountaineer in the annual period of semi-starvation through which he generally passes. Game at that time is scarce and wild, and is none too plentiful in these narrow ranges at any period. If these cabins and clearings were in

THE "POOR WHITES" OF THE MOUNTAINS 151

Oregon or British Columbia, there would be nothing singular about them; they would be the commonplace heralds of advancing civilisation. The men and women might bear the outward stamp of poverty, but hope and intelligence would be written on their faces, and the crudeness of their surroundings would be but a recognised and honourable phase in their career to prosperity. Here, however, it is all different; the squalor carries no hope with it, and is the outcome of the oldest civilisation in the Western world.

And yet civilisation and comparative prosperity through all these years has been within easy sight. There is hardly a bend in the road up the gorge of Rumbling Creek, from which if you turn in your saddle you cannot look down over the tree-tops upon the rolling plain of old Virginia, which means so little to the mountaineer. The very roofs of the plantation-houses, catching the sun ten or fifteen miles away, flash from point to point as the eye ranges far over the rich and glowing stretch of field and forest. The white smoke of a train goes trailing northward towards Washington. Senators, congressmen, merchants, millionaires, tourists from beyond the seas, are there likely, watching with admiration the ever-changing outline of the glorious crags upon whose sides we stand. But of the race who inhabit them, their habits and customs, the senator and the foreign tourist are in the matter of knowledge about upon a par; for all that one or the other knows of the population upon Rumbling Creek they might be Digger Indians.

What life is upon the head-waters of Rumbling

Creek, so with slightly varying conditions it is in the thousand other valleys of the Southern Mountains. Better land and more abundant game modify material conditions, but more or less all belong to the same primitive non-progressive class. They are out of touch with everything which the name of America suggests to the outside world. Books on Rumbling Creek are unknown, for there are no scholars. Pete can read, and the county paper once a week finds its way to that worthy, who transmits the news up the mountain. Nor is life absolutely without excitement. If wheaten bread is at a discount and hogsmeat at certain periods wofully scarce, there are weddings once in a while, when some buck from the north fork of the Creek crosses the mountain and brings back a barefooted bride from the further side of the range. There is a great picking of the banjos then and much " patting " and dancing of the mountain boys on the loose undressed planks of the cabin floors. And there is Pete to perform the ceremony if the wandering Baptist preacher from Juniper Creek, ten miles to the southward, cannot be found in time. A new cabin then runs up in some hollow even still more remote than the rough highway on which the old folks live. Another five or six acres of oak and chestnut, poplar and gum, maple and hickory are belted and killed, and become grim and naked skeletons amid the wilderness of verdure. And under these trunks and unsightly limbs another half-worked corn-crop will struggle with only partial success against bushes, squirrels and crows. As for funerals, that festival so dear to the negro, I had almost said that the people

THE "POOR WHITES" OF THE MOUNTAINS

in these mountains never die. In spite of hard winters, when for three or four weeks together, both forks of Rumbling Creek go choking and gurgling under heavy crusts of ice; when the rude grist-mill below Pete's house is silent, and what little corn there may be left on the mountain cannot be ground; and when the winter wind howls through the gaping chinks of the cabins, and drives the mountaineer close into his one luxury, a blazing hearth; in spite of these and many other annually recurring horrors, and in spite too of his lantern jaws, his parchment skin, his irregularly filled stomach, the native of the Blue Ridge seemed to me always to defy death. There are men of seventy in these mountains, wandering in summer time along the streams, who talk as naturally as possible about their "pa up yonder." And there, sure enough, at the cabin in the woods above you will find the veteran himself, seated probably on a straw chair on the shady side of the house, puffing at a long pipe and shaking his head at the very mention of time, as if it had long past his reckoning powers.

The population on Rumbling Creek live mostly in small settlements—clusters of half-a-dozen cabins more or less together, and between them long intervals of forest. These settlements in great measure represent different families, or at least clans of the same name. Feuds deep and bitter between clan and clan have not seldom agitated the mountains from top to bottom. The knife and the bullet have played their part often enough within the memory of even the middle-aged, and the county sheriff could tell many a tale of pursuit, generally fruitless, over these pathless hills. On such occasions indeed it is upon Pete that the majesty of the law leans. The most determined officer, in such a wilderness, would have a poor chance, unaided by local experience, of hunting down a transgressor. Pete feels his importance to the full on such occasions. It is pretty well known that it is he who decides beforehand in his own mind on the veniality of the "cuttin'" or "shootin,'" and arranges for escape or capture as seems good to his judicial mind. Pete belongs to no sept, so may be supposed to be free from all personal bias. From the very rare occasions on which an offender has been actually brought to justice we may conclude that he is not rigid in his views upon the use of deadly weapons in dispute. Few Southerners indeed of any kind are decided upon that point, and certainly no mountaineers.

The nomenclature on Rumbling Creek is amazing. The surnames are, of course, common English or Irish ones, but the Christian or "given" names, in which the local imagination has had full play, surpass in extravagance those even of the plantation negroes. Pete's immediate neighbours, for instance, consist of a father of eighty and three middle-aged sons. The former's name is Micajah, the latter are known commonly as Atch, Phil, and Pole. Such familiar abbreviations might pass almost unnoticed, if you did not chance to find out that they were short for Achilles, Philander, and Napoleon.

Co-operation of any kind has always been a difficulty on the mountain. A little way above Pete's house, by the side of the stream, the uncompleted log body of a house stands, and has stood, for years. Pete, at some former period, urged forward probably by his devout helpmate, decided that it was a disgrace to the mountain that its people had no regular church. Logs were cut and hauled, so many a-piece, by the various families. When it came to "raising" the house, however, and a general gathering of the clans was necessary, every attempt resulted, after a log or two had been put up, in what Pete denominates as a "fuss"— and a "fuss" in the South means a free fight. So the church, according to Pete's account—for it was a long time ago, and the logs have got by this time black and mossy—had to be abandoned altogether, and the wandering preacher continues his exhortations in Pete's living-room or under the arches of the forest trees.

The trout of Rumbling Creek have always been a leading item in the general economy of the mountain. I do not allude to them merely as an article of food. There are no sweeter trout in the world than these, but the native, as a rule, has been satiated with them, and has to be exceedingly hungry before he has any relish for what his betters consider a luxury. Of fishing, however, he never tires, and if he ventures out of the mountain to the nearest village store, it is generally to exchange trout for whisky or ammunition. The sport itself seems to exercise a fascination over these rude beings, and there is considerable rivalry of skill among them. Until quite recently the art of fly-fishing was unknown, and even now it is only a very adventurous sportsman among the mountaineers who attains to that pinnacle of science. Worm-fishing, however, in clear water is, as all anglers know, something of an art in itself, and in this art the rude fishermen of Rumbling Creek excelled. Pete claimed always to be the best fisherman of the mountain. Deep and almost bitter was the rivalry for pre-eminence between him and old man 'Lisha, who lived near the top of the pass. Through many a long spring day, when April showers have been driving the wild cherry-blossoms in clouds on to the river-banks, have these two champions, when they ought to have been ploughing their corn-land, wrestled for the biggest "string" of fish.

Trout, in these latitudes, cannot live away from the forest shade and the cool waters of the great mountain ranges. Before the war, with the exception of the mountaineers and an occasional farmer in the country adjoining, scarcely a trout-fisherman could have been found in the whole of Virginia. The mountaineers themselves appreciated the superiority of trout-fishing over the kind of angling for coarse fish in vogue in the lowlands, and prided themselves vastly on the accomplishment. It was a momentous day indeed when the first fly was thrown on Rumbling Creek. So much so that I have thought it worthy to be recorded later on in a chapter to itself.

THE VIRGINIA QUAIL

No finer game bird flies than the American or Virginia quail, which must on no account be confused with the little migratory bird that one associates with toast and the Mediterranean, or notes as an occasional "etcetera" in an English game-book. In fact, one feels much more inclined even in print to follow the people of the Southern States and call the *Orty Virginiana* a partridge, for such, indeed, to all intents and purposes, it practically is.

Though the bird does not get much notice in English literature which deals with American sports, it is, nevertheless beyond all comparison the most important, and far the most valuable item on the American game-list. One half of the cartridges that are loaded in the United States are probably fired at quail; and taking the older States alone, a much larger proportion even than that. It is the one domestic game-bird of the Americans in the sense that the partridge is with us; and not only fills the place of the latter most admirably, but may almost be said to do duty in a certain fashion for the absent pheasant as well. As to other American game-birds, the prairie chicken or grouse recedes more or less before civilisation, is not easily preserved, and is much more easily killed. The woodland or ruffed grouse, though widely distributed, is nowhere plentiful, and has an objectionable partiality for the tops of trees. The woodcock is partial and scarce, and an inferior bird to the European species, while snipe and wildfowl do not come within the range of our comparison.

But the quail has neither a hankering for the wilderness nor a dread of man. On the contrary, he clings to cultivation, and is only too anxious to remain there if given anything like a chance. In former days the comparative scarcity of sportsmen was sufficient guarantee for the maintenance of the stock of birds. Since the improvement in guns, however, and the immense increase in the number of sportsmen, not merely the game laws but the sense of private property in game have acquired more stringent recognition. And it is a notable fact that, with the exception of a few thinly settled Western districts, some of the best quail-shooting in America is to be had in regions that have been occupied for over two hundred years.

There is neither space nor occasion here to go into geographical detail as to the wide range of the Virginia quail. More than half the area of the United States, at any rate, carries a greater or smaller stock. It is sufficient to say that in the colder Northern States they are either extinct or too scarce for serious consideration; and efforts at re-stocking have, I believe, not been wholly successful. In Canada there are scarcely any left; Western Ontario, their only breeding ground, is almost denuded. And, indeed, extreme winters and clean farming together are, generally speaking, too much for the quail. It is in the Southern States that he really thrives to perfection; and, though still more numerous, for obvious reasons in thinly settled districts of the new South-West, there is nowhere that he shows finer sport than in the older parts of Maryland, Virginia, and the Carolinas. For here there is always that proportion of open country and woodland, of stubble fields and rough pastures and straggling thickets, that makes the birds, from a sporting point of view, show to the best advantage.

I have ventured the remark—which no one qualified to judge will, I am sure, dispute—that no finer sporting bird exists than the Virginia quail. I am almost tempted to go even further, and wonder if there is another bird that for dash and pluck and versatility is quite his equal: and this with no lack of respect, by any means, for a rocketing pheasant or a driven partridge. Heaven forbid, too, that one should even touch on that profitless but perennial controversy between the old style of sportsman and the new, since each of them are the product of circumstances beyond their control.

But I do think most of us like shooting over dogs; and by this I do not mean putting pointers into a turnip-field where birds are known to be, or over a country where they could be walked up to with equal or greater advantage, merely for the sake of seeing them work. When the dog ceases to become indispensable half the charm of his assistance has surely gone. But in a country like England once was, or like a few outlying corners and nearly the whole of Ireland still are, it is different. Yet, when birds are so scarce and lie so close that dogs are necessary, it is almost sure to mean that most of the shooting is too simple to satisfy a first-class performer. It is here that the Virginia quail comes in, and seems to me to stand as it were alone among game-birds. For none call out to a higher degree the qualities of the setter or the pointer: none lie better to the gun; but when the quail rises at short range, instead of presenting three times out of four a "pot shot," he will so contrive that something like that proportion of the chances he so boldly gives to his pursuers shall tax their marksmanship to an extent that would satisfy the most exacting sportsman of this proficient age. And this is possible from the fact of the covey scattering, as a rule, when first flushed, and the single birds seeking covert of a sort such as enables them to offer a really smart shot to the gun. The English partridge seeks safety from the guns by rising wild or out of shot. The Virginia quail first challenges the quality of the dogs, and then, more often than not, the shooting qualities of their master. He gets away with lightning speed. He generally contrives to have some obstacle handy to his hiding-place which will assist his escape; and of this, whether it be tree, or bush or fence, he knows how to take advantage with a nimble dexterity and tortuous flight unknown to any other of the gallinaceous tribe. He leads you into every variety of covert; tests your dogs in open stubble, in briary thicket, in silent, leaf-strewn woodlands; and there is no conceivable class of shot that in the course of a single day is not presented by this plucky, saucy, resourceful little bird.

"The Virginia quail," says that celebrated sportsman and charming writer, the late Mr. Herbert ("Frank Forester"), "is probably the hardest bird in the world to kill quickly, cleanly, and certainly. He gets under way with the speed of light. Before the wind he goes like a bullet from a rifle, when he has once fairly got on his wings. He flies as fast in the thickest covert, which he affects, as he does out of it. He takes a heavy blow, and that planted exactly in the right place, to bring him down; and, above all, he has a habit of carrying away his death-wound, flying as if unhurt until his life leaves him in mid-air."

Out of the many seasons during which with much ardour and enthusiasm and in various places I pursued the Virginia quail, or partridge as he was always called in the South, it is not easy to select a particular stage upon which to introduce him to the reader. But most prominently perhaps of all these memories there rises one of a roomy old mansion set right in the heart of what is known as "the bright tobacco belt" of Virginia. The landscape here lies in pleasant undulations, with little rivulets babbling down the valleys towards the greater rivers. The whole country except the strips of valley land is astonishingly poor, but possesses at the same time peculiar virtues for the production of the highest quality of tobacco. For this is a concentrated crop and takes up little space, and is here forced up by stimulants to a yield whose moderate quantity is more than compensated for by surpassing quality. The main bulk of the country is an alternation of ragged weedy stubbles of wheat or oats, of rough pastures and large maize-fields, of stately forest or scrub woodlands that have covered abandoned lands. It was an ideal country for birds and an ideal one to shoot them in, and well preserved withal. November and December were the two quail-shooting months, and it was almost always some evening in the second or third week of the former that used to find me, after a drive of forty miles over the worst type of Virginia road, approaching the hospitable portals already briefly alluded to. Within these dwelt one of the most accomplished sportsmen it was ever my privilege to know. I will call him the Major, because every one did so—on the principle perhaps that if he was not a soldier he ought to have been, and had mistaken his vocation—which was possibly true.

The Major was, I am proud to say, a Briton. He had purchased this plantation after the war, and if the cause of his exile was in part too great a devotion to horse and hound, he at least found much consolation in so fine a field for gun and dog. The Major was as popular as he was celebrated for his shooting prowess. The district was remote from towns, the farms were large, and my friend had practically the right of shooting the whole country for a dozen miles round, and nearly every one was only too glad to see him kill, or help them to kill, their birds. I have qualified this statement because the Major was possessed of a somewhat fiery spirit and a most formidable frame and pair of fists. So, if there was a little bit of country here and there "posted" against him, it was quite sure to be in connection with some such passage of arms that had occurred between the owner and himself. That the latter had never been shot was the marvel of his friends and those who knew the code of that country. One misguided man had once let fly at him, but was imprudent enough to miss, and before he could get in a second barrel, the pistol was spinning one way and its owner another. As there was little chance of the local law as then administered consigning the offender to prison, the Major took care he should at least have to go to the hospital for a considerable period. But by the time the Major and I used to shoot together he was a grandfather, and by far the most nimble grandfather I ever saw. No hours were too early, no day too long, no pace too great, no bird too quick, no colt too devilish, no negro too intractable for the Major.

What a month of months was November, or at any rate most of November in Virginia! The summer heats had gone; sharp night frosts had stricken the rank greenery of field and thicket. The tints of the open country were all brown and yellow, save the dark green of the pine woods and the brighter glow of the freshly sprung wheat. The forests were ablaze with red and gold. A great lull rested over all things; crisp mornings and balmy sweet-smelling days, with floods of sunshine tempered often by the dreamy haze of Indian summer skies, followed each other with little interruption. If you were a loafer, you could loaf to perfection; if you were a sportsman, you could walk or ride for ever. It felt a good thing merely to be alive. And when you knew that in every stubble there were huddling coveys of the little brown fast-flying birds waiting to be shot, the cup of happiness used to seem in these gorgeous seasons to be entirely full.

We used in that district generally to shoot on horseback in the old Virginia fashion, not because we were lazy, but because the beats were very large, and we could by this means cover more ground and handle more coveys in the day. We had often, too, a long way to ride in the morning before commencing operations, and a still further distance to travel home at night. It might be supposed that relays of dogs would be a necessity, particularly as the weather was occasionally as warm as an English September and the country rough to a degree. I can only answer that they were not necessary, and that our native-bred setters and pointers stood up to these long days three, and occasionally even four, times a week without apparent difficulty.

The Major's own property was about a thousand acres, a fourth of which, perhaps, was original forest, another fourth second-growth timber of pine or scrub oak on abandoned lands, while the remaining half would be equally divided between wheat, oats, and corn, or rough knee-deep pasture divided into large fields by snake fences, themselves half buried in woodland growth. Here and there were strips of clean, well-cultivated land, whose recent occupation was indicated by the rows of tobacco stalks still chequering the loose black soil. Here in these ten- or twenty-acre patches the pulse of the whole estate really throbbed. To them were tributary the greater area of ragged stubbles and bristling corn-stalk fields that covered hundreds of the surrounding acres. For them existed the tall, sharp-gabled barns that dotted the landscape, full now to bursting with the fragrant leaf. The strings of mules, the groups of whistling darkies, the rows of cabins at the homestead, everything centred in the one word—"tobacco." It was the burden of every conversation—the end of all human aims. It was in the very bone and blood of the people. Its fragrance was upon every breeze.

Such in outline was the Major's plantation, and such were the dozen or so others around it over which we had the privilege of shooting. This privilege, however, when their owners happened to be sportsmen, was saddled with the very natural condition of their company in the field. They were capital fellows these shabby-coated planters, if not perhaps exactly the style of men you would have selected to swop horses with. They were not of the same social stamp as our old friend Colonel Broomsedge of Locust Grove, but they were frank and hospitable, and with the genial friendly manner that places such a gulf in this respect between the countryman of the South and his equivalent of the North or West. They were all used to firearms, of course, but it was only a very few that were professed partridge shots and kept "bird dogs." But these few were very good performers and very keen, and to any one who shared their tastes they opened freely their hearts, their hearths, and their stubbles. They were a bit wild and dangerous, it is true, and something jealous; for rivalry enters into the American's field sports with a candour that an English sportsman might consider somewhat indecent. There was no particle of malevolence in the hearty way they would "down" your bird if the chance offered at fifteen yards before you could pull on it, or claim with unblushing promptness the entire merit of a simultaneous shot; but it made you like them much better with a pipe and a glass round their own fire at night than upon the opposite side of a fence during the day. The Major and I, however, used to utilise their spirit of rivalry by suggesting as often as possible the separation of our forces, for which there was plenty of room—he and I taking one beat and our native friends another, so that while we could thoroughly enjoy the day after our own fashion, our local companions were generally quite zealous to engage in what partook of the nature of an international competition. But some of our hosts were of the forest-hunter variety—deadly at sitting shots—men who could "bark" squirrels, or shoot the heads off turkeys, or circumvent the wily geese that cackled in big flocks on the new-sown wheat-fields, but "took no stock," as they would have said, "in shootin' on the wing"; and if leaving out the terminal "g" helps to make a sportsman, as we are led in England by inference to suppose, they did this to perfection and without any effort too. They were always delighted, however, to see us kill their birds, and hovered about all day on our rear and flanks with fearsome single barrels of prehistoric build. There was no getting away, of course, from these gentry by any appeal to their bumps of competition, for they did not profess "wing shooting."

They were out to enjoy themselves, and skirmished around with their long guns, talking farming, and cracking jokes, and now and again taking a promiscuous and generally futile shot at a hare stealing back, or even at a bird swinging round them. You never knew where you were with these cheery casual souls, or from what quarter the explosion might come, or in what direction their cannons might be pointing. The latter when at rest were generally covering some man or dog; for after the manner of the type, they generally carried them "at the trail," with the hammer down upon the cap, or at full cock—the happy medium having with these old guns usually ceased to work or else arrived at a condition that was more dangerous than either. It was holiday time too, now; the tobacco was housed and fired, and, though temperate men as a rule, both the season and the occasion seemed to demand some little token of festivity. So in the tails of their coats there nearly always lurked a small bottle of ten-horse-power whisky, with a corn-cob stopper. And by afternoon our hosts were sometimes a little merry; and when the men at the end of those long guns got merry, and took heart, and pressed up to the dogs, and came seriously into action, and let fly when the air was full of wings, or worse still, when birds were darting in the woods, it ceased entirely to be a laughing matter, however humorous it may seem in the long ago. Even the good shots were astonishingly indifferent as to what objects were in the line of fire. There were very few sportsmen of that country who did not carry shot about in them somewhere. I have always regarded it as a special dispensation of Providence to have survived so many campaigns without so much as a scratch, or even a horse shot under me. And I use this latter phrase in no figurative sense, for the horses used often to get badly sprinkled, particularly when they were standing about hitched to trees, while a scattered covey was undergoing treatment. The horse, however, did not as a rule stay on these occasions to get the second barrel, as may readily be imagined, but carried away the balance of his owner's cartridges, and possibly his lunch, leaving only the broken ends of a bridle behind him.

There was usually no pleasanter day in our annual programme than the one on which we shot the Doctor's place. It was four miles away, and as our medico had it rented out, and lived upon the other side of the Major's, he used on these occasions to stop and breakfast with us on the road. He generally brought with him as a fourth gun a dilapidated individual of some local notoriety—a landless, feckless, middle-aged bachelor, redeemed from utter disrepute by his cunning in every kind of sport. This individual rejoiced in the name of Rat Morgan; and no inverted commas are needed in this case, for the suggestive prefix was no nickname, but the short for "Rattler." And Rattler was a famous hound who flourished, quite early in the century, and was practically the god-father of our dilapidated friend. He had, at any rate, been solemnly called after him by a fond parent—a substantial yeoman, wholly given over to fox-hunting, of little education, and no religion, and considerable eccentricity. Rat's brothers had also been all called by hound names; and no minister, it was said, had ever been asked to assist at the family baptisms. Rat Morgan was fifty at least when we used to shoot with him, and had as yet taken no steps, so far as I ever heard, to remove the scandal, though there had been much competition among the rival parsons of the neighbourhood to bring him to some kind of font and remove such a heathenish stain from their midst. Rat's signatures was chiefly utilised upon promissory notes of trifling amount, as I have reason to know. If, however, he had possessed a bank account, his cheques would most certainly have carried the name of his father's favourite hound, for he had no other. Rat, however, had acquired a breechloader by some mysterious means, and was a first-class shot. The Doctor was profoundly respectable, both in birth and standing, and "rode," as the local saying went, professionally, the whole south side of the county. He was a keen sportsman, however, and I don't think that on such occasions as this the most violent epidemic would have kept him on his professional beat.

I dare say we should have looked a strange party, the four of us, all mounted—Rat Morgan usually on a plough mule—as we turned out of the Major's gate and went clattering down the hard and rough red highway. Half a dozen setters and pointers of the native stock ran at our heels, for the pedigree Laveracks and Gordons that were then finding their way into the country couldn't have faced our long days or stood up to the briars. Each of us had saddle-bags slung over our McClellan saddles, and behind two of the party at any rate was seated a negro boy, hanging on as best he could to his precarious perch

Nor was there any trouble here about dividing our forces when we came to the scene of action, for the Doctor and Rat held us in deadly and traditional rivalry.

Quail, like English partridges have their good and bad breeding seasons, dependent upon the weather, though it is not so easy with the former to tell what the year may bring forth till you are actually in the field with gun and dogs. They are late breeders, not pairing till the month of April; and the nests are well concealed in rough pastures or fence corners, though sometimes, unfortunately, they are made in clover or mowing-grass. The old birds themselves, however, are infinitely tamer than the partridge in the nesting season. For at that time—and, indeed, throughout the summer, till the broods are hatched— they will come out and perch on roadside fences or garden palings and fill the air with their cheery piping of "Bob-white! ah-bob-white!" And at such periods even the very negro with his old army and other vermin musket respects the trustful, handsome little bird. Their natural enemies are numerous— hawks, crows, and foxes; but the opportunities of escape are considerable in so much covert. I remember a sportsman's association once upon a time was founded in Virginia with a view among other things to the suppression of vermin, and a reward of fifty cents was offered for every hawk's head forwarded to the secretary. Times were bad, and every loafer and schoolboy in the country went out hawk-hunting. Flour barrels full of hawks' heads came up from remote counties, it was said, and descended upon the association's headquarters in Richmond. It was perhaps fortunate we were not an unlimited liability company for the well-intentioned fund to which we had subscribed was cleaned out in about a week, and there were unpaid creditors it was said going to and fro like raging lions in back country districts to whom five dollars were five dollars, and hawks' heads were hawks' heads. The committee were popularly reported to go about Richmond armed for some time; and it was jocularly suggested in the press that the office should be put in a state of defence. However this was twenty years ago and no attempt so far as I know against the Virginian hawk has ever been made since. The quail cock is as pugnacious as he is handsome, and his size is about two-thirds that of an English partridge. By September the young broods, usually numbering from sixteen to twenty birds, are hatched, and one oftens hears them scuttling in the dry thickets by the roadside, or occasionally even startles them into the air like a cloud of grasshoppers on their tiny wings.

October is the last close month, and it is not only that the birds then are usually not fully grown, but the country, untouched by serious frost, is too green and dry and tangled for successful shooting. Nor is there as yet any particle of scent, and quail-shooting without scent would be a vain hope indeed. But by November some sharp night frosts, following, perhaps, on heavy rains, have killed the last lush rankness of summer, and turned the landscape into a vast patchwork of varying autumn tints. The covert is so all-pervading that it would be hopeless to hunt it promiscuously; but the experienced sportsman and even the experienced dog knows by instinct what fields are likely and what are not.

The habits of the birds change slightly as midwinter approaches; and as they are, moreover, always liable to eccentricities in their movement, there is ample demand upon the intelligence and experience of the sportsman. Their favourite haunt is wheat stubble, which by November is knee-deep in brown, frost-killed "ragweed." And where little streams fringed with brushy alders and wild vines course through the stubbles, there will, in all probability, be found the greater part of your coveys, till real winter sets in with December, and they are forced to wider rambling in their search for food.

There was no better line of country in Virginia than the one upon which the Major and I used to start on these propitious mornings, as the darkey boys unceremoniously threw a panel of the roadside fence down to let us through into the waving sedge grass that covered the ridge upon which we gave our dogs the word to " Hie away ! " (the American equivalent for " Hold up ! ") As nothing is I think, more tedious than a detailed account of a day's shooting, I will but venture to ask the reader to accompany us just so far as to see where and how a bevy of quail is found, and in what manner it is handled. I may remark, however, in passing, that we didn't call them " bevies of quail." Rat Morgan would have wanted to know " what in thunder we were talkin' about.'

The Doctor would have grasped the meaning, but resented the term as "a d——d Yankee notion." However, let us ride down the slope of this long ridge, the tall yellow broom sedge brushing our stirrup-irons, while the dogs run off their first excitement—though, to be sure, the seven-year-old pointer is much too wise to waste her strength over such indifferent ground. Below us lies the valley, whose course we shall more or less follow all day; and we can see the brown stubbles stretching away upon both sides of the brushy stream that meanders down their midst. Here, too, the eager setters, young dogs, both of them, range wider over the deep stubble; which is quite right, for the birds might possibly be away from the watercourses. It is not very likely, however, this warm morning, so early in the season; and this the old pointer knows full well, as she trots leisurely along in the ranker growth, through which the rippling brook burrows its hidden way. In a few minutes there is a sensation—for we can't always see her—that the old dog has come to a stop. "Hi, dar she is!" pipes a shrill Ethiopian treble in my ear. "Dar she is, Marse Major—stannin' right plum in de bresh!"

And so she is. The setters are whistled up, and with a timely caution are soon backing their senior in pretty style right out in the field. The alders and willows here form a thicket ten or fifteen feet high, and it is a case of a gun each side of it. We are soon off our horses and abreast of the dog, who begins to crawl slowly on, the setters creeping after her. The birds are running, and we can hear them scuttling over the dry leaves. They soon rise, however, with a great commotion, seventeen or eighteen of them, and the air above the alder tops seems for a moment alive with glancing wings; and from the far side it is not child's play to pick out two outside birds and plant two effective shots before they have dipped out of sight—most of them to swing past the Major in the direction of the forest skirting the valley, the rest to dash on further down the stream, scattering, probably, as they fly.

If it can be avoided, it is as well not to follow a scattered covey instantly, as the birds, either voluntarily or involuntarily, give out but little scent for some time after they have squatted. So, with good prospects of a fresh covey within a few hundred yards, leaving our horses, we hunt onwards down the stream. We are not disappointed, and the former scene is re-acted with those pleasing variations incidental to shooting a sporting bird in a sporting country over dogs. In a quarter of an hour this second covey, taking the same flight, is for the most part in the forest, some single birds, as in the first, taking an independent line and being haply marked.

We have now two coveys scattered in the woods, which are perhaps four hundred yards off, and towards the spot where the first one entered we now bend our steps. A large corn-stalk field with yellow pumpkins lying about and a broom sedge pasture sprinkled with small pines have to be crossed, where we pick up a lagging bird that had been marked and knock over a hare or two—the Brer Rabbit, this, of Uncle Remus, whose diplomatic victories over

Brer Fox are by now classical or ought to be; and the turkey buzzard, who was also, it will be remembered, so notably out-generalled by that long-eared practical joker, hangs above us in mid-air, his broad wings silhouetted against the blue sky.

As we enter the woodland it is desirable to make a wide cast round so as to get behind the birds, and drive them, so far as you can drive a quail, back into the open. If you have a heady dog on your string, it is well upon such occasions to leave him with the horses, for steadiness over this crackling carpet of dead leaves, where the birds are squatting singly or in twos and threes, is essential. The forest is open, and at this season of the year a veritable fairyland. Oak and chestnut, poplar and hickory, rise like vast grey columns from the russet carpet beneath to the fluttering roof of red and gold, of saffron and burnished copper, illumined by floods of sunshine and broken by patches of cerulean sky. There is no sound but the tapping of the woodpecker and the gentle rain of acorns and chestnuts on the leafy ground, or the light scraping of a grey squirrel as he leaps from tree to tree. But here is the first of the birds, a whirr of wings, a momentary vision of a brown streak, disappearing behind a monster oak, and Ponto, who has flushed him, sitting on his haunches and gazing wistfully into space with an expression of countenance that most unmistakably declares, " That was not my fault." And in all probability it was not. But of the rest of the scattered birds, in whose midst we soon find ourselves, the dogs, for the most part, are able to give us timely warning. This, indeed, is the very cream of quail-shooting—I had almost said of all shooting. It is beautiful to see the dogs, with all their senses wrought up to the highest tension, working carefully over the bare woodland floor, and dropping suddenly and without a second's warning into every sort of rigid attitude known to the setting tribe. Sometimes a fallen tree, sometimes a heap of leaves, blown against standing saplings, yields a patch of covert, but as often as not the little brown bird is squatting on the open ground not three feet from the quivering nostrils of his discoverer. And what a dash he makes for his life, rising even with so timely a warning from your very feet, must be seen to be believed. Leaving the ground with the speed of a snipe and the noise of a partridge, he rushes through the forest trees, twisting and corking like a woodcock, only a woodcock on double speed. Sometimes he shoots straight up like a rocket for some opening in the leafy roof, at others he tears along not a yard above the dark ground. Often, too, on such occasions a bird is flushed by the other gun, and comes rocketing down over your head like an arrow from a bow. And perhaps when you have emptied your right barrel at him, a second, with cunning instinct, has allowed you to walk over him, and now, thinking the time has come, rises at your back, and gives you an instant's snap-shot through the trees with your left. Many of the birds find their way back into the open, and drop in sedge fields, or in thickets, and occasionally in the open stubble, and are marked, in part, at any rate, by our sable horse-keeper. But there is no necessity, with so much country before us, to be too exacting from each covey. So, emptying our pockets into the game-bag, we mount our horses and canter over some half-mile or so of unlikely country, till the next stubble fields spread themselves before us. It would be tedious to pursue further on paper the incidents of such a day, varied and delightful as they are in actual practice. We are baffled now and again by the plump of a covey into the dense scrub pine woods that here and there cover abandoned fields. Now and then, too, one escapes us in that mysterious, unaccountable way sufficiently familiar to the English partridge-shooter. We kill a woodcock or two and a good many hares, and eat our lunch where some big sycamore or beech spreads its arms above a bubbling spring. And all the afternoon the cheery work goes on through stubble, thicket, woodland, and pasture. The negroes, driving their waggons through the crackling corn-stalks, or hauling fence rails from the woods, tell each other that the " Major's bird-hunt'n'," with many strange ejaculations that imply it's a bad day for the " patridges." The shadows are long, indeed have almost faded, before we turn once more into the main road and head for the Doctor's buildings. The western sky is one entire blush of crimson, and that incomparable after-glow which succeeds these autumn sunsets in the South spreads a strange and lurid flush over the many-tinted earth. The negro women are calling up the cows. The axe is thudding from the wood-pile of cabin and farm-house. The scattered birds are piping in the stubbles, and the frogs from brook edges are proclaiming that the winter of their silence and their discontent is not yet quite at hand.

The Doctor and his henchman have got their bag spread out upon the porch floor of the overseer's house, and when the Major and I reckon up our spoils and find them to amount to twenty-five brace of birds, besides extras, our shooting host has to confess that once more he has been "bested" by the Britishers, though not, indeed, by much. He has, however, a most excellent excuse—for to Rat, it seems, was thoughtlessly entrusted the whisky-flask, and the natural result of such misplaced confidence had occurred; the greater part, that is to say, of the Doctor's share, had leaked out in some mysterious fashion, though it was not into the pocket of his faithless partner, it is to be feared, that the precious fluid found its way. The Doctor, however, merely remarked, and with some justice, that so unequal a division of the refreshment should fairly account for the difference of five brace in our respective bags.

MAR'SE DAB AFTER THE WAR

IT was fortunate for Dabney Carter Digges that he came out of the war with the well-earned rank of Captain, as he stood badly in need of some handy title for use on formal occasions. For by nearly the whole of the negro population, in spite of the tendency to drop, after the war, old *ante-bellum* terms that denoted servitude, he was still, for some reason or other, universally spoken of, and to, as Mar'se Dab. This was partly, no doubt, an unconscious tribute to the local fame of his family, as if, perhaps, it were due to these latter not to snap the old times quite so abruptly as in ordinary cases, and partly, no doubt, to accident. Nor, indeed, was this a unique survival of old habits; it was simply a rather exceptional one. So I think the reason that made those of us who were the Captain's immediate friends and neighbours speak of him generally, and in frivolous moments to him, as " Mar'se Dab," must be sought for in the humorous contrast between the great man's impressive personal appearance and the curt juvenility of this particular *sobriquet*. At any rate, it is as " Mar'se Dab " that my old friend's image comes most forcibly to my recollection, and it seems natural to recall his peculiarities, or to attempt to do so, with the familiar appellative upon the title-page. With regard to the subject of this sketch, I have so far used and shall continue to use the past tense. I don't wish the reader to suppose Mar'se Dab is dead. Far from it. But because the industrial system he pursued with such vigour proved so much less profitable than picturesque, he is now, I regret to say, an exile from his native land. The old acres, fortunately for them I fear it must be added, know him no more.

Mar'se Dab, in short, "burst all to pieces" many years ago, as his neighbours, with that kindly interest people take in their friends' futures, used always to prophesy he would. Not even a fragment from this aforesaid explosion remained wherewith to start him in a new land-killing enterprise. So he, poor man, scarcely past the prime of life, had to accept an offer from his wife's brother, who kept a store far away in Western Kansas. The Captain was not, I think, a proud man. He had not so much pride in matters of this kind as most of his class. But what he had he was compelled to swallow, when circumstances forced him behind the counter of a western country store. For those who had known Mar'se Dab on his ancestral acres, it required a mental effort of no ordinary kind to imagine him tying up packets of sugar and coffee for Teutonic or Scandinavian homesteaders. Indeed, it is distressing even to think of the Captain in such a place or at such an occupation.

To attempt a Virginia sketch without at least a genealogical allusion would not merely be unpardonable,—it would be impossible. It was an instinctive feeling that this had to come which I think prompted me to open this chapter with the Captain's full baptismal name. For the English ear, neither the names of Dabney, of Carter, nor of Digges have any particular significance. Distinguished individuals may possibly have borne them, but the names themselves are by no means distinguished. In Virginia, however, it is otherwise; for they are all three written large upon the pages of her past. There are, no doubt, plenty of people in Virginia possessing one or other of these names who are no connection whatever to the old colonial families who have given to them their local lustre. The Captain, however, was a representative in his own person of these three illustrious houses, respectively. For his mother was a Carter of Birley, and his grandmother had been a Dabney from the shores of the Rappahannoc, while as for the Diggeses, are they not written in the chronicles of Berkeley county from generation to generation?

Mar'se Dab himself, however, never appeared to take much stock in the genealogical advantages he enjoyed. In many respects, indeed—more particularly in the superficialties of life—he by no means did credit to his courtly progenitors. It used to be a common matter of criticism in the more aristocratic circles of Berkeley county—among the ladies particularly—that "Cousin Dab was a mighty rough man for his raising." But then, as these fair critics would go on to remark, it was not so much to be wondered, seeing of what "very ordinary stock" his wife came. Now, as I have said, the Dabneys, the Carters, and the Diggeses were among the very first families in the State. If all their members were not educated and polished men, they ought to have been. But the Thackers, from whose family the Captain took his wife, neither were, nor ever had been, people of education and polish. They were not, it must be understood, mere common farmers. They owned plenty of land, and before the war had acquired almost as many negroes as the Diggeses themselves. Nevertheless they were upon quite another social plane.

The Thackers, in short, belonged to that very numerous class which came between the real gentry of the south and the poor non-slave-holding whites. Politically a part of the great compact "slavocracy," numerically and its greater part, but socially, and for obvious reasons, inferior. Not a harshly defined inferiority, it is true; that would never have done among people whose somewhat precarious interests were identical, and who were all members of a dominant political caste, with most of the world against them. But the division was the unavoidable one between people with the habits and customs of gentlefolk, and those whose existence was quite devoid of such refinements, who were, in short, at the best, intelligent farmers, and nothing more. These things were managed very well. The Diggeses and the Thackers had been accustomed to interchange calls regularly every year. The phraseology of the most perfect equality had always been maintained when they met, but there the fiction ended. Human nature could do no more, as I am sure you would have said if you had paid a visit first to the old Digges's homestead, and then gone on to the family mansion of the Thackers; and the Diggeses and the Thackers were only types, and very good ones, of what, to apply English terms, we may call the gentry and the yeomanry of the South.

So when the war was over—though old prejudices and social barriers were a good deal shaken—Mar'se Dab was looked upon as having rather let himself down when he married Amanda Thacker. Southern rural society, however, though by no means destroyed in that district, was greatly shattered. People were too poor and too busy, and too sore with the outside world, to be very ill-natured about such trifles. Still social traditions that are founded upon common-sense and natural forces cannot be destroyed in a moment. So, as I have already remarked, the ladies of Berkeley county used to say in after years, that it was not altogether to be wondered at "Cousin Dab had got so rough."

Mar'se Dab's social position is then, I think, sufficiently well depicted. I once heard him airily described, by a jocose Canadian who was staying in the neighbourhood, as "a dilapidated blood." The Captain's friends rather resented the phrase; but when he heard it himself some time afterwards, he laughed so loud that you could have heard him all over the plantation, and so long that his wife got anxious about him,—Uncle Ephraim, however, who was standing by at the time, reassuredly remarking, "That's 'zactly how Mar'se Dab useter laff befo' the wah."

When I first knew the Captain soon after the close of the war, he might have been five-and-forty. His lung power was in keeping with his powerful frame. He did more shouting and shouted louder than any man I ever heard of on his plantation, standing about on hilltops and sending his orders echoing far and wide to his numerous and widely scattered dependants. The negroes on the place used to declare that " Mar'se Dab could go in two hollers to Shucksville." Now Shucksville was the county town, and as it was thirteen miles off, this remark must of course be regarded as an Ethiopian illustration of a purely allegorical nature.

Mar'se Dab's military title was no bogus one, such as Captain Topfodder's, for instance, who kept the store at Digges's Mills, and took his rank from a freight barge he had skilfully navigated for many years on the James River Canal. On the contrary, the fact that it was not more important may be attributed to the Captain's own reckless gallantry. If valour alone—and of course I allude to the Civil War—could have regulated rank, our friend should by rights have been a general of division at the very least. For it was always said—said, that is to say, in Berkeley county—that Dab Digges was the bravest soldier in the whole Southern army. His valour, however, was of such a hopelessly reckless kind, and his contempt of discipline so profound, that even the command of a regiment would have been out of the question. So as a captain he started in the 20th Virginia Cavalry ; and a captain he remained till the second year of the war, when he was taken prisoner.

Those of his brother officers who survived the struggle used to say it was extraordinary that Cousin Dab (for the regiment was raised in Berkeley, and most of the officers were his relations) succeeded in escaping death or captivity, or even a wound, so long. "There was no man in the war," they said, "that tried so hard to get killed as Cousin Dab, and that wrought such havoc in the ranks of the enemy; or," they sometimes added in the strictest confidence, "got his men so often into 'tight places.'"

I gathered that it was upon the whole considered by no means an irreparable calamity when Mar'se Dab, the fire-eating captain, was harmlessly removed in the second year of the war. The climax came about in this wise. It was in one of the great battles of that year, I forget which, that the 20th Virginia Cavalry were ordered to charge a regiment of Massachusetts infantry. It was a misty day, and it was not until the horsemen were within a couple of hundred yards of the enemy that an overwhelming body of cavalry was discovered to be drawn up in their rear. At any rate the retreat was sounded, and the 20th Virginia wheeled about. Not so, however, Mar'se Dab! That big voice which the negroes declared would go in two holloas to Shucksville, was heard sounding through the fog and smoke that its owner would be d——d if he'd retreat. And that was the last that was seen of Mar'se Dab for two years.

From evidence that filtered out afterwards, it appeared that the Yankee infantry were amazed upon that day to receive the charge of a solitary horseman, who came down upon them out of the fog, from whence they never rightly knew. They supposed it to be a runaway horse till it got so close they could see that the rider was spurring for all he was worth and shouting like a madman, as they then took him to be. Not a rifle was raised, but when Mar'se Dab arrived among the enemy's ranks, so far from appreciating the forbearance, he laid about him with such zest that if his sword had had an edge on it, several people would have been badly hurt. As it was, he was knocked off his horse with the butt-end of a musket, and sent to a Federal prison on Lake Erie.

Here Mar'se Dab chafed for nearly two years, picking up various and useful accomplishments hardly worthy, perhaps, of a Digges. Among these he learnt how to bake bread, to cut hair, and to pull teeth—studies forced upon him partly by the *ennui* of his position, and partly by the necessities for making a little money out of his fellow-prisoners, with which to procure those cakes of chewing-tobacco which were the solace of his life. Again and again, in the piping times of peace, has Mar'se Dab joked to me of these accomplishments. Two of them at any rate he carried with him into private life, and practised (in a friendly way of course) during his few spare moments, with an enthusiasm that I am afraid somewhat victimised his neighbours. As for hair-cutting, it was at least a harmless if a somewhat singular hobby. The Captain was indeed in great request in the neighbourhood as a trimmer of locks. As a puller of teeth, Mar'se Dab's popularity was nothing like so great. He used an old-fashioned key, and for the rest trusted only to his herculean strength; so the hesitating attitude of the neighbourhood towards him on the tooth question may be partially understood. There were some people of an economical turn of mind who were tempted to call in once the gratuitous services of the Captain. But I never heard that the most desperate sufferer from toothache or the most penurious individual ever repeated the experiment. Living near, as I did, I have heard sounds occasionally proceeding from Clover Hill that the negroes declared was Mar'se Dab at work upon some confiding countryman's jaw.

I was only once, however, a witness to one of these operations. If, as the negroes said, Mar'se Dab "could go to Shucksville in two hollers," I am prepared to swear his patient upon that occasion would have reached the local metropolis in one.

When I first knew the Captain he had just come to live at Clover Hill. This was not actually at the close of the war, but it was at the close of those few years of chaos—political, social, and financial—which ensued in war-worn Virginia after the surrender of Lee and the abolition of slavery. It was the period which marked the first conflict of new conditions with old ideas—that reluctant struggle of an old civilisation based on a kindly picturesque domestic slavery, to adapt itself to an altered state of affairs; a change from the obligation for food, clothing, lodging, and protection, to a business compact between master and servant, terminable at any moment.

Clover Hill was an average Virginia homestead of the better class. It had no pretension, of course, to compare to "Newtown," the old Digges place at the other end of the county, where the Captain's eldest brother still lived at that time. There, indeed, at Newtown were many heirlooms and old sideboards, and antediluvian bedsteads, and a good deal of old silver, and family portraits that, whatever their defects may have been as works of art, represented at any rate ladies and gentlemen. Newtown was quite a famous place in Virginia; but Clover Hill was nothing of the kind. For that reason, perhaps, it was all the more typical. Till the Captain took possession, the place had been occupied only by an overseer. Seed-wheat had been stored in the parlour. The best bedchamber had been for years devoted to the storage of dried apples and washed wool, and the walls were coated thick with entomological specimens that had danced in the sunny rays of a half-score of departed summers.

With the Digges advent this was of course all changed. But the house was furnished distinctly upon Thacker and not upon Digges lines. As Amanda Digges was an only daughter of old man Hiram Thacker, she had inherited his household gods. Among these, too, there were family portraits of a kind—daguerreotypes and black paper silhouettes framed in fircones or varnished oakleaves, caricaturing the last generation of Thackers in merciless if unconscious fashion.

The house at Clover Hill, though not so venerable nor so large nor so hallowed by traditions as Newtown, had been built nevertheless as a gentleman's residence in the early part of the century. The Captain's great-uncle, Randolph Digges, somewhat prominent in his day as a Whig politician, had been its founder and its occupant for a great number of years. The instalment of Amanda Thacker and her family household gods at Clover Hill was an improvement on the overseer interregnum. Still it did very little, I am afraid, to restore to Clover Hill the aristocratic tone that was said by old people to have marked it when that venerable patriarch "Uncle Ran" over his madeira used to make its walls echo to post-prandial denunciations of Jefferson, infidels, and Frenchmen. The building was of red brick; it was two stories high and perfectly square. A wide corridor ran straight through it below, and another with the same direct simplicity pierced it above. Upon the ground floor there were three rooms upon each side of the corridor, all exactly the same size and exactly alike. Upon the upper floor, too, there were three rooms upon each side of the corridor, also all of the same size and exactly alike.

It has never been rightly decided which was the back and which the front of the Clover Hill house, for at either end of the corridor there were big porticoes, supported by the same number of high white fluted columns, and approached by the same number of half-decayed wooden steps. The up-stair corridor led through doors on to the roofs of these porticoes, from whence, under the over-arching leaves of aged oaks, could be seen glorious views of woodlands, fields, and distant mountains. In Uncle Ran's time, you may be sure, no such things would have happened; but in the utilitarianism of Thacker tradition it was no uncommon thing, after washing-day, to see the family linen hanging in graceful festoons over the carved railings, and fluttering in the wanton wind.

The doors and the windows of the Clover Hill mansion may possibly one day have fitted tolerably, though even in an old Virginia house of the most approved kind such a condition would have been hardly orthodox. Now, however, they had sprung at their lintels, and gaped at their hinges to such an extent that Mar'se Dab used to swear that the house was not merely not weather-proof, "but it warn't hardly dog-proof."

From the early spring to the late fall of the year, however, there were few more charming spots in all Virginia than Clover Hill. Mar'se Dab could then boast with justice "ther was 'ar stirrin' thar" (for he had dropped hopelessly, I am sorry to say, into the vernacular), "when the heat elsewhere was enough to kill a mule."

To nature's charms, however, I fear Mar'se Dab was almost insensible. He was not devoid of sentiment of a kind. Indeed it was partly that, I think, that made him so reactionary. But it was a sentiment that hugged insensibly all time-honoured Virginia rural customs—a sentiment that made him cling obstinately to old-fashioned ways, to be happy among big gangs of negroes, to love the very sight of a tobacco-field, to put up almost cheerfully with roads bottomless for mud, with gates that would not swing, with barns through which the rain-storms soaked, with houses through which the winter winds blew.

When the Captain took up his abode at Clover Hill, the land was in very fair condition. The overseer, who had had it in charge so long for the Digges family, had been a skilful and thrifty farmer. Being too old to be drafted for the army, he had remained at home all through the war. The estate had never been too heavily stocked with negroes, and had been seeded largely to grass and clover, the very acme of high farming in the South of those days.

When slavery and capital together were swept away by the war, and the conditions of southern life practically revolutionised, most sensible men recognised that a different system of farming must be pursued. Numbers of the upper class flinched from the prospect, and went into business. Others set to work with good resolutions, and kept them. Many, again, made the resolutions, but did not keep them. Mar'se Dab, however, when he came to Clover Hill after the war, not only showed no inclination whatever towards agricultural reform, but he did not even make any profession of such intentions. He did even more than this. He openly and emphatically repudiated any such course, and declared that the style of farming that had been good enough for his fathers was good enough for him. He was too old, he said, to start raising clover and grass, when he'd been all his life trying to kill it in the corn rows. So Mar'se Dab "went into terbaccer." He collected double as many free negroes on the place, both renters and hired hands, as there had been slaves before the war, and commenced that enlightened course which finally reduced Clover Hill from tolerable fertility to absolute barrenness.

Mar'se Dab, moreover, was more fortunate than

many of his neighbours; for when he married, he got with his wife five thousand dollars of hard money, which, in old man Thacker's thrifty hands, had somehow or other survived the general wreck of war.

Clover Hill was a picturesque property, undulating enough to give happy variety to the landscape, without too great abruptness for cultivation. The prevailing colour of the soil was red, which gives such a warm look to fallowed hillsides when contrasted with the green of woodlands and growing crops. Of meadow-land there was plenty in former days—snug flats of rich alluvial soil between the hills, whose fertility was sufficient to resist, without deterioration, the average treatment of the old Virginia "rip and tear" system, which was saying much. In the overseer's time, and probably in the time, too, of old Uncle Ran, waving timothy grass and rank clover had flourished there and glistened in the heavy dews of the bright June mornings. When I first knew the place the backs of the negroes in hay time used to bend low, and the perspiration pour from their ebony faces as they swished their mowing blades through the heavy growth. Little tinkling streams all overgrown with alders and grape-vines, coursed their way down the valleys; and very troublesome they grew in flood times if treated, as Mar'se Dab used to treat them, with contemptuous neglect.

At the far end of the place where Buffalo Creek, which bounded it on one side, crossed the high road to Shucksville, which bounded it on the other, there stood a venerable wooden edifice which, together with the hamlet attached, was known as Digges' Mills

Here the corn and wheat of the neighbourhood had been ground ever since there had been any to grind, which was a good long time. From an Old World standpoint, perhaps, it was not very ancient, but at any rate it looked it. While the hum and drone of the wheel and the flashing of the waters over its black and sodden timbers, and the spray that sparkled on the mossy rocks beneath, and the rustic bridge of chestnut trunks that crossed the stream, and the huge weeping-willow from which it swung, made a picture that on sunny summer days it was both cool and pleasant to behold. Besides the mill there was a store, where Mar'se Dab had, in his earlier prosperous days, a ready and extensive credit with Captain Topfodder the merchant. In the days of his too evident decline, he had an account even greater still, whose remote settlement agitated greatly the waking hours of that worthy ex-commodore of canal-boats. Mar'se Dab's wages to his hired hands, and the advances to his tenants, came more and more, as time went on, in the shape of little notes on the torn leaf of a pocket-book, written in pencil, to the long-suffering Captain. There were whole files of these scrubby little remnants stored away in the desk behind the counter, running after this fashion mostly :—

"To Cap. TOPFODDER.—Please supply Chris' Johnson with goods to am^t $1.75,—Y^r friend, D. DIGGES."

The Captain began to wish he hadn't been quite such a friend to Dabney Digges. As he sat tilted back in his straw-bottomed chair on the store porch, squirting tobacco-juice over the railing and calling to his customers, as they rode past, to "lite and set awhile, he ruminated over the possibilities of how upon earth at this late date he could alter matters without appearing unneighbourly. The Captain did get so far as to say in public that "Dab Digges was the hardest man to git money out of in North Berkeley." Besides the mill and the store there was a wheelwright's shop, whither ploughs and waggon bodies and dilapidated buggies retired for repair for indefinite periods, and grew weather-scarred and almost mossy from long hope deferred. There was the forge, too, of a blacksmith, who was always out of coal or " gone away to 'tend his crap," and an Episcopal church, that had of late years found it exceedingly difficult to procure, or at any rate to retain, the services of a parson.

Mar'se Dab was a man rough of speech, as has been implied. He didn't say negro, nor even nigro, but always used the word " nigger," which is a variety that, strange as the statement may appear to outsiders, is seldom used by well-bred Southern men, and never by ladies. "Those durned niggers!" Mar'se Dab used to be fond of saying, "ought to be put right back in slavery,—a triflin', no 'count parcel of scoundrels."

This was of course mere verbosity. The Captain would have been miserable if he had not been surrounded by his dusky crowd. Most people in the neighbourhood agreed, in a great measure, with the sentiments so baldly expressed by Mar'se Dab; but they acted up to their opinions, and dispensed as much as possible with Ethiopian assistance. But the Captain did nothing of the kind. As I have already stated, he collected all he could lay hands on, and established them upon the Clover Hill plantation. When he was remonstrated with upon the African centre he had set up, he used to reiterate the vices and the worthlessness of the dusky race with much greater warmth of feeling than the subject required, and then would suddenly break out, "Dawg my skin! I must have a big force of these scoundrels, if I am going to make any terbaccer worth speaking about. I tell you, sir, folks may talk about grass, and stock, and fruit, and suchlike. Terbaccer made old Virginia, not termaters, and, by golly! I'm goin' to hold on by it any way."

Now Mar'se Dab did really understand the science of tobacco growing and curing. It was the management of free labour, and the keeping in heart, by judicious cultivation, a limited amount of land, that beat him.

Now, in Virginia, it is generally estimated that a labourer is required for every 20,000 hills of tobacco. As the Captain used to aim at planting 400,000 hills, or about 80 acres, it will be understood that he was compelled to have about him what was a large force of hands for these later days and a limited estate. For it was not only the tobacco, but the 300 or 400 acres of maize, not to speak of the wheat he had to grow "to bread his folks," as he would have said, and to keep his horses and mules, and milch-cows and hogs.

When I first knew the Captain intimately his

system was in full blast. I have mentioned that he recommenced his life with some ready money, as he did also free from debt. Now there were two or three years, about that period when prices were exceptionally high, for artificial reasons that originated with the war. Mar'se Dab's credit was good, and he seemed for a time to be actually prospering in spite of his defiance of economic laws. He came to believe in himself more than ever. He ridiculed his neighbours who sowed clover and agitated themselves on the subject of the improvement of stock. His loudest and most tremendous laughs were got off at the expense of a cousin of his wife's, who had set out fifty acres of apple-trees in the mountains. When I last saw that cousin he was netting 4000 dollars a-year from his orchards, and poor Mar'se Dab was in Western Kansas! Well, as I was saying, "the pitching" of a great crop was the main idea in those days, not only on Clover Hill, but on many other plantations too. The negroes in the neighbourhood would flock to Clover Hill before Christmas-time to try and rent a bit of land or hire out to Mar'se Dab. Many too of the regular old Digges servants from Newtown again united their fortunes with the family in this manner.

It was noticed, however, that these last seldom stayed more than a year. The true reason of this may perhaps best be given in the words of old Uncle Ephraim, one of the most attached of the bunch. It was a confidential communication, it is true, and delivered across the boundary fence which separated my own woodland from the tobacco patch on Mar'se Dab's land, which old Ephraim was working. After all these years, however, there could, I think, be no sort of objection to recalling some of the old man's remarks.

"Mar'se Dab," said the patriarch, "is a mighty good man, but he ain't like his pa. I bin raised with quality folks, and knows what they is. Thar ain't no fambly in the State as held therselves higher or more 'sclusive than our folks done useter. But Mar'se Dab! Lor'! he don't seem to have no respect for hisself or fambly. It make me feel mighty bad to hear him cutt'n up, a rippin' and a swarin' an a hollerin' roun' like the ordinary white folks at this upper 'een of the county, that ain't had no raisin' wuth speakin' 'bout. I was a bit of a chap down at the big house when Mar'se Dab wur borned, an' when I heern him lettin' hisself down an' gwine on in sich a way, I feel powerfully moved to say suthin. But he's a rough man, Mar'se Dab, an' like as not to burst me all to pieces. It 'ud go mighty hard with the ole Miss' if she wur alive and know'd. She'd get after me, too, fur cert'n and sho', if she thote I 'lowed Mar'se Dab to run on without speakin' any. I'll be powerful oneasy when I see ole Miss' at de judgment, when de hearts of all men * * *."

The asterisks represent one of those exhortations to which Uncle Reuben, since he took religion, had been addicted. But sound as was his doctrine, and eloquent as was his language, there is no space for even a sample of it. Upon this occasion, however, it was cut short, and the venerable man's attention turned somewhat abruptly to earthly things, by his mule, which he had left standing in the tobacco-rows, getting his leg over the trace-chain, and showing a disposition to leave the field, plough and all.

"Stan' still, sah! What you warnt to be cutt'n up fo'. It look like to me yo' oughter hev movin' roun enough, and be prepar'd to stay quiet once in a while, and study over yo' foolishness."

Unc' Ruben's mind, however, was not yet unburdened, for he returned upon another count.

"It ain't Mar'se Dab only. 'Spite of the rumpus and fuss he raises 'roun him, thar ain't no kinderhearted man north of Jeems river, or dis side of the Blue Ridge. I could put up with his rearin' an' pitchin' roun', for the 'spect I bar to the family, but, bless grashus! the niggers that Mar'se Dab's c'llected on this yer place! No one ever heern' me say a word 'gainst nobody; but I swar de solemn truth that the cull'd folks on dis yer plantation is de meanest, no 'countest, crowd of niggers that Gord ever made. I ain't *all*together 'sprised, for I know'd what this yer north end of the country wur befo' the war. I don't hold as what some o' these yer plain white folks warn't mighty good masters to their servants; but then a cull'd man as ain't belonged to a good fambly, whar is he? He don't know nuthin' 'bout manners or 'spect for hisself. Now, sah, I bin *raised*, I has! I bin *raised*! I ain't growed up like a sassafras bush in a ole turn'd-out field anyhow! Thar's a heap o' difference 'tween white folks, an' thar's a heap o' difference 'tween cull'd folks, too. Fur a gen'leman as has bin raised among cull'd folks, Mar'se Dab beats anythin' I ever seed. He don't seem to know more 'bout 'em than ef he wur a Northern man. He don't study neither character nor princerples. Everybody layed out to git on this yer place, as they know'd it war a good plantation, an' that Mar'se Dab had right smart money by his wife an' a good force of mules. Dis yer nigger or dat ar nigger cum 'long about 'hirin'-time, an' talks big to Mar'se Dab 'bout the wuk he'll do if de boss 'll guv him a house an' land for de comin' year. He runs on mightily maybe about how he's bin mindin' a team for his ole mar'se since de s'render, an' how as his ole mar'se was jes fit to kill himself at losin' sich a good hand; but how his wife took sorter ailin, an' a whole parcel of foolishness which Mar'se Dab takes stock in. Den dis yer nigger tells Mar'se Dab he'll be satisfied with half the terbaccer an' a third of the corn; an' as Mar'se Dab's bin givin' half the corn, he thinks he's makin' the finest kind of agreement, not studyin' neither character nor princerples.

"Gord knows whar sich niggers wur raised—up in de mount'ns as like as not." (The supreme contempt at such a source of origin, expressed by Uncle Reuben's shrug of the shoulders, could only be thoroughly appreciated by a local expert.) "Dar's bin a heap o' folk an' a heap o' house-buildin' on dis yer plantation since de war. Dar soon won't be a house-log stanin' or a board-tree left in the woods. Dar's bin land clur'd so nat'ral po' it 'ud skeercely sprout a black-eyed pea in the first crap. I mind the time when I usetest to come up 'yer in busy times. It wur a fine place, an' de craps wur powerful heavy den. The wheat wuz so rank I jes told the Jedge—Mar'se Dab's pa—that ef he warnted me to go up cradlin' wheat to Clover Hill, he'd jes have to trade me away fur some one who could do it; for my rheumatics was too bad, an' I couldn't an' I warn't agwine ter do it, not if he cut me in pieces fur it. Now, bless grashus! the heads ain't within hollerin' distance of one another.

"Yes, sah, dar's a heap too many folk on this yer plantation, an' mighty poo' kind of folk, too. It look like to me as if Mar'se Dab had been ridin' round the country fo' a yer or two an' skeered up all the meanest niggers 'twixt here an' the big mount'ns, an' sot 'em plum' down in a muss. Sich a stealin' an' lyin' an' cussin' an' rippin' an' rearin' an' tramplin' roun' never wur seed, an' yet thar's mo' talk 'bout 'ligion here than most anywhar. To see 'em scufflin' up to the mourners'-bench on preachin' Sundays—O-o-o-o-ēē!

"I laffed fit to kill myself las' Sunday when Brer Moses from Poplar Creek was guvin' a open-ar preachin' for the noo church fund. Well, sah, when Unc' Mose' had got through de preachin' he tuk off his felt hat, an' axed me to sukkerlate it roun' for the c'lection. Fo' Gord, sah, that ar ole hat of Brer Mose' passed aroun' from han' to han' o' that bowdaciously 'ligious crowd, and nar a quarter nor a ten-cent piece, nor even a nickel, wur drapped in the crown of it. I saw Brer Mose' face wukin' powerfully as the empty ole hat were comin' roun' to him again, an' I could see he wur pretty mad. When it got to the man as wur stanin' next him, he reached out his han' and grabbed dat ar hat in de biggest kind of a hurry—sorter makin' out as if he wur skeered he wouldn't han'le it agin. Well, sah, Brer Mose' in front o' all de folks fust looked at one side of de hat an' den at de other, an' den he crams it on his head, an' hollered out, 'Well, bredren, you isn't showin' yo'selves by yo' deeds 'preciative of all de blessins showered upon yo', but tank de Lord I'se got my ole hat back anyway,—dat's somethin' in these yer hard times.' In all yo' born days, sah, you never seed a crowd of niggers look so mean. No, sah; I reckon I'll git on down to the old place agin. Mar'se Ran, so long as he's thar, 'll give me a house an' terbaccer patch. I ain't suited to these times nohow. A heap a hurrain' an' fuss was made 'bout dis yer friddom[1] an' that; but I b'lieve I'd as lief things had stayed as they wur."

Uncle Reuben was, of course, a privileged person. His years, loyalty, respectability, and "dignified manners" procured for him a licence and liberty of speech that are submitted to, the world over, in ancient and faithful domestics.

"Durn that old man Reuben!" said Mar'se Dab to me one day not long after this.

"What's he been up to?" said I. "He's the best hand you've got."

"Oh, Lord, yes! He's a good enough hand; but I'm blamed if I stand his nonsense any more! He's just been spoiled down at home by our folks, and got to think I can't live without him. What d'ye think he did yesterday? He came up to the house 'bout sundown and said he wanted to speak to me. I thought, of course, a horse was sick or something, and went out to him; and I'll be dorgonned if he didn't

[1] Freedom.

stand and lecture me for a half hour, and would have gone on for two hours if I'd 'a let him. He run on about my cut'n har, and said no Digges had ever cut har before ; and that my pa and ma would get up out o' their graves and ramble roun' in 'straction if they thote I was goin' on so. As sure as I stand here, if the old scamp didn't go on to tell me he was afeared I hadn't any o' the old Digges dignity, and Lord knows what, till I took up a swingle tree and told the old scoundrel I'd burst his head open if he gave me any more of his sass! 'Oh, that's right—that's right, Mar'se Dab,' says he. 'Kill me, sah—for Gord's sake kill me! I bin yer in this wicked world, long 'nuff anyway. I'se made my peace, an' am ready to go right away. I'll suttenly go straight to the ole mar'se and missus, an' tell them how yo' cutt'n up an' swarin' an' rippin' aroun'. Yes, knock me on de head, Mar'se Dab ; I ain't keerin' much anyway. Folks' ways these times ain't my ways. I nussed you, Mar'se Dab, when you was so small you hadn't hardly commenced to notice. I shuk down apples for you, Mar'se Dab, befo' ever you put pants on. Go on, Mar'se Dab ; kill me, sah ! You're mad now an' jes' think I'm sassin'. One d'ese yer fine days you'll say old man Reuben warn't sich a fule as I thote.' If you'd heard the old fellow, you'd have been powerfully tickled. I shouldn't have cared, but the old man raised such a fuss, a lot of the hands came round to listen."

So Reuben, the last of the old generation, went, and Clover Hill continued on its downhill course. The Captain's notions of the capacity of land were drawn from no human standpoint. He ploughed up the hillsides; he ploughed up the bottoms. Noble groves of oak and chestnut fell before the destroying axe on ridges infertile for cultivation, and that the commonsense of two centuries had left intact. So it was year after year, red-land and grey-land, upland and bottom, turned and heaved unceasingly beneath the recklessly-driven ploughs. Year after year the axe rang, and the toppling trees crashed for new tobacco-ground. The negroes sang and shouted, and Mar'se Dab holloaed and stormed, happy in the pandemonium he had created, and hugging even closer, as their evil fruit became apparent, the worst traditions of the past.

Tobacco, tobacco, wheat, wheat, corn, oats, wheat, oats, corn, corn—— This, I think, would fairly have described Mar'se Dab's method of rotation. This amazing tax upon the soil was not modified by any outside assistance. Some phosphate or stimulating fertiliser of a like kind was dropped in the hill with the second crop of tobacco; but the Captain's favourite dictum was that "commercial fertilisers would break any man." There was, however, an immense bank of barn-yard manure accumulated round the stables, scorched by the suns and bleached by the rains, it is true, of many years, but still by no means valueless. Never, Mar'se Dab declared, when twitted by his friends upon the subject, could he find time to devote his waggons and horses to such a secondary matter.

The rotation above formulated with tolerable accuracy covers, it will be noticed, some ten years. This was about the length of Mar'se Dab's reign at

Clover Hill, the year of collapse, when the long-suffering soil at last gave out in indignation, and absolutely refused to bear further the burden so unjustly laid upon it, and the property, in the estimation even of the most reactionary Ethiopians, was "run clean out." The corn-stalks had shrunk to the size of your little finger, and, save in the rich hollows by the streams, produced nothing but "nubbins."[1] The wheat-straw was so miserably short, and the ears so scanty, that Uncle Reuben's forcible illustration as to their being scarcely within hollerin' distance of one another, was by no means so far-fetched. The oat-crops had grown so weak that the briars and bushes, rioting in the filthy soil, simply choked them out of existence; while the fierce winter rains had cut gullies down the hillsides, which the thunderstorms of summer rent into ravines so deep that men and mules nearly disappeared from sight when they floundered through them.

Mar'se Dab "died fighting." It was the extraordinarily dry year of 187— that finished him. The sight of the crops on Clover Hill that year made venerable agriculturists weep who remembered the glories of the past. Mar'se Dab believed in tobacco till the last, nor was there anything unreasonable in his faith, considered in the abstract. It was his mode of applying it that was wrong. His tobacco he managed admirably. His plant-beds were burnt in good season. When the spring frosts cut other folks' young plants, or the fly got them in cold, dry weather, Mar'se Dab had always a plentiful supply. When

---
[1] Short deformed heads.

"planting out" came in June, the Captain always had his land ploughed, harrowed, and hilled up, ready for the first good "season," and everybody in the plantation had ample warning of the coming rain. For so long as Uncle Reuben was there, he was better than fifty barometers. The signs had never been known to fail. When "de mis'ry" took that venerable henchman "in de left shoulder, there'd be fallin' wedder befo' day, cert'n and sho'."

No growing crop was better tended than Mar'se Dab's tobacco; and if some of the tenants' houses "cured up a little blotchy or ran some" during that critical period, it was because the boss, "rustler" though he was, couldn't be everywhere at the same time. But while Mar'se Dab's tobacco was well done by, everything else was neglected; and economic laws were defiantly and aggressively flouted. Clover Hill was not quite in the real tobacco-belt—that group of counties where the highest grade of leaf is produced, and where other crops may be safely made subservient to tobacco culture. These are technicalities, however, that would only bore the non-agricultural reader. I will simply quote once more that oracle, Uncle Reuben, who was fond of declaring that "any one who put his main 'pendance on terbaccer in North Berkeley, 'ud git inter the porehouse sho'." Mar'se Dab put his 'pendance on tobacco. He didn't go to the poorhouse, because he had a brother-in-law in Western Kansas of a kindly turn of mind; but the latter alternative was, I fear, only one degree removed from the former in the Captain's mind.

I can recall his figure, as it were but yesterday,

sitting on the roadside fence on a hot June morning, looking wistfully towards the west for the long-expected rain that would enable him to plant out his tobacco.

One glance at Mar'se Dab was sufficient to discover that he ignored the assistance of the tailor even more completely than he did that of the manure-merchant. But there is method and not madness in this. In his patriotic fervour, Mar'se Dab swore that he would wear nothing that was not manufactured in old Virginia. To a man who was fastidious about his personal appearance, such a resolution would have amounted (in those days anyway) to an astonishing pitch of self-denial. It was very praiseworthy in Mar'se Dab, no doubt, but I don't think it weighed oppressively upon him.

He had yellow homespun pants, the cloth of which had been woven by an old lady of colour up on the mountain, who still possessed that disappearing art, while the cut forcibly suggested Mrs. Digges's sewing-machine. His boots were made by Uncle Reuben, who solaced himself in his cabin during the long winter evenings with shoemaking and the weaving of baskets. I once had a pair of boots from Uncle Reuben myself; but we will draw a veil over the recollection, and hasten on. Mar'se Dab despised a waistcoat, even in cold weather. His coat was always out at both elbows: whether this was because he got the cloth by the piece from the new woollen mills at Barksville or not, I can't say. It was, I think, a kind of defiant tatterdemalionism that the Captain liked to hug as a sort of mute undying protest against the disruption of the South's old institutions. For however great his financial difficulties might have been, they were not on a scale so trifling as to necessitate an exposure of both elbows. When his neighbours joked with him about his ragged edges, he used to say, "times were too durned hard for fancy dressin'." Mar'se Dab's hatred of Yankees was conspicuous even at a period when sectional bitterness was extreme. It made your flesh creep to hear the pains and penalties to which he consigned in fancy his fellow-citizens north of Maryland. At election gatherings his defiant shout was the terror of Republican stump-orators and carpetbaggers. At the same time, I am perfectly sure that if a Connecticut man, even though he were loaded down with wooden nutmegs, stood in need of a dinner, and Mar'se Dab had only a crust, he would have shared it with him.

There is something, I think, in the culture of tobacco, as pursued from time immemorial in the Old Dominion, that appeals to the patriarchal instincts of the conservative Virginian. The innumerable waggon-loads of wood that are set to blaze upon the new plant-beds in midwinter, to kill the germs of weeds and prepare the woodland soil for the tender seed; the crashing and tumbling of the forest-trees when "new grounds" are being opened; the cheery shouting of the negroes, and the unwonted energy that any momentous undertaking, more especially if it is connected with tobacco, calls forth; the excitement and rush of transplanting from the beds to the field in early summer, when the necessary rain, perhaps, is scarce, and opportunities consequently few.

Then there is the pleasure of watching, through the hot days of July and August, the gradual growth and expansion of the broadening gummy leaves to the sun, and all the risks of shattering hail-storms and of early night-frosts in September catching the "crinkley" ripening plants before they are fit to cut. Then the critical period of curing; and lastly, the long journey, plunging through the mud to the market, where the interests of master and man, of landlord and tenant, are absorbed for a short and exciting period in the yellow-labelled heaps upon the warehouse floor, which the auctioneer is knocking down to local and foreign buyers. Perhaps it is in the rapid fluctuation of the prices bid for tobacco and the speculative flavour thus imparted to its cultivation that forms a leading attraction.

Everything to do with tobacco Mar'se Dab loved with a hereditary devotion to the time-honoured product of his native land. Still the making of tobacco, in his estimation, had gone to the dogs. The very seasons had altered since the war; the sun seemed to shine less brightly; the moon to shed a dimmer light (and Mar'se Dab believed in the moon); the summer dews to fall more sparingly than of yore. So at any rate Mar'se Dab was thinking, when we left him just now sitting upon the roadside, looking westward at the thunder-clouds.

The tobacco-land is hilled up, but scarcely half of it as yet planted, though the young plants in the beds are actually pushing one another out of the ground from their size and vigour. The earth is dry and parched, and in ten days it will be July—and upon

July-planted tobacco, everybody in Virginia knows, no 'pendance, as old man Reuben would say, can be placed. The great black cloud comes nearer and nearer; woods and mountains are absorbed, and vanish into the approaching gloom, while from the inky void there breaks gradually upon the silent air the hoarse roar of waters dashing upon a myriad leaves. Mar'se Dab's hopes have ceased to have even that slight element of uncertainty that is inseparable from the word. "It's come this time, any way," says he, as he turns homeward, full in his mind of the big crop he will now pitch. The very spray of the coming storm scuds on the newly awakened breeze that is flying before it; and the red dust of the turnpike, as if its last chance for a frolic had come, whirls this way and that in the changing currents of the thunder-laden air. Everywhere there is the hurry of preparation for the coming storm. The Clover Hill domestics are hard at work rushing the family linen and mattresses off the front portico. Aunt Judy is racing after the young turkeys; the negroes have unyoked their teams from the corn-rows, and are hastening up to the barnyard, singing tearful dirges for joy at the "prospec' of a season." The spring calves in the yard are galloping hither and thither with their tails in the air, like quadrupeds demented; and old Uncle Reuben, at his cabin-door, is reminding Aunt Milly that "he'd bin lookin' fur weather" (inspired of course by the sensations in his shoulder), "but hardly reckoned it would cum befo' sundown."

Here, happy in the prospect of at any rate planting out one more tobacco-crop, we must leave Mar'se

P

Dab. If he was obstinate and prejudiced, there was no kinder-hearted man, as Uncle Reuben said, " north of Jeems river." If he was loud-mouthed and boisterous, and stormed at his hands in a way that made him conspicuous in a place where these peculiarities are not common, it was, at the same time, the confiding fashion in which he supplied these very dependants with the necessaries of life in advance from year to year that hastened his downfall. His inability to refuse security for all the bacon and corn-meal, the cotton dresses and "pars o' shoes" that the inmates of the twenty cabins on Clover Hill wanted, or thought they wanted, at Captain Topfodder's, no doubt swelled greatly the obligations that finally crushed Mar'se Dab. How the gallant Captain came out among the creditors I never heard, and was most happily spared the harrowing spectacle of the sale. The details of this great occasion, however, were of course fully communicated. There was twelve months' credit given, and the prices were accordingly quite fabulous. How much was actually collected at that remote period is of course a matter I know nothing about. But, so far as paper went, the bidding was so brisk and the prices so unprecedented that Major Hogshead, the famous auctioneer from Shucksville, had twice to go behind the stable for a drink—his feelings were so much overcome.

Poor Mar'se Dab, however, benefited from none of these things. His chief creditor, a local Jew with a Scotch name, took over the place, and here is the advertisement of sale, cut out of the local newspaper of that date, and kept all these years as a memento :—

"FOR sale, on terms to suit purchaser, 13 miles from Shucksville and 1 from school, store, and mill, situate on the old Richmond Pike, 924 acres of fine rolling land, 100 acres original forest, 50 acres bottom-land ; fine brick Mansion, with all necessary Outbuildings, and 16 Cabins. Price $9,500. Apply at the Office of this Paper."

TWO EPISODES ON RUMBLING CREEK

I

IT was just about twenty years ago that the art of fly-fishing first dawned upon the sportsmen of the Southern States of America. It is well known that the latter have for all time been devoted to the chase, but the gentle art, in any sense worthy of the name, has till recently held no place at all in their sporting calendar. No countries are better watered than the five States which, from Maryland to Georgia inclusive, face the Atlantic. No rivers were ever better stocked with fish of the coarser variety than those which rise in the Great Alleghany ranges, at the back of all these States, and flow eastward to the ocean. But of the three sporting fish of America, the salmon, black bass, and trout, the first is not found in the South, the second is a recent importation, while the last, though indigenous and abundant, is confined entirely to the aforesaid mountain ranges. And these latter, which form the Western boundary, roughly speaking, of all the South Atlantic States, have been always far removed, both geographically and socially, from the ordinary spheres of Southern life. In the countless clear streams which furrow the wooded sides of the great

TWO EPISODES ON RUMBLING CREEK 213

Alleghany system trout have been always indigenous and more or less abundant. But most of this romantic country has only been opened within the last decade or two to the knowledge of even Southerners themselves. It has been inhabited, to be sure, for a century and more, but mainly by the wildest, most ignorant and lawless types of that class which generations of slavery cast up upon the rough and waste places of the land. We allude to the Poor Whites of the South, a people despised and shunned by all ranks of the old slave-owning class, and even by the very negroes themselves; a folk who may be said to have lived from generation to generation amid aërial forests, and to have been born, married, and buried in a mountain clearing. These, however, till comparatively recent years, were the only trout-fishers in the South, for the very excellent reason that it was only in the wild and romantic territory they inhabited that the trout was found. The thousand streams that babble so temptingly through Virginia and the Carolinas are, so far as that gamest of fish is concerned, entirely barren when once they have left the forest shades of their native mountains. Under the hot suns of the South the shallow waters of these mountain brooks take on a temperature too high for trout to flourish in; and the fish that, before civilisation opened the lower country, no doubt were content to abide there, are now exclusively found in high latitudes where beneath unbroken forests the streams run cool and clear.

When I say that Southern landowners in old days were not fishermen, this does not mean that the brook or river which was certain to run through or close by every plantation was not utilised. There were coarse fish of various kinds everywhere, and the planter or farmer occasionally angled for them in a desultory fashion with clumsy tackle, as did, with perhaps greater zest, his boys and girls and his negroes in their spare hours. But fishing was not a sport, as it is in England, and not one Southerner in a dozen had ever seen a trout or stood upon the banks of a trout-stream, though both were to be found in such abundance in a portion of every Southern State.[1]

But the half savage mountaineers were inveterate and even enthusiastic trout-fishermen. They fished for sport, they fished for food, and they fished to secure the wherewithal to barter for powder and shot, coffee and sugar, at the nearest country store. They used the worm only, but each valley had its champion fisherman, who was most jealous of his reputation, and who could tell tales of trout that would have put to the blush the greatest Ananias that ever sat in a chimney corner of an Angler's Rest or Fisherman's Arms in Scotland or Wales. They fished up stream did these unkempt, illiterate children of the woods, with short lines fastened to the end of hickory poles fifteen feet long, and a worm on a single hook. They were not mere pot-hunters, either, but were fond of the sport and recognised in their rough fashion that trout-fishing, even as they followed it, was altogether a superior affair to catching chub and cat-fish and horney-heads with a float in the low country rivers.

[1] Many of the "summer resorts," it is true, were among the mountains, but the mode of life there followed by most visitors was not conducive to an intimacy with the surrounding country

They firmly believed that there were no trout anywhere else in the world but in their mountain gorges, and consequently that no other people in the world knew anything about catching them. They were Anglo-Saxons, or Irish for the most part, by origin ; they had no standing and no money; their principles were of the most lax description, and they could rarely read or write. They seldom went off their mountains into the very moderate civilisation that lay close at their feet except to vote, and nobody from civilisation in those days ever paid them a visit but a sheriff's posse on the search for whiskey-stills, an odd cattle-drover, or a refugee from justice.

It is my firm and well-founded belief that, in the year 187-, I assisted in the very first invasion of the Alleghanies south of the Potomac ever undertaken with fly-rod and tackle. If we were not actually the first party in the whole South to make such an assault, we were most certainly the first that struck what was known as the Windy Gap section of the Blue Ridge mountains. And what consternation and astonishment our advent created upon the now familiar waters of Rumbling Creek I propose to make the subject of a brief reminiscence. Our base of operations for this notable campaign was the town of Bunkerville, a place celebrated, I need not say, for the manufacture of tobacco ; and it was moreover the home of the three other sportsmen who with myself composed the party. These three gentlemen we will call (and this indeed without much departure from accuracy) the Colonel, the Doctor, and the Judge. As Southerners, though keen sportsmen otherwise, they were as a matter of course at that time novices in the art of fly-fishing; but the Colonel and the Judge had recently paid a visit to Scotland, and there utilising their leisure in acquiring some practical insight into the noble science, had returned home great enthusiasts. Their enthusiasm they had transmitted to the untravelled Doctor, and he had been duly entered, and carefully coached, upon the barren surface of the Colonel's mill-pond. Most people at so short a distance from the Blue Ridge, for it was little over forty miles from Bunkerville, knew that there was a good store of trout hidden away somewhere among those great forest-covered peaks, that could be just seen on clear days like faint blue clouds above the horizon. But the Colonel's great ambition was to inaugurate fly-fishing as a Southern sport. He had brought a large assortment of tackle from Mrs. Hogg's famous little repository in Edinburgh, and, as he was a man, who did nothing by halves, had paid fifty dollars in New York for one of the then newly invented split-cane rods. He talked trout all day on the main street to audiences who had never risen above a languid interest in chub and a float, and half the night upon his porch to his family, who could not very well get away from him.

The train would take us about halfway to our destination. The remainder of the distance we were to drive in the Colonel's ambulance, which his old coachman Caleb, with tent, provisions, and the rest of our baggage, was to take forward the previous day to the point where our route left the railway. Bunkerville was but a country town, and excitements were both scarce and mild. So it was almost a matter of course that its weekly organ should indulge in sundry jests at the expense of our venture. The Colonel was recommended to take revolvers instead of "fishing-poles," and he was congratulated, I remember, on his foresight in "securing the services of the first medical man in the community," which it was hinted he would be likely to need. But old Caleb, the Colonel's coloured coachman and gardener, who had been included in the expedition as part of the establishment, took it much more seriously. The Colonel had owned him before the war (not then so very long over), and now it was jokingly said he owned the Colonel; at any rate he was one of the old and privileged sort. Now there was nothing a well-constituted Southern negro despised and dreaded so much as rough wild scenery and rough low white men. Caleb did not fancy this job at all, and confided to me at some length his sentiments on the subject. He declared that there were more mean men upon those mountains than there were hairs upon his own head. It passed his understanding, moreover, that any civilised white men should deliberately precipitate themselves into a wilderness inhabited by savages and bears. He had heard, upon the very best authority, that the mouth of hell was situated in the neighbourhood of our proposed operations, and that every dark of the moon the devil himself, with live coals for eyes, rode astride of a big black bear along the summit of the Windy Range. Fox-hunting and partridge-shooting Caleb accepted with approval as the sport of gentlemen, but these new-fangled ideas of the Colonel about trout-fishing gave the old henchman the utmost concern, seeing the places and the company into which they would lead him. And all this, too, when the mill-pond at home was full of chub, and the Colonel could sit on the bank, with his fishing pole resting on a fork, and have his meals regular, and boys to bait his hook, and an iced julep whenever he felt in the humour for refreshment. No—Caleb could not understand it; and more particularly as he had to go himself, he condemned the whole business in most unqualified terms. If this is what came of emancipation he, for his part, would recall the days of slavery with the utmost pleasure; though considering what a much greater personage Caleb had been before the war, the concession, it must be confessed, was not such a great one as it might at first sight appear. He finished the long speech, of which this is a summary in plain English, by displaying a single-barrelled pistol he had purchased that day for a dollar, "jes ter skeer off the bars," he said. And when two days later he met us at the station with the waggon and our baggage, and confided to the writer that he had it loaded in his coat-tail pocket, I could not help feeling that a terror much more real than the old negro's imaginings had been added to our journey.

We were not indeed launching ourselves upon the mountains entirely without an introduction. For it so happened that an old sergeant [1] of the Colonel's ragged, but valiant, regiment was a sort of headman among the mountaineers of the valley for which we were bound. He could write a little, or, as he expressed it, "could scratch some," and had sent word to his old commanding officer to come along whenever he felt like it. "I'll be mitey glad," he

[1] See page 143.

wrote, "tu teche you alls how tu cotch trout." He little thought what we were going to teach him.

We drove for twenty miles through a rolling arable country whose bright red soil showed off to exquisite perfection the rich greens of the growing crops and the freshly mantling woodlands. As we approached the mountains the fields turned gray, the homesteads grew humbler, and the red unmetalled roads changed to stony tracks, strewn with boulders and crossed continually by impetuous streams fresh from their mountain home. Old Caleb, in a steady half audible monotone, cursed the country, as his horses, unused to rocks, slipped heavily on to the pole, or lunged forward on their collars with spasmodic and uneasy jerks. "You an' me, Charley," we heard him growl to his near horse, who had almost been on his nose, bin used ter travellin' on roads not to crawlin' up, the bed of a creek among wild Injuns."[1] By the time we reached the actual foot of the range, where the ex-sergeant's house, we had good reason for believing, was situated, the sun had sunk behind the great wall of mountains which here towered above us to the height of some 4,000 feet; but against the crimson trail that it had left we could plainly see the outlines of the stunted pines and wind-swept chestnuts that crowned the topmost ridges. All below, however, was rapidly merging into a black chaos. Of the terrors which that vast void contained Caleb was no doubt thinking when his horses halted abruptly in

[1] It may be worth noting, lest Caleb should be taken too seriously, that even a hundred years before the date of our visit, the noble red man was but a memory on these mountains.

their tracks, and the old man, calling out that there was a bear in the road, begged us to take the reins while he extracted the pistol from the depths of his long coat-tails. It was not a bear however this time but Pete Robison, who, it must be confessed, was remarkably like one. We must leave to imagination the cordial greetings that passed between him and the Colonel, and merely remark that he piloted us safely to his log-house, which stood upon the bank of Rumbling Creek, just where it issued from the mountain. Here, on Pete's circumscribed grass plot in front of his house, we unlimbered, lit our fire, pitched our tent, and with the invaluable help of the Sergeant made everything snug for the night. It was late before we had finished our supper, and sitting round the camp-fire smoking, began seriously to discuss operations with Pete. The latter was a middle-sized, but powerful and sinewy man, with a head and face so covered with masses of tangled black hair, that Caleb might have been almost excused for mistaking him in the dark for a bear. He was now, too, in high good humour, for, though better off than most mountaineers, he rarely tasted good wheat bread, butter, sugar-cured ham, or Mocha coffee, and still more rarely all at one meal, with a glass of old Bourbon whiskey afterwards. "You've brought a right smart chance of whiskey along with you, I hope, Cunnel?" said he.

"Two gallons," said the Colonel, pointing with his pipe-stem to a demijohn (not old Bourbon) within the circle of light; "why?"

"Them mount'n boys is apt to be a bit techy with

strangers," he answered, jerking his thumb up towards the dark masses above us.

And Pete then proceeded to explain that scarcely any strangers were ever seen upon the mountain, except a sheriff's posse hunting horse-thieves or whiskey-stills, and that our presence, even as fishermen, might excite suspicions which he would find it necessary to allay. But he declared that his intervention would be greatly simplified if he had a good supply of whiskey at his back. In any case, he proposed to cut us some fishing-poles the first thing in the morning.

The Colonel's reply was to reach over for the bundle of rods that happened to be near him, and pass them to Pete.

"Well, I'll be dorgonned," said the electrified backwoodsman. "Is thar a jinted pole in each o' them gray bags?"

"There is," said the Colonel.

Pete seemed overcome with an emotion too deep for words. He had only once handled one of these strange weapons it appeared, and that was when he was away in the army. But many a time and often had he descanted upon that notable incident to his brother fishermen in the mountain. It was not, however, he declared, till he had thrown one or two scoffers into the creek, that they had consented to believe in his tale, and in the existence of such fabulous implements. And now, behold, on his own river, and right under his very nose, lay a whole bundle of them!

But Pete was to be much more astonished than

this before the night was many minutes older. "Cunnel," said he, when he had recovered from this first shock, "I reckon' you'll be lookin' for me to dig you some worms in the mornin'."

"Worms be hanged," said the Colonel. Pete was perhaps a little surprised, possibly hurt, at the warmth of the Colonel's tone, but still unsuspecting, he replied that he *had* heard people used crayfish, maggots, and even paste in the low country, and suggested that we might have brought a supply with us.

It was a great moment this for the pioneer of the noble art of fly-fishing in the South, as he opened his fly-book by the light of the cedar-log fire, and displayed to the confused eyes of the champion fisherman of Windy Range the dainty treasures of Mrs. Hogg's repository.

Pete rubbed his eyes for a moment with the back of his hand in deep perplexity. "Them hooks is a heap too small, Cunnel, to carry a bait, and with all them feathers and truck on 'em too."

"They ain't intended to carry a bait," said the Judge striking in; "the feathers are the bait."

"Good Lord ha' mussey, you ain't proposin' to cotch Rumblin' Crick trout on them ar fool things?"

"Yes, we are, and a heap of 'em too," said the Colonel with much dignity.

The mountaineer's face was in shadow and, unfortunately, I could not catch its expression after this astonishing announcement, but we heard a familiar click and the sound of a solid projectile hitting the side of the tent, and then rolling gently down its dewy surface. We knew it was a quid of tobacco, and understood the mingled feelings which prompted the discharge.

"Well, gentlemen," said the Sergeant, after a brief but significant interval of silence, "I believe I'll say good-night. I reckon I'd better get them worms in the mornin', and see if I can't scare up some hooks."

I should like to dwell for a moment on the splendour of the sunrise on these Southern mountains, and endeavour, if only in some inadequate fashion, to recall the manner in which the golden glory, driving before it the dark shadows and the light vapours of early dawn, steals downwards over this vast sea of many-tinted dew-laden leaves. But space forbids, and Pete, true to his word, had come provided with a tin of worms, and some fearsome-looking hooks attached to a foot or so of coarse gut. We duly and properly expressed our gratitude, and declared that we would gladly fall back on his supplies if our own methods failed, but in the meantime we should try those first. "Well, gentlemen, you alls is out on a frolic anyway (a frolic indeed!), and it ain't no business of mine; but when you git tired flicken' them feather-hooks aroun' I reckon you'll find the worms come in sorter handy."

To say we had absolutely no qualms about the fly-taking inclinations of these trout would be untrue. But there was nothing whatever in the surrounding conditions here to keep them from following their natural instinct, and upon the whole we felt tolerably confident.

There were perhaps ten miles of available fishing on Rumbling Creek above our camping-ground.

Below, the trout grew rapidly scarcer, till, after a short neutral territory which they shared with various sorts of coarse fish, they disappeared altogether in favour of the latter. In the high mountains, however, they admitted no inferior species to share their glancing rapids and swirling pools of crystal water. They were the ordinary American brook-trout, the *fontinalis*, silver in colour, red of fin, and pink of flesh; and here, as one would have expected, they ran small, sometimes three, more often four or five to the pound, with a thin sprinkling of what Pete called whalers, fish, that is to say, of a pound or more.

Every mile or so up the river were small clearings in the forest, where scanty crops of corn, oats, or tobacco struggled with weeds and briars in stump-strewn enclosures, or beneath the giant skeletons of what had once been living trees, killed by girdling to save trouble to the indolent occupants. In each clearing stood three or four cabins of unhewn logs chinked with mud, and flanked by rude chimneys of sticks and clay. We must not pause here to introduce the reader to the angular sallow-faced matrons who sit at their spinning-wheels inside, or to their equally sallow, but more nimble, bare-footed daughters in big sun-bonnets, hoeing in the poor garden-patch or washing the scanty family linen in the stream below; or yet to the old crones blinking over their knitting-needles on the shady side of the house. They are nearing their hundredth year some of these old witches, and have known no other life since they can remember, nor is it likely that the girls at the brook, except by an accident, will ever know any other.

TWO EPISODES ON RUMBLING CREEK

And there is nothing incongruous in dropping into the present tense as we find ourselves doing here, for twenty years has made no difference on Rumbling Creek. There is, perhaps, no drearier existence led by any Anglo-Saxon females in the world than that endured by these mountain women. What to them are the everlasting hills and the fairyland of leaves and glancing streams among which they are immovably fixed? Not much, indeed, at any time, and least of all when fast bound in the icy stillness of fierce winter, or even later when in the dawn of spring the biting March winds roar through the naked forests and whistle through the gaping chinks in their crazy cabins. For the men there are many compensations. They fish, and hunt, and fight, and get drunk, and that, too, more often on whiskey that pays no tax. But for the women it is different. American travellers profess amazement at Connemara, but we fancy the Connemara woman, upon the whole, suffers no more deprivation, and most certainly leads a cheerier life, than the wives and daughters of a considerable portion of these Southern mountaineers.[1]

It was probably eight o'clock in the morning before we got to work, and long before that hour news had sped up the mountain that there was "a parcel of low country folks, camped down below and fixed up for fishing." Natural curiosity, and an instinct for whiskey, soon provided us with an

---

[1] This description, it should be understood, is not applicable to the inhabitants of the limestone or natural grass regions of the Alleghanies, who, though rough and unsophisticated, are generally prosperous enough in their circumstances.

audience; and while we were yet completing our preparations, half a dozen woodlanders had solemnly ranged themselves before us, and with lack-lustre eyes, and jaws working mechanically on the inevitable quid, were with great deliberation trying to take in the situation. Three of them had fishing-poles, fifteen feet long at least, over their shoulders; another carried a long brass-mounted Kentucky rifle. Pete now presented us to them in due form. He explained that we were not a sheriff's posse, nor were we surveyors come to inspect their ever precarious titles, nor were we cattle-men, or anything else unpleasant, but merely harmless individuals from Bunkerville out on a frolic with a demijohn of whiskey, and "a sorter notion of tryin' the trout." To this low level did Pete's eloquence reduce us, and at the word *trout* he gave such a prodigious wink at his friends that it could have been seen halfway up the mountain. Three of the natives had smooth, yellow faces with receding chins, and sloping shoulders, the other two were short and squat, and apparently covered with hair. They wore coarse cotton shirts and homespun trousers tucked into long boots, one or two of them, however, being bare-footed.

The whiskey was brought out, and having shaken our hands all round in flabby and fish-like fashion, they declared they were mighty glad to see us, which at the moment was beyond a doubt sincere. They also remarked that there were plenty of trout in the creek, adding significantly "for them as knowed how to cotch 'em." Old Caleb in the meantime was moving fussily about, with much parade of anxiety, and with a most solemn face, picking up stray articles, and putting them ostentatiously into his waggon. The drift of his movements became apparent when he touched our elbow in passing and remarked: "Yo' keep yo' eyes, sah, set plum on them thar men. Them kind'll steal the teeth out'n yo' head befo' you knows whar you is."

Pete now brought out our rods for general admiration, which was freely accorded by our new friends; but that feeling was soon sunk in an amused contempt for our ridiculous "featherhooks." Though much the youngest in years of the party, I was a veteran compared to the rest in the matter of fly-fishing, and proceeded to explain that I had myself in England killed thousands of trout in this fashion. "England, oh Lordy!" said one of the little men. "Why, that's the country whar there's a king as takes a tenth of all you raise, ain't it?" The name seemed to stir a chord too in the memory of one of his attenuated companions, who, rubbing his forehead as if to quicken thought, drawled out: "That thar's the place Grandma useter run on 'bout so, away out yonder t'other side of everythin', ain't it? Her folks come from out thar, when she was a bit of chap."[1]

"Well," interrupted the Judge, "it's where all our folks came from some time or other, that's as sure as shooting. So come, let's get to work."

But the Colonel had yet another surprise in store for the mountain. As we have said, he was a man who did nothing by halves, and while in the old

[1] Vernacular for *child*.

country, had not failed to provide himself with waders and brogues. In these he now appeared, and fairly paralysed the rude audience. It was a great sight to see him thus attired, with a new basket hung on his back, a landing-net in one hand and his gorgeous rod in the other, descend into the pellucid shallows of Rumbling Creek. Such a spectacle could never have been conceived even by the wildest imagination on the mountain. But the Colonel, honest man, looked proudly conscious of the solemnity of the occasion, and maintained a dignity befitting the inauguration of a great sport. As he waded into the streamy tail of a most beautiful pool, one could almost fancy him consecrating the waters, before proceeding to open this new epoch in the history of Southern angling.

The mountaineers stood in a row upon the bank, with eyes and mouths wide open in amazement at such a spectacle, Pete with his baits in reserve at their head.

The Colonel was not a great expert, but he was quite good enough for the trout of Rumbling Creek, that had never seen an artificial fly in their lives, and there was moreover a breeze behind him. As he let out his line and made the usual preliminary casts, there was an audible stir among the spectators. The first two or three serious throws up the pool provoked some stifled merriment; but at the next—heaven and earth!—up went the point of the Colonel's rod and a six-ounce fish, fast on his tail-fly, leaped a foot into the air. Never shall we forget the excitement among those lethargic mountaineers. They fairly danced upon the shore. "Heist him out, Cunnel!" they yelled. "Fling him on the bank, or he's a gonner, sho'."

But the Colonel did nothing of the kind at this supreme moment. With rod at the perpendicular, in the most approved manner taught him in Scotland, and his spare hand on the reel, he proceeded with the most admirable presence of mind to wind up the game little fish, and in the most collected manner possible, to humour his struggles, and finally to bring him head up into his landing-net. In less than a minute he had another fish on, and successfully repeated the same operation, the mountaineers in the meantime keeping up a chorus of ejaculations not found in Webster.

When the pool had been thoroughly fished, the great pioneer waded leisurely to the bank, and taking off his hat began to wipe from his forehead the signs of that emotion which he had so admirably in other ways suppressed, and thus delivered himself to the amazed mountaineers: "There, gentlemen, that is the way to catch trout. I hope to see the day when not a bait or a worm will be dropped into this beautiful stream on whose banks you have the good fortune to live." As the Judge said, the Colonel looked as if he had just been elected President of the United States. If the thrill of the performances of which this was the inauguration did not shake the United States, it shook these mountains from end to end. Men, who had believed themselves the only trout-fishers in the world, were knocked flat upon their back, so to speak, by strangers whose apparent greenness in the art had provided for the mountain a brief interval of unqualified delight.

Exactly how many dozen trout we took on that day, and on the two next, is of no consequence. For ourselves, and accustomed from childhood to the brushy streams of the West of England, it was simple work killing these unsophisticated creatures. The Colonel, too, though so recent a convert, proved a most efficient one. The Judge contributed his dozen or so each day, and the Doctor, after spending two days, as he declared, in climbing trees, was quite rewarded on the third and last by half-a-dozen fish.

The news sped up the valley like wildfire, that there were strange fishermen below, and that "one big man in gum pants was trompin' up the middle o' the crick with a dip net, flickin' a silver pole about like a buggy whip, and rakin' out the fish like ole Scrat." Many a mountaineer that day left his corn-row unhoed and his tobacco-hills half finished upon distant heights. And as we pushed our way up stream through avenues of forest trees, and groves of cedar, and blazing banks of rhododendrons, some gaunt son of the mountain was always hovering near by in a state of curiosity almost too great for words.

Our camp fire on the second night presented a very animated scene. Caleb had piled a waggon-load of wood on the fire, and the flames leaped high heavenwards. Conciliation being so vital a point, we had brought half a sack of flour and a bag of coffee, and nearly a dozen mountaineers assisted at the greatest trout-fry, as Pete said, that had ever been known in the mountains. The theme of conversation as they sat round and smoked their long pipes well into the night can be easily imagined, and after two rounds of the whiskey they began telling stories of trout and bear against each other of a kind that would make the post-prandial performances of the ordinary British fisherman seem tame in comparison.

We parted on the fourth morning upon most friendly terms with the whole mountain, and they were profoundly grateful for a souvenir of a couple of dozen "featherhooks," which all disappeared in a single day, so Pete told me afterwards, in tree-tops and snags.

As with our third day's catch carefully packed for sceptical friends in Bunkerville, old Caleb once more got his team off the rocky mountain roads on to the old red highways, he gave a great sigh of relief. "Praise de Lord," I heard him say, "I'm done wid it fur dis year anyway." He little knew what was going to happen the next year; and how much truer his estimate of the mountain-men accidentally turned out to be than his master's.

II

IT only remains now to narrate as briefly as possible what actually did happen on this next occasion, when the Colonel, the Doctor, the Judge, and Caleb, the first three being full of pleasing anticipations, ventured on their second expedition to Rumbling Creek. It was an episode too that created so much excitement, and gave rise to so much misplaced mirth, at the expense of the adventurers, I had myself much cause for satisfaction that circumstances had prevented my making one of them. The only person, indeed, who came well out of the affair was Caleb, who, it will be remembered, held views with regard to the mountaineers that nothing could shake. He had already been too much given to regarding himself as the fountain of all wisdom and the embodiment of all sagacity, but after this second campaign he became so intolerably puffed out with self satisfaction that it almost caused a total breach between him and his master. That the whole trouble, too, arose from an irresponsible newspaper paragraph made the fiasco all the more grievous to those concerned. Now it so happened that this next spring my own plans would not fit in with those of the Colonel's party. Moreover, I lived in another county, and approached this particular part of the Blue Ridge from an entirely different angle. I decided therefore to go alone, early in May, and, abjuring tents, waggons, and other encumbrances, to travel on horseback, and take my chance of such hospitality as Pete's log house at the forks of the creek afforded. It was a bright May morning when, bound once more for Rumbling Creek, I mounted my horse, with no incumbrances but a pair of well filled saddle-bags and a fishing rod. Owing to the badness of the roads and sundry delays, it was nearly dark before the fifty miles was accomplished, and I arrived at Pete's door. Nothing, however, need be said about my own visit, except that it was uneventful and successful, the sport being good, Pete's accommodation sufficient for the circumstances, and the mountaineers entirely friendly. But upon the third and last evening of my stay, on returning to the cabin, I found Pete, with a newspaper in his hand, surrounded by mountaineers, all of whom, by this time, I more or less knew personally. My host was then almost the only man on the mountain that could read, and he now had on his horn-rimmed spectacles, looking both solemn and important. The other men dropped away in rather unusual fashion. There was no banjo playing or fish stories that night. But as we were busy after supper cleaning and slightly salting the last catch of fish for transportation home the next day through a hot sun, I took very little notice of the incident. Before bed time, however, Pete called my attention to the paper he had been reading. It was the Bunkerville *Sentinel*, and had been forwarded to one of the mountaineers with a paragraph marked, and the deciphering of the paragraph had been of course entrusted to Pete. "These boys," said he, "are mightily put out at a piece that's sot down on that thar paper; I told 'em it was all foolishness, and thote I'd cam'd em down some, but they's right techy." The paragraph ran thus :—" Our esteemed fellow townsman, Colonel D——, was so delighted with his fishing experiences last year on Rumbling Creek, he is reported to have made arrangements with the State Fish Commissioner and the actual owners (who live in Richmond) of the large but profitless mountain tract through which these waters run, to reserve both the North and South forks of the Creek. These are to be kept, it is said, as a nursery for stocking depleted or barren streams in other parts of the State, and the Colonel is to be granted the sole right of catching trout therein. The Colonel, we all know, was a gallant and brave Confederate officer. But we should have thought he had had, like the rest of us, enough fighting, and we are really surprised to find the veteran once more upon the war path." Part of this was evidently due to some suggestions that were in the air for making experiments in stocking accessible streams, the rest was, of course, more or less of a joke. I don't suppose the Colonel thought twice about it. I am quite sure I did not, and rode home the next day. "Yes," said Pete, as I shook his hand at parting in the morning, "I wish them mount'n boys hadn't seen that thar all-fired newspaper foolishness. They'se mighty ignorant and powerful techy, and if they take a notion inter their heads no crowbar won't drive it out."

It was some three or four weeks after this that, on opening the Bunkerville *Sentinel*, which circulated through the adjoining counties, I found myself confronted by several flaming headlines. "*Brutal assault on peaceful anglers. Party from Bunkerville savagely chased out of the Windy range. The Colonel says he has had enough of trout-fishing, but refuses to say more. The Judge goes back on Isaak Walton, and gives it as his deliberate opinion that trout-fishing is not the recreation for a contemplative man—not on Rumbling Creek anyway.*"

"*The doctor declines to commit himself, but he has intimated to his friends that he proposes in future to confine himself entirely to the homely chub and cat-fish of civilisation.*"

"*Uncle Caleb is to-day the biggest man in Bunkerville, and talks of nothing else but his trout hunt. He says he told his master all along that it warn't safe for no gen'l'mens to go among them white trash in the mount'ns.*"

The story, as I have remarked, went all through Virginia, and even got into the Philadelphia and New York papers, as an evidence of the barbarism of the Southern mountaineers. It appears that, in driving up in the same fashion that we had done the year before to Pete's house, my former companions noticed a certain depression in that great man's manner, which he accounted for by saying he was "pestered by a jaw ache." This of course I heard afterwards. But they had intended in any case to drive a little way up the stream, and camp in an open spot that had been noted down the previous year. This they proceeded to do, and pitched their tent on a strip of turf, lying between the creek and a steep wooded slope. The fire was lit, supper cooked, and the big demijohn of whisky set out ready for the expected company. But, with the exception of Pete, who was anxious and mysterious, none came. Nothing suspecting, the three fishermen rolled themselves in their blankets, and Caleb, as before, retired to his waggon, to his gloomy anticipations, and his single barelled pistol.

As Caleb was the first of the party I happened to meet after the adventure, running across the old man on the cars one day, I may as well, in as brief a form as possible, give the full and true account of the matter as he gave it to me.

"Well Suh," said Caleb, "it mout have bin twelve,

and then agin it mout have bin one o'clock, and the gen'le'men's was asleep in de tent and snorin' right good too. I was sorter wakesome myself. What with the fuss the crick raised on the rocks, and what with listenin' fur bars, and the lonesomeness of the location, I couldn't git no sleep. All at onst, I thote I heerd a trompin' and stirrin' roun' way up on de mount'n above my hade. Well Suh! befo' I knowed anythin' mo', a whole pile of rocks come leapin' and tarin' down the hill, crashin' agin the trees, some on 'em, and others pitchin' doun on ter the grass-lot by the tent, and hummin' on par'se de waggon tur'ble. Two of 'em hit de waggon spang bang, and at the same time I let out a holler that fotched the Cunnel, the Doctor, and the Jedge skippin' out 'n the tent in the biggest sorter hurry. The Doctor who was the hindermost wern't hardly clear of the ropes, when a rock as big as my hade, lit plum on de tent, went spang through it and bust the tree of the saddle which he'd bin usin' for a piller. I dun seen this arterwards, an its de solemn troof fur sho'. Well Suh the rocks cum pilin' doun that grass lot tremenjous. The gen'l'mens couldn't see good fur to dodge 'em, and got right smartly bruised, till they crep right in under the ridge of the crick bank.

"I lep' up den in de waggon an' fired my pistol right at de mount'n, an' ther was the biggest yellin' you ever hern from up dar in the sky like, an' three or fo' rifles went off, makin' streaks of fire up agin the dark wood. I jes heard Mar'se Robert shout: 'Damn you, fool nigger!' when I hollered out I was shot, an' rolled over in de waggon, an' laid thar studyin' on de day of judgment, an' thinkin' to myself, 'Dis yer's trout-fishin', is it? It look to me a heap mo' like de war come back.' Presently I begun to think it wur a bit o' rock, not a bullet, that had struck the side o' my hade; an' I felt mighty thankful it hadn't fotched me on a wuss part.

"Presently the rumpus guv over, an' the gen'l'mens crep' out from under de bank. The Doctor had got his arm mighty nigh broke, an' the Jedge was bleedin' from the face, and had been mashed by a rock on de shoulder. The ole Cunnel he hadn't bin teched nuthin' to speak of, an' he begun shout'n an' cuss'n he'd clean out them mount'ns, if he had to bring out the whole State melesha. I b'lieve ef the Doctor an' the Jedge hadn't bin crippled, the Cunnel would have charged up that thar mount'n wid his fishin'-pole, as we hern the survidges whoopin' an' hollerin' an' darin' us to come up.

"'But,' says I to myself, 'the very fust thing we've got ter do is to git from yer.' Praise de Lord, too, de horses was hitched clar out'n the track o' them rocks' An' while the Cunnel was holp'n the two other gen'l'-mens, I jes lit out quietly, without sayin' nuthin', an' had the whole tent an' truck flung in de waggon, an the horses hitched up in the worst hurry you ever saw.

"Mar'se Robert, I b'lieve, was layin' out to wait till sun-up and fight de mount'n himself. But I said: 'Look yer, Mar'se Robert, you an' me got other folks ter study. We kin come back an' attend to this fightin' business afterwards; but them two gen'l'mens aint fit to lie out in dese yer bushes no mo'.' The Cunnel sorter quieted down then, an' we holped the

Doctor an' the Jedge inter the waggon. Mar'se Robert he was 'bleeged to climb in afterwards. An' I tell you, Suh, when I got the lines in my han's, an' the moon shinin' good, too, I didn't wait fur de word go; an' by sun-up we was ten miles from de foot of them blamed mount'ns. The Doctor was sufferin' mightily, an' the Jedge was powerful stiff an' bruised. But the Cunnel was snortin' an' runnin' on turr'ble. He ain't a swarin' man, as you know, but, bless grashus! he did let out, as we went bumpin' home over them rocks.

"When, jes' arter sun-up, we struck the big dirt road once mo', I laid out to speak a piece o' my mind to him. 'Mar'se Robert,' says I, 'you rec'llect I dun warned you——' I didn't get no fudder. The Cunnel hollered out he'd pitch me dar over the fence ef I opened my mouf agin. Lordy, he wor powerful mad. He know'd thar'd be the biggest laff all over de county when dis yer frolic cum out, as thar pintedly was. Some even o' dese yer Yankee papers, I hern tell, got pieces in 'bout it."

And so they had, as I have already mentioned. The adventure was a nine days' wonder. Nothing could be done in the way of punishing the culprits, for there was no evidence as to their identity. But it confirmed the general impression of those days, that the mountaineers were dangerous, as well as barbarous. Those, however, who knew something about them, took a rather different view, and the truth gradually came out. The newspaper paragraph, I had seen them so perturbed about earlier in the season, gave the clue to the whole matter. It seems that from this they had contracted an idea that their streams were to be forcibly closed to them by some vague, newfangled piece of legislation, with which the Colonel's name had been so unhappily coupled. And it was evident that Pete, with his metaphorical crowbar had been unable to eject it from their heads. An illiterate, savage, clannish race, who were always half conscious of smarting under a social ban, they not unnaturally resisted, in their own wild way, this supposed attempt upon their liberties, looking upon it as an intolerable infringement of their most cherished rights. It was only a mere handful of us, however, who were interested in the practical side of the question, and to our ears there soon came rumours that these wild men had not only found out their mistake but were actually ashamed of themselves.

Pete, it appears, had known nothing definite of their intentions. Being a sort of link between the mountain and civilization, and, moreover, a leader who was quite sure to oppose disorder, as well as being a friend of the Colonel's, these hostile intentions had been kept back from him. He had only vague ideas that resentment was in the air. And being, after all, himself a mountaineer born and bred, he could not afford to see further than he was intended to among his own people. The next spring, however, he sent word to me that I could come up and fish the whole of both forks, and he would guarantee that not a soul would pester me or any of my friends. How I acted on his advice, and revisited his humble abode, not only the next, but for many seasons afterwards, has been indicated in a previous chapter.

But nothing would ever induce the Judge or the Doctor to go trout-fishing in the mountains again. As for the Colonel I have reason to think that old man Caleb in the end proved too much for him. Fortunately, however, just at this time, the larger rivers, which had been stocked with black bass, began to show great sport with the fly.

These were not dominated by mountaineers, but could be comfortably worked from hotels and such like resorts, so Caleb could raise no possible objection. It is probable that some compromise was arrived at, for the Colonel took vigorously to bass-fishing, and Caleb always accompanied him. Indeed, he frequently, so I was told, took a hand himself, and could be seen watching his cork float from under the shade of a willow or sycamore, while his master, with the same gum pants and silver pole, and dip net, that had so astonished the bloodthirsty mountaineers of the Windy Gap, waded out into the broad, streamy shallows, and performed miracles upon the, then somewhat unsophisticated, bass of the Greenbriar and the Upper James.

SOME PLANTATION MEMORIES

IN the whole of Virginia—and that is saying much indeed—there was no more glorious prospect than the one upon which our first plantation looked out. Around us spread, in pleasant undulations of fallow and forest, of tillage and pasture, the warm, rich coloured but ragged landscape where Virginian homesteads, gentle and simple, lay supinely amid their groves and apple-orchards. Behind us the incomparable peaks of the Blue Ridge Mountains lifted their heads many thousands of feet in to the sky. Before us a tributary range, scarcely less beautiful, if less majestic, spread heavenwards a boundless sea of woodland upon which the bloom of spring, the lush greenery of summer, the fire of autumn, the white terror of winter, proclaimed in a succession of splendid pageants the flight of our placid lives.

These mountains, however, had but recently looked upon scenes that were sufficently stirring. For it was in the period immediately following the war that the plantation known then as the " Old Robertson Place " came into our hands. From that vantage point we witnessed, and indeed partook in what may in one sense be called, the close of the old Southern life.

Historically and financially the long tale of the Slave States ended, as every one knows, with the surrender of Lee in April 1865. But for many years after that, the same families in most parts of Virginia, both white and black, that had lived under the "Institution" and fought in defence of it, were still upon the land. The blacks were free, the whites were ruined—in a sense—it is true. But the latter still had their property, and the negroes, though no longer slaves, were nevertheless there as labourers to work it upon terms that were, in fact, more favourable to all parties than slave labour. The actual paralysis that followed the war was over. Landowners had scraped together sufficient stock and implements, and made arrangements with the newly freed negroes to work their lands, and the same generation that had lived together in a kindly fashion as masters and slaves had settled down as master and servant. Above all, the prices of tobacco and grain were high, and the material outlook seemed upon the whole promising.

Our plantation (the very phrase nowadays is old-fashioned in Virginia) lay "'way back" from the railroad. Fifteen miles of a road such as no civilised community outside the Southern States could have even contemplated without dismay, lay between us and the station. No one but a Virginian, or some one broken into the Virginia attitude towards roads, would have dared, I think, to venture over ours upon wheels. And yet our neighbours had traversed it cheerfully for some generations, and saw nothing seriously amiss with it. The wrecks of waggons and bullock-carts, the fragments of wheels and broken shafts, that marked its course with such terrible significance, had no alarms for the native—they were all in the day's work. The Virginian of slavery days, east of the Blue Ridge at any rate, had never grasped the conception of what road-making meant. In Mashonaland, in the Rocky Mountains, in the far backwoods of Canada, a primitive highway is the natural accompaniment of the dawn of civilisation. But Virginia is the oldest community of Englishmen outside England. It is an ancient and even a distinguished province. For over two centuries it has had something like a territorial aristocracy living upon its soil. Their pleasures and their interests were wholly rural. No people have ever existed in the wide world to whom country locomotion was more important. And yet in most parts, not only till the Civil War but up to this very day, the two-horse plough has been the only factor in road-mending and construction. Over these unspeakable tracks of mud, pleasantly broken by slabs of rock and meandering tree-roots, it was not only the waggon of rural commerce that had to jolt, but the family coach itself to rock and stagger on its way to dance or wedding, to church or merry-making—and with what loss of dignity can be well imagined. These old relics of past splendour (using the latter word in its Virginian sense), with their leather springs, have long vanished now. But I can recall many a venerable specimen that survived the war, and can see them even now writhing in all the agonies of a bottomless mudhole, the negro coachman craning forward with loud shouts of wonderfully worded exhortations to his struggling horses. It was many years indeed before these rickety emblems of *ante-bellum* dignity disappeared entirely from the road. One after another however they made their final trip to the village wheelwright, to be hopelessly condemned even by that resourceful functionary, and left to rot upon the wayside amid the wrecks of humbler vehicles. Much sorrowful consolation, I have reason to think, used to be afforded by these bleaching skeletons to the whilom family coachman as he passed by with his mule or his ox-cart, and dropped the tributary tear to the ghost of the old domestic chariot, which he had once steered with such *éclat*. Some of these old carcases survive to this very day—in remote corners of barnyards and orchards—buried in briers and weeds, a harbour of refuge for the "broody" hen and roosting turkey. This road of ours, it was true, was perhaps the worst, if there could have been a worst, in the county. It was lifted for a considerable part of its course off the red clay of the lower country, and wound its tortuous way over the shoulder of mountain-spurs, where the winter rains did not stand, but tore into atoms every feeble effort that was made to soften the natural obstacles of rock and gully. It was a road that would have made even a Rocky Mountain teamster hold his breath. But our local patriots were quite equal to the occasion, and used to declare, when twitted by people who were fortunate enough to live off it, that it was, at least, a fine *winter* road. That is to say, you couldn't sink permanently into a mud-hole—if nothing smashed you eventually got over it. But then, again, it was almost as bad in summer; whereas in the lower country, when the mud hardened on the track, a reckless driver with a fast horse and a strong buggy could make six miles an hour with luck for a short distance.

Our neighbourhood was beyond doubt a bit isolated, and this perhaps accounted for the fact of oldtime ideas dying harder than in other parts with which I became afterwards familiar—particularly among the negroes. Of these, great numbers of the best of the old *régime* were still, at the time I write of, living and in their prime, and some of them were in every sense as reliable and as trustworthy as good English farm-servants. Their families, had generally got out of hand, but the older darkies were often the very models of industry, and even honesty. One old man in particular whom we found upon the plantation, renting an outlying cabin and a few stony acres in a mountain hollow, was in some respects of this description. So far as cleared land went, he had what he would have himself called "a mighty po' chance fur terbaccer," which at that time was the crop which dazzled and filled the eye of the emancipated slave. But old Uncle Archie had two or three stalwart sons who worked out for wages, and when he went into this dignified retirement he forgot that the patriachal era was over in Virginia—between parent and child as between master and slave. The old gentleman was quite surprised when his "chaps' showed a disposition to appropriate their own wages to their own uses. Archie had built this cabin himself after the war in a corner of the plantation, at the foot of a heavily timbered mountain, whence a crystal brook, breaking from the shade of the forest, went babbling over his patch of open tillage land. Upwards over this wide expanse of oak and chestnut foliage the old man had gazed with sanguine eye, and pictured the tall trees tumbling in every direction, and vast tobacco lands opening, beneath the sturdy strokes of his obedient and filial offspring—inspired, of course, and directed by the wisdom that lay beneath his own snowy brow. But Archie's "chaps" showed no disposition whatever to develop a family estate for their clothes and rations, when they grew to be worth ten dollars a month to any farmer in the neighbourhood. "I've dun frailed them chillern" (they were eighteen and twenty) "till my arms jes ache," the old man used to complain, "but it ain't no manner of use—these new-fangled notions of projeckin' roun' fust hyar den dar, there ain't no satisfyin' young folks these times."

So the forest above Archie's cabin continued to wave in all its pristine luxuriance, and to this day I have no doubt the wild turkey still leads her young in summer-time beneath its friendly shades, and the squirrel gambols amid its giant trunks, and the spotted woodpecker still wakes with cheery tapping its mysterious echoes.

Uncle Archie, it will be gathered, was a *laudator temporis acti* of the most pronounced kind. I think if he could have had his own way he would have reversed the issue of the war and put his whole race back into slavery again. The times, according to Archie, were all out of joint. The revolt of his sons sat sorely on his mind. He had been an industrious, hard-working man all his life, and had belonged to a kind but hard-working master—one of those thousands of small slave-owners of whom the usual literature on this subject shows its ignorance by taking no account. Rough, decent men, whose appearance, education, habits, and means were those of small working farmers, neither more nor less, who owned perhaps a single family of coloured folks, and not seldom laboured with them on the small farm that supported all.

Archie had looked forward to running a bit of rented land with his own family upon somewhat the same principles—inclusive of the whip, if needed. He was an ardent member of the Baptist Church, and had hoped, no doubt for a leisurely as well as a dignified old age in which he could pursue on fence-rails and at cross-roads that taste for religious discussion and controversy which his soul delighted in. Still he raised a tobacco crop of a sort, enough to prove, at any rate, that the filial instincts of Jake and Wash were not wholly dead; and his corn-patch supplied at least his daily bread. A pig or two, moreover, called him owner, and carried ruin and destruction in the point of their snouts all over the plantation; and a cow, which, even with a forefoot tied to its horns, could jump any fence in the neighbourhood, completed Archie's stock.

The old gentleman was quite as honest as he knew how to be. He never succeeded in paying any rent, it is true; but the desire to do so was the burden of many an eloquent harangue, which was something. Archie, however, as a weather prophet and as a character which memory is thankful for, was well worth the twenty-five dollars a-year which constituted his nominal tribute. He died in the odour of sanctity—

lecturing us all to the last on the degeneracy of the world since the "s'render," and foretelling the doom of Sodom and Gomorrah for a land where age and authority were getting to be at such a discount. We had a negro burial-ground on the plantation, and thither Archie's remains were dragged in solemn state by his neighbour William Henry Higginbottom's bull. There was snow on the ground, I remember; but it was a Sunday, and half the negroes in the county were there. It was always said that the patriarch would "walk," and "walk" he did, sure enough, for he was seen in the full moon of the April following his death sowing a big field near the house that had been fallowed for oats; for it should be remarked that he was the great grain-sower of the neighbourhood, and it was natural enough that his spirit should be restless while the dust of the harrows was actually flying over his new-made grave. He was seen again, too, in the same week by Lizzie, our cook, hovering in spectral fashion around the tobacco-plant-beds he had sown just before his death. We were, indeed, already somewhat overrun with ghosts—thanks to the possession of two graveyards, whose inmates, if negro tradition were to be believed, were of the most uneasy kind.

I may remark in passing that the ghosts, or, in negro parlance, the "hants," of our neighbourhood seem to have retained, even in the after-world, their devotion to agriculture. For whether white or black it was in the dawn of spring that they were always "looked for"; nor, like orthodox ghosts, did they haunt bedsides or passages, but were to be seen rather in the neighbourhood of corn-cribs, wheat-fields, or tobacco barns.

The mention of Archie's funeral obsequies recalls another of his neighbours and our tenants, who held a remote corner of the plantation, and this was the aforesaid William Henry Higginbottom. Most of the negroes after the war took their late masters' names, but no Higginbottom had ever been heard of in those parts. This was serious, it is true, but not unnatural, seeing that the bearer of so much name had come from the lower counties since the war, and was in some sort an alien as well as a suspect. Negro nomenclature was of a brief order as a rule, and it was probably in tacit disapproval of William Henry's personality, and of the sort of mystery attaching to him, that he was usually called by all his three names, and, in spite of his grizzled locks and furrowed face, never achieved the honoured *sobriquet* of "Uncle."

In face William Henry was the most forbiding, in form he was the most comical, negro I ever saw. We found him inhabiting a cabin close to the house, and thought at first his looks might belie him. It took about a month to find out from experience that they did not. Hence his removal to the slope of the mountain where he undertook to raise corn and tobacco on shares.

William Henry was, to use the vernacular of the neighbourhood, a "mighty low man"— in a physical sense, that is to say—for he was barely five feet, while he had a head upon him the size of a Missouri pumpkin. He could neither laugh nor could he joke like the rest of them. I never saw him even smile, but there sat upon his dark seamed face a perennial frown. In winter and in summer he wore a long tail-coat that had once been black; and if the front view of him was hideous, his reverse side was much the funniest in the whole county to look upon. But what made William Henry famous, even more than his whispered crimes and his grotesque appearance, was his bull, or in the local phraseology his "gentleman cow."

For when he moved to his mountain farm with nothing but his household truck, it seemed a problem to the neighbours how his stony acres were to be cultivated; but William Henry was equal to the occasion, and one fine day his establishment was seen to be augmented by a two-year-old bull that was as mysterious in origin as the owner himself. There was no direct evidence that our Mephistopheles was a great criminal, but he was said to be capable of any enormity. That he stole that bull I am afraid there was no doubt, and it was whispered that he drove it, with the help of the Evil One, whom he was supposed to resemble, in the night over the almost pathless mountains that divided the plantation from the adjoining county.

Wherever William Henry got his bull, he certainly made it earn its keep. He hitched it to his rude plough and his clumsy harrow. It pulled the rough hand-sled on which he hauled his fire-wood and his fence-rails; while on its broad back, behind a sack of corn, he himself might often be seen perched upon his way to the mill. Such spectacles as these, however, were not unfamiliar in the old happy-go-lucky Virginia life. But even in Virginia, so far as I ever saw or heard of, the bitting, bridling, and saddling of a bull was an unprecedented performance.

But William Henry was nothing if not unconventional. And it was with no sense of humour whatever, but in a solemn seriousness which heightened the sublimity of the spectacle, that he used to clap an old broken hunting-saddle on to the broad back of the patient ox, and seat himself astride thereon, and turn his face on Sunday mornings towards the negro church at Mount Hermon. Mr. Higginbottom, it is perhaps needless to remark, was no church member. The vacant seats upon the mourners' bench had no attraction for him, nor had the eloquent black forefinger or strident appeals of brother Moses ever moved a muscle of the scowling furrowed face. But, for some mysterious reason, William Henry was always to be found at Mount Hermon on a preaching Sunday—silent, inscrutable, and hideous in a back pew—while outside, hitched to a tree in the shade, stood the Durham bull, with its saddle and bridle, all unconscious of any indignity of treatment.

The first time we ever sighted this never-to-be-forgotten spectacle was, I remember, upon the Sunday on which Archie's funeral sermon was preached, in the summer following his death, and all the negroes in the neighbourhood had flocked to hear how brother Moses thought the illustrious dead was getting on in Paradise. We were sitting in the porch as the advanced-guard of the returning congregation came into view upon the highway. This consisted of those negroes who could either beg, borrow, or steal their master's mules for the day, or those who, being tenants at a money rent, had some attenuated quadruped of their own. As the capering, chattering crowd came along amid a cloud of red dust, William Henry Higginbottom could be seen holding a clear lead of several lengths, mounted on his bull, which was travelling at a steady, swinging trot that was thoroughly business-like. That its back was no armchair was evident, for William Henry's long coat-tails were flying in painful agitation, as, with a rein in each hand, he leaned back in approved Southern fashion till his short legs, which were short even for so " low " a man, came not far off the level of the straight horns of his extraordinary steed. The ordinary negro mounted on his master's mule, and attired in his full Sunday war-paint of black broadcloth and white shirt-front, was a sight entirely edifying; but William Henry Higginbottom, leading the queer crowd upon his bull, solemn and gloomy, without the faintest suspicion of any humour in the thing, was a spectacle to have lived for.

But there was a serious side to our plantation life of course, and John Jones, who was our largest tenant, took life very seriously indeed. He held nearly a hundred acres, and actually hired labour on his own account. Indeed he was justly regarded as " a 'sponsible man." He got a good house with his holding, built of squared logs and shingle-roofed, and a garden-patch, and the run for a cow, which, like Archie's, no fence could turn. John farmed his land on shares—we providing the horses and implements, he the labour ; and, like some of his kind, at that period he was an indefatigable worker. From dawn till dark he never rested except to feed his teams and get his meals, and I have even known him to work all night when the weeds in his corn or the suckers on his tobacco had got ahead of him. In spite of his practical qualities, however, John was as comical a character in his way as William Henry. He thought he could write, for one thing—an almost unknown, performance at that time—and he was inordinately proud of it. Furthermore, he had, as is rare among his race, a bad stammer with terrific facial contortions. This, as we know, is sometimes sufficiently trying in a Caucasian, but in a negro of quizzical appearance it is simply irresistible; and John's appearance was not calculated to bear any further embellishments of the kind. He was of the round, smooth, beardless, and oily type of Ethiopian, as black as a coal without a touch of cross about him. He was a stranger to the neighbourhood, and came to us, I remember, one autumn before wheat-sowing, which was the season of the year all over Virginia for making contracts, and wheat by the way at that time was worth not half a dollar but three times that amount per bushel. I can see him now as he stood at the foot of the verandah steps, with his mouth twisted nearly round to his ear trying to tell me who he was and what he wanted. His mania for writing, though it was in no way connected with hesitation of speech, came out instantly, and he insisted on being allowed to write down his late employer's name and address for reference. This was a great experience for us, so I fetched this phenomenal scribe a pen and ink and set him down at the office table while we watched the performance. It was a heroic struggle, and resulted in the most extraordinary specimen of orthography probably in existence. I have got it yet. John surveyed it himself with one eye closed for a few seconds, and evidently felt that it was a failure. "He'd got sort er onused to writing," he said, "since he'd been down ter the mines, but he'd jest like to mark down his own name on the paper lest he should forget it." This ceremony was got through with less execution, but it was as well I had not to depend on the result to save John's name and memory from oblivion. Still, the hieroglyphics stood for John Jones in their maker's estimation, and as a signature it was fairly uniform, though it was quite as like Thomas Evans or Henry Browne as it was John Jones. I never saw a man so devoted to signing his name. I believe he would have backed a stranger's bill for all he was worth, if he had been worth anything, rather than miss the opportunity.

When he settled on the plantation, I used to draw up agreements for all sorts of trifling transactions between us, to give John the pleasure of signing his name and myself the pleasure of seeing him do it. He would settle himself to the job as if to some weighty and solemn function. Slowly and with deliberation he would lay his left cheek down almost flat upon the table, and closing his left eye, which at such close quarters became unavailable for the purpose in hand, the squint of his right as it peered over the broad bridge of his nose at the objective point upon the paper was appalling. Little, indeed, but a big white eyeball was to be seen, and then after many flourishes of his pen above his head it descended on the sheet and left the fearful impress that signified John Jones. I generally managed to have a paper for John to sign when we had friends staying with us, and it was always voted much more entertaining than old Reuben's banjo performance, though Reuben was reckoned the best hand to "pick a banjer" in the whole neighbourhood.

The actual banjo of the plantation was not the stirring instrument it is in the hands of the Moore and Burgess minstrel, and a certain wild *abandon* it undoubtedly did possess in the cabin frolic after a wedding or corn-shucking, disappeared when introduced into the parlour of the "big house." Reuben, as has been said, was reckoned the best hand to pick a banjo in the neighbourhood. But when called upon to perform in private for our visitors he did not shine, and as an entertainment could not be compared for a moment to John Jones signing his name. Reuben, too, was a preacher—not a salaried, responsible minister like the dusky Boanerges who thundered weekly in the log church at Mount Hermon, but an amateur whose spasmodic exhortations formed a righteous excuse for his immediate neighbours to gather in his cabin on Saturday evening and work off their excess of religious zeal. Reuben in his hours of toil, which were not exacting, was a carpenter, and he occupied a cabin on the summit of a hill immediately in front of our windows. So on still nights we ourselves often had any benefit that was to be derived from the wild incantations of our eloquent dependant. This, I fear, would have been heavily discounted by the certain knowledge that Reuben could not have been trusted for five minutes with the cornhouse key, or for as many seconds within grabbing distance of the storeroom sugar-barrel; while John Jones, who had never yet "professed," might safely have been submitted to either trying ordeal. Reuben, however, did not confine his sermons to proper times and seasons, but his anxiety for the souls of men followed him to his intermittent labours. As he nailed the shingles on to the roof of a waggon-shed he seldom failed to hurl down misquotations from the Bible on the head of the man who held the ladder; and as he swung his cradle in the wheat-harvest amid the long line of reapers, the busy swish of the blades was often—much too often —accompanied by his fitful bursts of eloquence. The cabin that he then occupied acquired something of a clerical reputation, for no less than three of what for brevity's sake we may call lay brethren took it in our own time. Possibly the near neighbourhood of the graveyard, with its turfless mounds of red earth and its tangled unkempt clusters of grape-vines, briers, and sassafras-bushes, may have given the old log-house some sanctified associations.

People sometimes ask if the genuine plantation negro was as comical a person as tradition represents. I can only say that to me their quaint humours were an unceasing source of refreshment. They made up, or almost made up, for those lamentable shortcomings which grew worse as the war and "the s'render" faded further and further into the past. They have almost ceased nowadays to be a local peasantry identified with their native counties and districts, but are to a great extent a wandering race—here for a year, there for a year; first in a factory, then in a mine, then back again for a brief spell at farming. And this, though not to the advantage of their morals, has been distinctly so to their financial condition. Indeed, under the agricultural depression that has lain upon the Southern farmer for so many years, intensified as it is by oppressive tariff laws, it was inevitable that the negro of the rising generation should leave the land. He has been a greater success, too, as a navvy or factory-hand, than he was as a farm-servant; but as a man he is an infinitely more unpleasant and much less humorous person, as is only natural. Hundreds, too, who in the days I write of were unredeemed plantation hands, whooping and holloaing at the plough-tail without a thought beyond a corn-shucking or a cake-walk, are now sleek waiters in hotels, who know as much of the devilry of city life and the outer world as there is to know. Through whole counties in Virginia the exodus of the negro to busy centres can be easily seen in the roofless cabin or the solitary chimney standing by the brookside or the forest-edge amid the broom-sedge and the briers. However strong are the forces which remove an ancient peasantry from a not unkindly and certainly a racy soil, there must be a melancholy side to it with those who have seen the change.

In the days I write of no such exodus, in our part of the world at any rate, was thought of, and the Ethiopian, if unambitious, was at least cheery. Per-

S

haps he was seen at his best in the first warm days of spring, when his limbs after the cold winter got "souple and limber," and the whole country echoed with his rude rustic melody. We always recall the month of May upon our plantation as an ideal Arcady, —when through the lush and dewy nights the opening chorus of the tree-crickets and the plaintive call of the whip-poor-will welcomed the coming summer; when a sea of snow-white apple-blossoms caught the morning sun as he topped the hills upon the east of us, while upon the west the fresh greenery of summer was clothing with its leafy mantle the splendid masses of the Blue Ridge that towered above us. All around us glowed against the warm red soil the freshness and the lushness, the leaf and blossom, of dawning summer, and the cheery stir of rural life gave animation to a scene which nature had fashioned and bedecked with such unsparing hand. The one-horse ploughs ran merrily up and down the corn-rows. The harrows clanked cheerily along their dusty course. No wonder that in such a climate farmers were sanguine, and that even the oldest of them estimated their crop with a persistent optimism at double what it turned out to be. Hope animated every rural breast. The mating dove filled the orchard with melodious notes. The cock quail piped in the fence corner with tireless throat, while his partner hid snugly away in the adjoining clover-field the fifteen or twenty eggs whose products were in the still far-off crisp days of November to spring before our keen-nosed pointers.

Above all the pleasant echoes of field and woodland at that season of the year, used to ring the voices of the negroes. No people were more susceptible to stimulating atmospheric conditions than they. Nowadays, so small has the world—the English-speaking world, at any rate—become, that the field-hand is more likely than not to hill up his tobacco to the accompaniment of "Knock'd 'em in the Old Kent Road," or even "Tommy Atkins." In those days, however, a mighty gulf lay between Virginia and the world outside her borders: the old plantation songs were still the sole music of the plantation, and I can in fancy even now see Reuben's son Gabriel, as he swung his plough round on the headland, lifting his shiny face skywards and bulging out his chest as he roared—

> " O—O my lovely Lemma,
>   I—I do love you so ;
> " I—I love you better tha-a-n
>   I ever did befo'.
>   O-oh—O-oh."

Then from the dewy low ground, where some rival swain in leisurely fashion was slaughtering the bushes that at this season threatened the very existence of the Virginia oat crop, came an answer to the vocal challenge :—

> " O—O my lovely Lemma,
>   I—I know you of old ;
>   You got all de money,
>   All de silver an' gold."

Then from another quarter—far into our neighbour's domain—would roll the strident notes of that sonnet to "Scindy," which was the most popular air in our part of the world :—

> "Away up in de mountain
>   I took my horn and blow;
> I tink I hear Miss Scindy callin',
>   'Yonder come my beau.'"

But Gabriel, though three-quarters of a mile off, would be equal to the occasion, and catch up the second verse:—

> "O Scindy, do you love me?
>   She said she loved me some,
> An' I threw my arms around her,
>   Like a grape-vine round a gum."

If the dawn of summer in Virginia, when the fields grew gay in colouring and the shadows deepened in the forests, animated the Ethiopian breast, the autumn in dreamy, balmy splendour was by no means without consolation either to blacks or to whites, who lived, so to speak, with nature. The tobacco was hung up and curing in the barns; the crops, such as they were, were stored away—all but the Indian corn, which still hung its big heads from the bare stalk stripped of its leaves and its top fodder. The leanest of stock, too, had grown fat in the rank growth that covered pasture and stubble fields alike, and carpeted even the very forests.

All nature rested from its labours—and man, too (in Virginia), for the most part. There was plenty for all present needs, and weeks of bright, still weather often intervened before the chill breath of winter with its flurries of snow stripped the forests of their golden mantle, and the heavens of their long unclouded brilliancy.

The sunny days of October and November were

days of plenty on the plantations. The lean times were over. Hogs were fat, and the new crop of corn was ready to grind into meal for those hot cakes which were the Ethiopian's staff of life. The mill-wheels in the valleys were humming, and along the tortuous red roads went shambling work-horses or mules, whose backs presented the familiar spectacle of a bare-legged negro urchin just visible behind a big sack of meal.

How delightful, too, were some of these old water-mills in Virginia!—not very old, perhaps fifty to a hundred years at the most, but still venerable-looking with their weather-stained and spray-moistened timbers and big rumbling wheels, to whose music four or five generations at any rate had gossiped and fore-gathered as to a local landmark whose site nature had firmly fixed beyond the caprice of change or fortune. Pleasant places above all were these old-fashioned water-mills in the fierce hot August days; and how cool was the draught which blew up from the foaming caldron beneath the wheel as it churned round and round amid a white wreath of crystal water fresh from dark mountain hollows, where trout leapt between banks of flowery evergreens and beneath overarching avenues of beech and chestnut! And the millers, too, of Virginia—all that I ever knew, at any rate—were cheery beings of stout frame and well-powdered exteriors and strong lungs, who would crack jokes above the whirr and throb of their rude machinery with all comers, black and white, and tell stories of the gigantic crops that men made before the war in the brave days of old.

No living soul could look forward to an English autumn for its own sake with pleasure or recall it with tenderness. Certain enjoyments, it is true, belong to it, but that is wholly another matter. The season itself is one of sadness, of drippy decay, of blustering winds, of rarely unmitigated gloom. But October and November in Virginia, and indeed not seldom December also, are not merely the sportsman's saturnalia, but are largely composed of days in which mere existence is a joy, and every one worth living for itself alone—a dream of golden foliage and cloudless skies, of dewy mornings crisp and fresh, of balmy noons, of sunsets wondrous and incomparable. There is no breath of melancholy in the light and stimulating air, no suggestion of decay in the dazzling splendour of the woods: winter will come, we know, but it will fall like the curtain of a theatre on some splendid pageant which we have enjoyed till the last moment, and shall hope again to enjoy. Mid-winter, it must be said, had little to offer to the plantation-owner in Virginia. Without doors, there was snow and rain, cold and sleet, iron frost or red mud of a depth and tenacity beyond the dreams of Englishmen. Within, it is true, there were spacious brick fireplaces and big brass andirons, on which oak-logs of noble proportions crackled and blazed, throwing a cheery light over the wainscoted walls. Visiting was no longer thought of, farming was at a standstill, shooting was over, though the horn of the fox-hunter now and again woke the echoes of the gloomy mornings. The thud of the axe rang from the dripping or frozen woodlands, and spoke of the ceaseless cry for firewood that came from the draughty insatiable chimneys of cabin, farmhouse, and mansion.

The very mountains, that in the greenery of their summer dress and the gorgeous splendour of their autumn robes were beyond all description beautiful, looked now only savage and almost terrible, with their miles and miles of black and leafless woodland stretching over their snowy carpet to the cheerless skies. Worst of all these dreary weeks to the planter was that which intervened between Christmas and New Year, — that season which to other Christians with a white skin is a period of festivity and rejoicing. Here the negro had it all to himself, and male and female, leaving their master to get on as best he could, abandoned themselves to those social joys so dear to the Ethiopian breast. "Cake-walks" and frolics and preachings filled the cabins with sound and merriment; whiskey of a fearsome sort flowed freely, and stimulated with its unwonted fires the merry antics of the coloured revellers. Even William Henry Higginbottom once gave a party at Christmas, though to be sure it was one of those social speculations called a "pay-party," where every guest paid twenty-five cents at the door, the profits going to the genial host, who provided food and music. As for the cake-walks, who has not heard of them? — though that indeed is a poor substitute for the privilege of having witnessed the inimitable spectacle of the sable beaux and belles strutting in couples arm-in-arm before the judge, with solemn efforts to outdo each other in elegance of movement and dignity of bearing, and thus win the toothsome prize.

But volumes could be filled with the queer characters of both colours, the quaint customs and the unsophisticated ways that obtained in the country districts of Virginia in the days I write of. These days are gone for ever. Half the cabins in the State have rotted away or been burnt for firewood. Agriculture of a large and careless sort is almost dead. The negro still in a measure follows the plough or wields the hoe, but more often, as I have already remarked, is a factory-hand, a miner, a waiter, or what not, and wears on Sunday a covert coat and a pot-hat, while his wife struts at his side attired in a caricature of the latest New York fashion.

A TURKEY HUNTER

NOBODY ever quite knew what the Captain took his rank from, though that was a trifle in Virginia. It was said that at some remote period before the war he had navigated a batteau on the rapid waters of the Staunton river, and had carried tobacco and grain for the planters in days when railways were distant and high roads, as now, the worst in the Anglo-Saxon world. So though an expert only in the handling of a punt-pole the Captain may be said in a sense to have been a member of the mercantile marine of his country. He had never in truth set eyes upon the ocean, nor had any desire that way; nor did he come of a people that were much given to going down to the sea in ships. In fact he would often tell us that he "had no use for so much water."

Four main roads met in front of the Captain's door, a circumstance which suited exactly his gregarious temperament. And they were roads indeed; roads such as only a Virginian would have faced upon wheels, or even calmly contemplated day after day as the Captain from the security of his front porch contemplated them. One of these red rutty tracks came toiling up from regions to the eastward wholly given over and sacred to tobacco; and if you had followed it on towards the sunset, and had not broken your neck or disappeared in a mud-hole, you would have found yourself eventually within sight of the Blue Ridge faintly outlined against the distant sky. The other came from counties lying to the northward that had seen much better days, and after passing the Captain's house shot off in a straight line regardless of obstacles for the frontier of North Carolina which was barely a dozen miles away. In fact the Captain, who was born just here at the forks of the old Bethel and Shuckburgh pikes, had, as you may say, a narrow escape of being born a North Carolinian, and that would not have done at all. For everybody in Virginia at any rate, knows that when a North Carolinian boasts of hailing from the Old North State he takes very good care to add if he can conscientiously do so, "but right close on the Virginia line." It is ill guessing what the Captain would have done if he had been born a North Carolinian, for he was a most ardent patriot, and a patriot in Virginia in those days meant a patriotic Virginian,—which is a highly intelligible sentiment.

The Captain had a strange domicile; he lived in the shell of an old coaching inn, and a very famous hostelry it had been in its day. First, however, came the railroads, and then the war with its chaotic ruin finally extinguished every spark of its ancient glory. For twenty years it had been slowly rotting, plank by plank, shingle by shingle. The Captain, however, reckoned it would last his time and would hardly anticipate nature by falling in upon him bodily. A rough board at the corner of the fence carried an inscription, rudely traced in lamp black, to the effect that the weary traveller could still get accommodation for man and horse; while upon the next panel was inscribed in still larger letters the much less hospitable notification, *No hunting or fishing here.* Such, it may be remarked, was the local and legal fashion of proclaiming that the proprietor was a game preserver; but of this anon.

As for the house, it was a rambling and now crazy edifice of wood from which every vestige of paint had long since faded. The main central portion still stood fairly upright, but the two wings lurched away on either side as if threatening to part company altogether with the parent stem. Long galleries ran around the outside of the queer structure both in the upper and lower stories, and helped, no doubt, to bind it together and prolong its precarious existence. Moss had taken hold of the twisting shingles of the roof. The tin gutter-pipes had shaken loose, and swung in strips from the eaves. There was hardly a pane of glass in the whole building except in the two or three rooms occupied by the Captain and his rare guests; and even there strips of the local newspaper did duty for many a vanished pane. Such of the Venetian shutters as survived swung loose, often upon only a single hinge, and with the dangling gutter-pipes made such an uproar on a windy night, that an abode which was ghostly enough by day was truly terrifying in a midnight storm. The Captain, however, cared for none of these things. The decay amidst which he lived never caused him, we will venture to say, even a passing pang. The very extent of the dilapidations paralysed perhaps any feeble spark of energy he may have possessed; and he lived as jollily as the proverbial sandboy amid his ruins. For there were rows of barns and stables in the oak grove behind the house, some of which had collapsed, the logs lying in a heap as they had fallen, while others leaned over at an angle that would have been impossible but for the heavy props that the Captain and his negroes had been absolutely forced to put up in self-defence. And this was necessary, for besides the pair of mules the estate still boasted of, an occasional traveller of the humbler kind from time to time sought the hospitality of the dilapidated tavern. The Captain, like every good Virginian, was greatly given to reminiscences, and his favourite theme was the animated splendour of the Plummer House in the old days when his father owned it. A somewhat notable rendezvous it had, in truth, once been, as was natural, seeing that it stood in the angle where the old highway from the Carolinas to the North crossed the route along which the planters from the regions lying eastwards used to travel in some rustic state towards the fashionable spas in the Virginia Mountains. Family coaches, dragged through the dust or mud by sleek horses and piloted by negro coachmen, were almost daily visitors in those halcyon times throughout the summer season; while gay young dandies on well-bred nags rode in and out of the shady yard by the score, drank juleps on the verandah, or flirted and danced in the now lonely rooms with the fair members of First Families who happened to be at that stage of their annual pilgrimage to the healing waters of the Alleghany Valleys. Never, perhaps, has highway tavern had a greater fall. The tobbaco-waggon, plunging and crashing onwards to the still distant market-town, is nowadays almost the only vehicle that ever pulls up before the deserted inn, and even the waggon-drivers in these hard times bring usually their own rations and camp, if benighted, on the patch of turf under the old chestnut tree at the cross roads. Still the Captain, who is gregarious and has long outlived financial ambition, gets some satisfaction, at any rate, out of their society. And sometimes a casual horseman, unduly reckless of his pocket and still more regardless of his inner man, would stay and face that nightmare of fat pork, soda-biscuit, and black coffee which the Captain's wife provided in exchange for a twenty-five cent piece.

Though the Captain would have registered himself as a hotel-keeper, as a matter of fact he was first and chiefly a turkey-hunter, and to support this inexpensive profession he owned, fortunately, about two hundred acres of land. Though the latter were perhaps as poor as any two hundred acres in Virginia, which is saying much indeed, the Captain's wants were so few and slight that when he had paid his taxes (amounting perhaps to some fifteen dollars), dull care may be said to have been wholly lifted from the establishment till the next visit of the tax-gatherer. The farm was cultivated in irregular and spasmodic fashion by a couple of negroes who worked it on shares, using the Captain's mules and giving their landlord half the tobacco, two-thirds of the corn, and three-fourths of the wheat and oats. In a dry year the whole lot of it could, we think, have been put into a waggon and drawn to market by a pair of stout horses even over the Shuckburgh pike. Only a portion of the estate would any longer produce even such skeleton crops as the Captain's negroes raised. The rest lay sick unto death with a sterility such as in any other countries known to man would be absolutely inconceivable where soil existed at all. Scrub pines and briars and sassafras and broomsedge had covered the corpse of most of the Captain's property in their not unkindly grasp; and for the rest it was a moot question whether they or the homestead would give out first. Even Uncle Moses and Jake Plummer (Jake had belonged in the days of slavery to the Captain) had begun to complain, and think that the residential advantages of their master's property were almost too dearly purchased. But the Captain troubled himself little about such things. For him the year had two seasons only: the one when it was possible to shoot, and the other when it was not. In the former few men were more active; during the latter, including of course the spring and summer, none probably ever took their ease with more unswerving deliberation. For every morning after breakfast, when it was not raining, the Captain carried his chair down from the rickety porch and set it against the rough trunk of a shady acacia tree, and as the shadow moved round with the sun the Captain moved his chair round with it. So that while the morning found him with his eye upon the lower road, the evening found that watchful orb surveying the approach from the Piedmont country. This was not so much for possible customers, who might or might not share the Captain's midday meal, for that great man was not in the least degree mercenary, but for such as might haply prove sociable and responsive to his urgent appeal to "get down and chat him some."

The Captain's notice that his place was forbidden to casual gunners has been alluded to. It may seem strange that such an ardent sportsman, who hunted the entire country for some miles round, should have been so churlish about his own little domain of two hundred acres. But the danger-signal on the fence was not hoisted for the benefit of the Captain's neighbours, who were rarely sportsmen, being small farmers mostly with large farms (if the seeming paradox be admissible), but against that type of humanity which our friend designated as "them city fellahs," and for whom he was accustomed with great warmth and frequency to declare he had "no manner of use." In former days the few gentry who lived in that neighbourhood had been wont to shoot partridges and rabbits in friendly unchallenged fashion over each other's and their humbler neighbours' land; but since the great upheaval social centres had wholly changed. What wealth and leisure existed was now in the towns, and it was from there that the gunners chiefly came. "Gawd knows who they are," the Captain used to say, as he sent a charge of tobacco juice at a sitting grasshopper, "or whar they come from, a-whirlin' over the country as if it belonged to 'em with ther brichloaders and neepaty, napity[1] dawgs,

[1] This was, we believe, an entirely original phrase of the Captain's, inspired by an occasional glimpse of the dainty, well-groomed Laverack setters that had been recently introduced into the country.

and fancy coats, and pants, and fixins. No, surr, I reckon no city chap'll fire a gun off for a right smart ways up and down this yer pike. I've fixed that, anyway." And so he had, for the danger-signal was upon every farm, though not against the Captain, for five miles round. Not being a "city fellah," I had no cause myself to complain of this; and indeed I often shot with the Captain's party, though never, if it could possibly be helped, upon the same beat with that great man himself, for he was not a pleasant companion after the partridges ("bird hunt'n," he would have called it), nor were his dogs shining examples to a young and heady setter in whose future you might feel an interest. He regarded you on such occasions rather as an opponent than a partner; and his great object was to bring down every bird wherever it might happen to rise, before you could pull on it, and so being in a position to boast of what he called "beating the crowd" when the game was counted out at the end of the day. As the Captain was only a very moderate performer at this work it resulted in his eye being wiped not seldom; and this he took so very much to heart that it was almost as distracting (for we had a great personal regard for the Captain) as having him cut down your birds as they rose in front of you or even upon your off side. I can see him now, in his big straw hat and flapping tail-coat, bustling up to the setting dog with elbows out, his gun at the ready, and an almost fierce expression of rivalry in his eye and general demeanour. His dogs would certainly not have been accused of being "neepaty, napity," for they were lumbering, poking brutes nearly as big as donkeys, with much more intelligence and nose than speed, till you unhaply knocked over a bird within range of their immediate vision, when they were fast enough in all conscience, and you would be fortunate indeed if you got there in time to save a wing-feather. The Captain had a gun, too, that was something worse than a curiosity. It may be unnecessary, perhaps, to remark that it was a muzzle-loader, but its ancient stock was a masterpiece of splicing and riveting; the barrels were worn as thin as a sixpence, and though they had so far withstood the Captain's "loads," as he called them, the nipples were accustomed upon occasions to blow off with a great sound, burying themselves in tree trunks or vanishing into space. This seemed in no way to disconcert the Captain himself; but it made his friends feel that it was almost as dangerous to be behind as in front of him. It was for every reason a good thing, when you arranged a day over the Captain's preserves, to make up a party of four, taking your own friend and your own dogs over one line of country, while the Captain and some third party, who either did not know him or was used to him, took another. And the spirit of rivalry was always strong enough to make this eminent sportsman accede most readily to such a plan. For not only was his method of shooting irksome and his gun dangerous in a mechanical sense, but his principles as regards safety of firing were hopelessly distorted. These latter, I recollect, were illustrated most forcibly upon a rather unfortunate occasion. A Canadian sportsman of some repute had come down to the

T

district for the best fortnight of the partridge-shooting, and we had included in our programme a day over the Captain's preserves. A party of four was as usual arranged, and it was easily contrived that we should separate, myself with the Canadian taking one beat and the Captain with his friend taking the other. We had a big stubble field, however, to traverse upon this occasion before the company separated, and in it a covey of birds was flushed wild, owing to the jealousies of our various dogs. Beyond the Captain at the extreme right of our line was his friend (not mine, thank goodness), and he had taken advantage of the brief halt to put his foot up on a fence, his back being towards us, for the purpose of adjusting a boot-lace. A lagging bird in the meantime rose before the Captain, and swinging to the right flew straight for the gentleman in question, who being about seventy to eighty yards off, neither saw nor heard it. The Captain, however, levelled his cannon with the greatest deliberation and fired. Down came the bird, and up sprang his friend with imprecations loud and deep, it is true, but not a whit too strong for the occasion, for he had received most of the half-spent charge in his person. "It's all right, squire" (the victim was a magistrate), sung out the Captain cheerily as he began calmly re-loading his gun; "I saw you had your back turned towards me." The Canadian who, as a matter of fact, was a British officer settled in Canada, an old and accomplished sportsman, was horrorstruck, not so much at the outrage but at the matter of fact justification of it. It seemed to him that he had struck a country where the less vulnerable parts of a fellow-sportsman's body were ordinarily regarded as a fair target if they happened to be in the way. He refused in most uncompromising fashion to go another yard with such an appalling prospect before him, and declared that if I did not get him out of reach of the Captain's gun at once, he would go home alone. It was fortunate for all parties that our paths here diverged. The story is, I believe, still told in Canada as an illustration of what to expect at a Virginian shooting-party.

It was at turkey-hunting, however, that the Captain really shone. At game-shooting he was a zealous but, as will probably be understood, a not very satisfactory performer; but at turkeys he was really great, the wild turkey, that noblest of woodland birds and wariest of feathered fowl, shows over a large part of Virginia few signs of extinction. So long indeed as the tall primeval forests, dense pine woods, and abandoned fields cover so large a portion of the country as they now do, the turkey will no doubt successfully defy the efforts of the few hunters who are sufficiently skilled in the art to menace his existence. For the Captain's friend, the city fellah, would never cause a single feather of that proud bird's to tremble; while as for the average sportsman, who has anything to do at all besides shoot, life is generally voted too short for a pursuit that consists wholly of woodcraft, contains so many certain blanks, and in which marksmanship plays so small a part. But for the Captain life was not too short for what was in fact its principal object. Partridge-shooting was only a secondary matter with him, as he, indeed, was in that art but a secondary performer.

It was when the first sharp frosts of October had fired the woods with the gorgeous splendour of decay that the Captain began to stir himself after his long siesta, and fetch down from over the mantel-shelf not only the double-barrelled fowling-piece already noticed, but the long Kentucky rifle that had belonged to his father and that he still used for squirrels and, upon certain occasions, for the noble turkey himself. His crops were housed, such as they were: his tobacco was being "fired" in the barn, such as it was, and coming out all the colours of the rainbow; and Jake and Uncle Moses for the fifth or sixth year in succession were vowing that they would quit farming. And it was at this season that the young broods of turkeys, who roamed the woodlands or picked their way stealthily through the sedgy fields, became lawful prey under the game-laws of Virginia, to those who, in the local vernacular, could succeed in "catching up with them." These flocks, or gangs, numbered as a rule from eight to fourteen birds, and by this time had grown to be nearly the size of the highly educated old veterans, their parents, who watched over their wanderings. In every great stretch of woodland, or where continuous belts of timber touched, or almost touched, each other, there one brood at least would be found ranging, always within certain more or less definite limits. Wherever, too, a mountain spur threw its wooded crest a few hundred feet above the low ground, it would be almost certainly frequented by a brood of the stately timorous birds.

The Captain had by instinct and experience a very accurate notion each season where to find the various gangs. But in addition to this not a farmer, nor even a negro, passed along the high road in August and September who was not ready to place the results of his local observations at the service of the "popular landlord of the Plummer House" as the county papers, when in a serio-comic vein, were accustomed to speak of our friend. For myself, though I made a point of having two or three excursions of this kind every year with the Captain, I could not boast of even the most elementary proficiency in the art. Life, as I have said, seemed too short, and such measure of skill as I possessed in stopping the rapid twisting partridge of Virginia would have been entirely thrown away in hunting the turkey. For when that noble bird could be induced to present you with a shot, it was usually a sitting one; and even when otherwise, the old familiar metaphor of a flying haystack was in such case almost literally applicable. But the essence of the mystery lay in securing the shot; and I am free to confess that, save when under the wing of the Captain and the shadow of his blunderbuss, the elusive tactics of the king of forest-birds were too many for me.

The chief and vital accomplishment, without which you could not hope to be a turkey-hunter at all, was that of imitating the call of the wily keen-eared bird. This sounds simple enough; but as a matter of fact it was about as difficult, or seemed to me so, as learning the violin, and not nearly so useful for general purposes. The implement used for this nice deception was usually the wing-bone of the turkey itself, which seems surely the very refinement of guile. It was by no means difficult with a little practice to imitate the *tuk ! tuk !* of your intended victim entirely to your own satisfaction, and to that perhaps of some inexperienced friends; but if you could not convince the turkey to an absolute certainty that you were one of his relatives, or should he suspect for a moment that there was treachery in the note, you might just as well, so far as getting a shot was concerned, have fired off both barrels at once into the air; even better, for sometimes a great alarm, such as the rush of a barking dog towards a flock, will act upon it in a paralysing or stupefying fashion. Indeed, many turkey-hunters, the Captain included, kept a small dog trained to run in and bark after the shot for the purpose of scattering the birds. The Captain's "tuckey-dawg," as he called it, was a singular looking animal, being what was generally known in Virginia as a "fyce," and the term, which, I think, is Elizabethan English, was applied in the South to every species of small dog indiscriminately. The Captain's fyce was of a yellow shade, with the head of a fox, and curly tail of a squirrel, and the legs of a turnspit. He would, in short, have been locally described as "a bench-legged fyce." His chief mission was to tree squirrels, and to bark up the trunk till the Captain with his long small-bore Kentucky rifle arrived upon the scene. For this great sportsman took sometimes what he called "a spell of squ'rl hunt'n'," the large gray squirrel being a popular luxury on the tables of the Virginia country folk.

We used to start generally about sunrise on those glorious autumn mornings. So far as my own feelings were concerned there was none of the gravity and responsibility of a campaign against the partridges. I was out to enjoy myself in an irresponsible fashion, to revel in the gorgeous colouring of the woodlands, to drink in the fresh, balmy, resinous air of early autumn, and take any bit of luck that came with thankfulness. But the Captain, I need not say, was very serious indeed on such occasions. I can see him now climbing stealthily up the broken surface of the rudely cultivated or abandoned fields that stretched up to the edge of the forests clothing the ridge and summit of the mountain, his keen and experienced eye searching everywhere for some faint print on the red clay or black loam that tells of the recent wanderings of the gang and the direction in which their footsteps have been bent. It is not, however, till we enter the forest above the highest line of cultivation that the time arrives for absolute silence and the extremity of caution. There is up here little underbush or covert in which birds might be taken unawares, for the tall gray trunks of chestnut, oak, and poplar shoot up from a smooth carpet of dead leaves, while far above our heads, broken here and there with patches of bright blue sky, hangs the now motionless canopy of leaves, one gorgeous blaze of scarlet and gold. Slowly and cautiously, about a hundred yards apart, we steal along between the tree-trunks, up the long ridge of the mountain which, dipping slightly here and there in its ascent, gives a possible chance of coming unawares upon the turkeys in some hollow or beneath some ridge. The Captain has his celebrated gun loaded with heaven knows what, for to-day he carries his shot in a medicine-bottle and his powder in a mustard-tin, the well-worn flasks, as very often happens, being laid up for repairs ; and the fyce dog, with its bushy tail curled over its back, prowls along behind him.

We are already very high up in the world, and the silence of the Indian summer in these lofty forests is intense. The bark of a squirrel, or the hoarse call of a crow, seems to make the whole air tremble. Far away below us lies the many-coloured rolling plain of old Virginia, basking in the sun with its red fallows and now golden forests and dark splashes of pine wood. The white gleam of a homestead shows here and there, while a score of scattered smoke-wreaths mark the site of tobacco-barns where the newly-gathered leaves are slowly curing. A faint gray outline rolls along the western horizon ; it is the Blue Ridge, the first outwork of the Alleghanies. The song of a plough-man, the bark of a dog, the thud of an axe come up faintly from far below us ; but where we are walking the mere snapping of a twig makes a noise like a pistol, and has at all hazards to be avoided if I would hope to keep on good terms with the Captain and catch, perchance, the wary turkey napping below yonder ridge. There is little other game or even bird-life in these silent altitudes. The woodpecker taps as if he revelled in the noise he made ; the gray squirrel, safe to-day at any rate from the Captain, leaps from tree to tree or scuttles up the horny trunks ; Brer Rabbit (for this, it must be remembered, is the land of Uncle

Remus) is much too sociable to mount so high above civilisation, though his old friend, the fox, now and again on these occasions steals across one's vision. It is just possible too that a brood of ruffed grouse, rare though the bird is east of the Alleghanies, and almost as shy as the turkey itself, might haunt these wooded hilltops. But should one of these grand birds, by some strange freak, get up under the very muzzle of your gun, refrain, as you value the Captain's alliance, from yielding to temptation; for so far as turkeys are concerned, a shot in these silent, echoing woods would most certainly ruin everything for the day, or at least for the morning. It is well, too, to keep an eye upon the leaves over which you are carefully treading. For the Captain at any rate would notice in a moment the slightest disturbance of their surface, and can tell at once whether it is the work of turkeys, and almost estimate the length of time it is since they were scratching among them.

Suddenly from just beyond the ridge, a hundred yards or so to the left, a sound like an explosion of dynamite seems to shake the whole mountain. The Captain has fired off his gun, and he never fires at anything less than a turkey on these occasions. A hasty flank movement of a few yards brings me in view of the situation, and a sound as of heavy wings flapping follows the concussion of the shot. The fyce dog, with tail well curled over his back, is charging along and yelping in a state of great excitement. The Captain is reloading his piece from the medicine-bottle and the mustard-tin, with a sheet of the county paper for wadding, and it is perhaps needless to remark that his left barrel remains at full cock during the operation.

The whole gang have risen, it appears, at long range from behind some old panels of a boundary fence. The Captain fired, it seems, with a view to scatter the birds, though he declares he crippled one. It may be added that he has never yet been known to admit missing anything clean; and indeed, "the Captain's cripples" have passed as an expression into the local phraseology.

And now comes the really serious part of the whole day's proceedings. The birds are thought to have been at any rate partially scattered, thanks to the noisy efforts of the bench-legged fyce well supported by the Captain's artillery, and also to the fact of their having been taken unawares. It now only remains to select a favourable position upon the ridge where we can both shelter ourselves from view and at the same time command all the likely approaches. A great chestnut trunk, fallen prone and dead these three or four years, favours our design and offers an excellent ambuscade; so sitting down behind it we possess our souls in patience for a time and discuss the situation in a low tone. Then in the fulness of time the Captain prepares to play upon his little pipe, and with lips compressed and cheeks distended the performance commences. *Tuk, tuk, tuk, tuktuk!* But the only answer comes from some solitary hoarse-voiced crow, or the *rat-tat-tat* of a woodpecker; and in the pauses between the Captain's efforts the silence is only broken by the dropping of acorns and chestnuts round us or the light scrape of a squirrel on the leaves. It may be a long time before my companion's industrious and careful piping is rewarded, or it may indeed be, as the song says, for ever. In this case, however, response comes at last to proclaim that one, at any rate, of the scattered birds is moving on the slope of the mountain below us.

Now the exciting period begins; we cease to speak even in whispers; the fyce dog lies low and, cocking his short ears, watches wistfully the rugged, hairy face of his master, which is certainly something of a study, as he holds treacherous converse with his unsuspecting victim. These, as may be imagined, are far the most serious moments of the Captain's life. A false note might mean ruin, and it is evident from the answers that another bird has now joined the first one; we no longer dare show our noses even above the log, and can judge of the birds' approach only by their answering notes. In ten minutes or so the *tuk, tuk*, gets very near; the birds must be almost within shot. The Captain's veins fairly swell, and the perspiration stands out on his forehead with the responsibility of piping correctly at so short a distance. We can now hear their feet actually treading on the dry leaves, and it occurs to me how disastrous were a sneeze at this moment. The turkeys are now beyond a doubt within easy shot. The Captain is to give the signal for action, and he grasps firmly his big gun, with five drachms of powder in each barrel if there's a grain this time, I'll warrant. It is not a pleasant gun to be at close quarters with, and for my part I do not like it. "Now!" says the chief, and at the word we both spring into a kneeling position above the log. A couple of big gobblers fill our horizon. They have just time to lift their heavy wings. The Captain does not take my bird this time: it is too serious an occasion; and we fire simultaneously.

There is a sensation for a moment as if the drum of my ear is broken, and my head sings like a tea-kettle. A cloud of smoke hangs like a pall over everything for a second or two, for the Captain not only uses black powder in such large doses, but buys it at the country store. Both birds are dead, of course; nothing but the equivalent of "buck fever," and we are neither of us likely to suffer from that, could produce any other result. The Captain has fallen back on his elbow for the moment; most people would be flat on their back from such a shock. "Dorgonne it, that ar blamed nipple has blowed off again!" And so it had. Still, no one is hurt, except the turkeys, and we go home rejoicing under the weight of our somewhat heavy spoils; while I seriously turn over in my mind whether it would not be worth while for the Captain's friends to raise a fund among themselves for providing him with a gun that would stand his "loads," and be less of a trial to his shooting-partners.

THE END

RICHARD CLAY AND SONS, LIMITED, LONDON AND BUNGAY.

BY THE SAME AUTHOR.

WOLFE

With a Portrait. Crown 8vo, 2s. 6d.

["*English Men of Action*" *Series.*]

DAILY TELEGRAPH.—"Mr. A. G. Bradley, the author of this admirable memoir, has only done justice to its subject by executing a faithful and elaborate word-picture of a man whose disposition and conduct were not only faultless, but supremely noble."

MORNING POST.—"In entrusting this volume to Mr. Bradley the editors have done wisely, and their wisdom has been rewarded by a charming biography. . . . Mr. Bradley's style is especially engaging. His descriptions are graphic without being in the least extravagant. This book is in every sense worthy of its place in an admirable series."

TIMES.—"It appears to us to be very well done. The narrative is easy, the facts have been mastered and well marshalled, and Mr. Bradley is excellent both in his biographical and his geographical details."

NATIONAL OBSERVER.—"Mr. Bradley has brought to bear a dramatic sense and a literary power—athletic, easy, always in measure to the topic—and a faculty for visualising scenes and events, that altogether make this volume notable even at a time when amongst our ablest men there is a rivalry in the making of little books."

ARMY AND NAVY GAZETTE.—"Mr. A. G. Bradley's *Wolfe* will rank among the best volumes in the 'Men of Action' Series. . . . There could be no better literary portrait of him in brief form. It is at once careful and accurate and well balanced, filled with the evidence of sound judgment, and conveyed in a terse and clear literary style."

ST. JAMES'S GAZETTE.—"It is a most interesting life clearly and ably described."

DAILY CHRONICLE.—"A military biography is apt to be full of wearisome detail and technicalities which bore the reader. This work is absolutely devoid of any such defect, and yet with all its beauty it is not sketchy, but very thorough, the history of Wolfe's times being well set forth, and withal style has not been sacrificed."

GLOBE.—"There is no more interesting volume in the interesting series of which it forms a part."

THE GRAPHIC.—"It makes the eyes glisten and the heart glow."

WESTMINSTER REVIEW.—"Mr. Bradley has done full justice to the subject, and we are sure the book will be widely read."

BRITISH WEEKLY.—"Every reader of this sketch of Wolfe will agree that it is difficult to imagine how it could be better done. Could all history be taught in lessons so brilliant, fascinating and instructive, the dullest boy might be won to attention."

PALL MALL GAZETTE.—"Mr. Bradley's life of James Wolfe is a welcome addition to the 'English Men of Action' Series. The history of the extraordinary campaign, ended by the glorious victory and death of the conqueror on the plains of Abraham, is one to be read with breathless and enthralling interest. . . . A delightful monograph."

WESTERN MORNING NEWS.—"For interesting reading few books of its size surpass it."

EDUCATIONAL REVIEW.—"Mr. Bradley is to be most warmly congratulated upon this book. He has put excellent work into it, and he writes with a restraint and sane use of words which go far to raise a facility of language into the distinction of style. . . . We are indeed greatly pleased with this book; it is not only delightful to read, but almost equally delightful to handle and look at. It is quite one of the best of the series."

REALM.—"In his life of Wolfe Mr. Bradley has added an altogether admirable work to an already excellent series. The story never loses its interest. One feels inclined to pray to be neither interrupted nor told the end of the story. . . . In this book Mr. Bradley has undoubtedly given us one of the most interesting of all the short biographies of famous men recently published."

SCOTSMAN.—"It was time to give Wolfe a place among 'English Men of Action.' He has now found a good place and had his life's story finely told and his noble character admirably presented by A. G. Bradley."

CANADIAN GAZETTE.—"The tale (Quebec) has often been told, but it bears retelling, and Mr. Bradley retells it with singular spirit and power."

SPEAKER.—"Mr. Bradley's able monograph is a just and needed tribute to the memory of a military genius as great as that of Marlborough and a career far nobler."

BLACK AND WHITE.—"Mr. Bradley's contribution to the 'English Men of Action' Series is perhaps the first adequate presentation of a gallant soldier and lovable man. . . . The author has taken a view of his subject at once comprehensive and sympathetic, and has given it full expression."

MACMILLAN AND CO., Ltd., LONDON.

The Eversley Series.

Globe 8vo, cloth, 5s. per volume.

The Works of Matthew Arnold. 6 vols.
    ESSAYS IN CRITICISM. First Series.
    ESSAYS IN CRITICISM. Second Series.
    EARLY AND NARRATIVE POEMS.
    LYRIC AND ELEGIAC POEMS.
    DRAMATIC AND LATER POEMS. | AMERICAN DISCOURSES.

Essays by George Brimley. Third Edition.

Chaucer's Canterbury Tales. Edited by A. W. POLLARD. **2 vols.**

Dean Church's Miscellaneous Writings. 9 vols.
    MISCELLANEOUS ESSAYS. | DANTE : and other Essays.
    ST. ANSELM. | SPENSER. | BACON.
    THE OXFORD MOVEMENT. Twelve Years, 1833-1845.
    THE BEGINNING OF THE MIDDLE AGES. (Included in this Series by permission of Messrs. LONGMANS and Co.)
    OCCASIONAL PAPERS selected from *The Guardian*, *The Times*, and *The Saturday Review*, 1846-1890. In 2 vols.

Emerson's Collected Works. 6 vols. With Introduction by JOHN MORLEY.
    MISCELLANIES. | ESSAYS. | POEMS.
    ENGLISH TRAITS AND REPRESENTATIVE MEN.
    THE CONDUCT OF LIFE AND SOCIETY AND SOLITUDE.
    LETTERS AND SOCIAL AIMS.

Letters of Edward Fitzgerald. Edited by W. A. WRIGHT. 2 vols.

Goethe's Prose Maxims. Translated, with Introductions, by T. BAILEY SAUNDERS.

Thomas Gray's Collected Works in Prose and Verse. Edited by EDMUND GOSSE. 4 vols. Poems, Journals, and Essays.—Letters, 2 vols. Notes on Aristophanes and Plato.

Works by John Richard Green.
    STRAY STUDIES FROM ENGLAND AND ITALY.
    HISTORY OF THE ENGLISH PEOPLE. 8 vols.

The Choice of Books, and other Literary Pieces. By FREDERIC HARRISON.

Poems of Thomas Hood. In 2 vols. Vol. I. SERIOUS POEMS. Vol. II. HUMOROUS POEMS. Edited, with Prefatory Memoir, by CANON AINGER. [*In the Press.*

R. H. Hutton's Collected Essays.
    LITERARY ESSAYS.
    ESSAYS ON SOME OF THE MODERN GUIDES OF ENGLISH THOUGHT IN MATTERS OF FAITH.
    THEOLOGICAL ESSAYS.
    CRITICISMS ON CONTEMPORARY THOUGHT AND THINKERS. 2 vols.

Thomas Henry Huxley's Collected Works.
    METHOD AND RESULTS. | DARWINIANA.
    SCIENCE AND EDUCATION.
    SCIENCE AND HEBREW TRADITION.
    SCIENCE AND CHRISTIAN TRADITION.
    HUME. With Helps to the Study of Berkeley.
    MAN'S PLACE IN NATURE : and other Anthropological Essays.
    DISCOURSES, BIOLOGICAL AND GEOLOGICAL.
    EVOLUTION AND ETHICS, AND OTHER ESSAYS.

Works by Henry James.
    PARTIAL PORTRAITS.
    FRENCH POETS AND NOVELISTS.

MACMILLAN AND CO., LTD., LONDON.

The Eversley Series.

Globe 8vo, cloth, 5s. per volume.

Letters of John Keats to his Family and Friends. Edited by SIDNEY COLVIN.

Charles Kingsley's Novels and Poems.
WESTWARD HO! 2 vols.
HYPATIA. 2 vols.
YEAST. 1 vol.
ALTON LOCKE. 2 vols.
TWO YEARS AGO. 2 vols.
HEREWARD THE WAKE. 2 vols.
POEMS. 2 vols.

Charles Lamb's Collected Works. Edited, with Introduction and Notes, by CANON AINGER. 6 vols.
THE ESSAYS OF ELIA.
POEMS, PLAYS, AND MISCELLANEOUS ESSAYS.
MRS. LEICESTER'S SCHOOL, and other Writings.
TALES FROM SHAKESPEARE. By CHARLES and MARY LAMB.
THE LETTERS OF CHARLES LAMB. 2 vols.

Life of Charles Lamb. By CANON AINGER.

Historical Essays. By J. B. LIGHTFOOT, D.D.

The Poetical Works of John Milton. Edited, with Memoir, Introduction, and Notes, by DAVID MASSON, M.A. 3 vols.
I. THE MINOR POEMS.
II. PARADISE LOST.
III. PARADISE REGAINED, AND SAMSON AGONISTES.

John Morley's Collected Works. In 11 vols.
VOLTAIRE. 1 vol.
DIDEROT AND THE ENCYCLOPÆDISTS. 2 vols.
ON COMPROMISE. 1 vol.
BURKE. 1 vol.
ROUSSEAU. 2 vols.
MISCELLANIES. 3 vols.
STUDIES IN LITERATURE. 1 vol.

Science and a Future Life, and other Essays. By F. W. H. MYERS, M.A.

Classical Essay. By F. W. H. MYERS, M.A.

Records of Tennyson, Ruskin, and Browning. By ANNE THACKERAY RITCHIE.

Works by Sir John R. Seeley, K.C.M.G., Litt.D.
THE EXPANSION OF ENGLAND. Two Courses of Lectures.
LECTURES AND ESSAYS.
ECCE HOMO. A Survey of the Life and Work of Jesus Christ.
NATURAL RELIGION.
LECTURES ON POLITICAL SCIENCE.

Sheridan's Plays. In 2 vols. With an Introduction by MOWBRAY MORRIS. [*In the Press.*

Works by James Smetham.
LETTERS. With an Introductory Memoir. Edited by SARAH SMETHAM and WILLIAM DAVIES. With a Portrait.
LITERARY WORKS. Edited by WILLIAM DAVIES.

Life of Swift. By HENRY CRAIK, C.B. 2 vols. New Edition.

Selections from the Writings of Thoreau. Edited by H. S. SALT.

Essays in the History of Religious Thought in the West. By B. F. WESTCOTT, D.D., D.C.L., Lord Bishop of Durham.

The Works of William Wordsworth. Edited by Professor KNIGHT.
POETICAL WORKS. 8 vols. | PROSE WORKS. 2 vols.

The Journals of Dorothy Wordsworth. 2 vols.

MACMILLAN AND CO., LTD., LONDON.

www.ingramcontent.com/pod-product-compliance
Lightning Source LLC
Chambersburg PA
CBHW032053220426
43664CB00008B/982